GOTTY AND THE GUV'NOR

GOTTY AND THE GUV'NOR

by

A. E. COPPING

Introduction and Appendix by John Leather

MALLARD REPRINTS
LAVENHAM SUFFOLK
1979

973009

910·45

First published by E. Grant Richards 1907
Published 1979 by Mallard Reprints
ISBN 0 904623 98 X

Printed in Great Britain at
THE LAVENHAM PRESS LIMITED
LAVENHAM   SUFFOLK

CONTENTS

INDEX OF ILLUSTRATIONS

INTRODUCTION

by JOHN LEATHER

ARTHUR Edward Copping was born in London on 22nd July
1865, the son of Edward and Rosa Copping. Edward was author
of several books including *Aspects of Paris* and essays. Rosa's father
was J. Skinner Prout, a watercolour painter. There were two other
sons; Harold who became a well known illustrator of books and
bibles and Bernard, who was for a time an actor.

Young Arthur Copping attended the North London Collegiate
School but is believed to have had an unhappy childhood, during
which his mother died and his father re-married. He left home as a
youth to become an office boy on the staff of the *Daily News*,
commencing a lifelong career in journalism.

Arthur Copping rose from office boy to a reporter with the paper
and developed a talent for accurate observation and impression of
people and places. He became well established with the *Daily News*
and remained a correspondent with the paper from 1884 until 1906.
He married Miss Nancy Knaggs, a doctor's daughter.

Their daughter Betty, now Mrs Betty Fletcher, remembers her
father as a man of very strong convictions whose hobbies were
gardening and carpentry yet who at various times throughout life
travelled extensively, at times in remote countries, where he had
some unusual experiences. He was an ardent advocate of temperance
reform and had considerable sympathy with the work of the
Salvation Army, also contributing to their publications. He seems to
have had great interest in people, particularly ordinary people and
their ways of life, conditions of work and home life, problems and
outlook. His first book, *Pictures of Poverty*, published in 1905,
reflected his concern and interest in working people and probably
brought him in contact with the fishermen of Leigh, then a small
and sturdily individual community on a creek off the lower Thames.

After leaving the *Daily News* in 1906 Arthur Copping became a
freelance journalist and received commissions to write books for
publication. He then lived at Westcliff, immediately to the west of
the seaside resort of Southend and desirably residential for travellers
to London by train. Copping's first meeting with "Gotty," a Leigh
fisherman, is revealed in the first chapter, the dullness of which

serves only to emphasise the vigour and humour of those following. "Gotty" was the nickname used by Copping in his books for Alfred Boynton, who was known to his friends and neighbours as "Ponto". Arthur Copping first accompanied him for a pleasure trip fishing for whitebait in a bawley probably named the *Breadwinner*, perhaps as a reporter seeking copy for an article on the fisheries of the Thames mouth. Soon after, Gotty was dismissed as skipper of the bawley, which he did not own and was unemployed; a serious matter in those days. Copping's sympathetic suggestion that Gotty should seek to own a bawley resulted in the *Jane* being found for Copping to buy and Gotty to fish. She was one of the fleet of eighty or so then sailing from Leigh. Copping renamed her the *Betty*, after his daughter. He had never before owned a boat or had any interest in sailing but he appeared to enjoy at least two cruises in the *Betty* and some fishing, mainly trawling for shrimps.

Geographically Leigh lies on the foreshore and hillside adjacent to the equally old Essex village of Hadleigh and four miles upstream along the Thames foreshore from Southend, a seaside resort beloved by Londoners and others since Victorian times and whose population growth and suburbs have gradually overrun the intervening districts of Chalkwell and Westcliff and also spread eastwards to Shoebury, via Thorpe Bay, to form a conurbation with the population of a city. All this was far off when Copping met Gotty in the old village of Leigh, with its narrow High Street running parallel to the creek, with brick and weatherboard houses jumbled along its sides and alleys. Steam trains of the London, Tilbury and Southend Railway whistled, puffed and rumbled through the village on the line from Fenchurch Street to Shoebury. Big glistening tank engines painted an improbable white drew coaches filled in summer with London's East End trippers, bound for the pier, the Kursaal, ice creams and shingle beach of Southend, with probably a view of its noted, muddy sand flats at low water or, if lucky, a sail at high water in the big, beamy, centreboard beach boats such as the *Prince of Wales* or *Britannia*. Although these visitors had little in common with the inhabitants of Leigh, their seaside tastes included eating shrimp teas; a delicacy sought by visitors to the many holiday boarding houses in Southend and at most other seaside towns in Britain. Many of these shrimps were trawled by Leigh fishermen with their bawleys and for over a century this trawling has been a part of the Essex fishermen's summer work and they were still being landed in quantities during the 1960s, though the supply has since diminished.

When Copping bought the bawley she was the *Jane*, registered at Maldon but working out of Leigh. She may have been built at Maldon, on the Essex river Blackwater, or at Burnham on Crouch, which shared the same registration. He had her name changed to *Betty* and port of registry to London, in keeping with most other Leigh craft. She was probably a typical bawley of the period 1870-1914; beamy well canvassed and generally heavy to work. When Copping wrote the book, about 70-80 bawleys fished from Leigh under sail. Motors afloat were only known in small yachts and service launches. Even these were only beginning to emerge from an experimental stage and it would be some years before one was fitted in a Leigh bawley. Stephen Frost of Leigh is credited wth starting the local shrimping trade in 1830, which brought a major part of its living to Leigh for over a century. In 1850 one of the Cotgrove family of Leigh put a brickbuilt boiler in the hold of his *Secret* and boiled the shrimp catch on board, an innovation enabling the catch to be landed ready for market. The term "boiler" may or may not have caused the name bawley, no-one knows. Shrimping grew quickly with the Victorian popularity of seaside holidays and by 1872 was the principal fishery of Leigh, employing about 80 vessels of which transom-sterned bawleys around 32 feet overall were the largest. These early Leigh shrimpers used a type of small, primitive trawl. This evolved into a triangular net with its mouth spread by a beam which was towed along the bottom by a trawl warp and bridle. The mouth was extended by a vertical post in the centre of the beam and this had a light, horizontal beam at its top, making a quadrilateral mouth. As the size of bawleys increased, they towed more nets until by the 1890s, a 35-footer worked four nets; two boomed out from the hull abaft the mast. When shrimps were scarce some Leigh fishermen sailed to Harwich, 40 miles down the Essex coast, in May, to join the fleet of smacks and bawleys working out of that port, returning in September. Sometimes, in bad seasons, the Leigh craft worked on the south coast, using Shoreham, Sussex, as a base. Occasionally they ventured to Holland, Belgium and France and the Channel Islands in search of shrimps to trawl and shellfish to dredge. Although shrimping formed their major work in later years, some Leigh bawleys carried on the earlier fisheries for sprats and whitebait and at odd times a few worked peter nets or stop nets for flatfish, seines for smelts and whitebait, or long lines for cod, though these activities do not significantly appear in the Gotty story.

Arthur Copping and his brother seemed to enjoy trawling and spent many amusing days with Gotty and his crew, working in the

Thames and its estuary. Arthur's wife Nancy and their daughter Betty were sometimes taken along for a sail, but as both were indifferent seafarers, frequently feeling ill from the motion of the sturdy *Betty* and no doubt from the rich fishy smells which clung to her tarry hull, their sails were of short duration. Betty, now Mrs Fletcher, recalls frequently meeting Gotty at that time and describes him as "strong and gentle, with nice manners and appeared to be exactly as he is shown in the book". Perhaps it was Gotty's own strength of character which provided most enjoyment in Copping's ownership of the bawley and enabled the uneducated fisherman and the journalist to find common ground.

Alfred Boynton, alias "Gotty" or to use his real nickname "Ponto", was born at Leigh in 1853 and was sailing and working in bawleys from a very early age. His two days schooling did not interfere with his more extensive practical studies and when a youth he became well known at Leigh and Southend as the champion walker of the greasy pole in regattas. For fourteen years Gotty won the pig given as a prize for walking the pole at Southend regatta and received a silver medal to prove it, besides taking similar prizes as far away as Mistley, in Essex and Gravesend, Kent. In 1912 he reckoned that he had won over fifty pigs, fifteen in sixteen years at Southend alone. He lost count of the ducks then given as second prize for this event, still popular at Essex regattas but with less exciting prizes. Ponto excelled at swimming, rowing or sculling races and was strong. He was in one bawley which sank suddenly in shoal water. Ponto and his two companions climbed the mast, which just showed above water and he held them both on his shoulders, up to his neck in water, until rescuers could sail down from Leigh. His short white beard, fine cut head and massive shoulders complimented his strong and fearless character, which Arthur Copping caught well in this book, along with an accurate rendering of the Leigh men's speech; a mixture of Essex and cockney dialect.

Gotty was tough. An onlooker recalled seeing him come flying out through the swing doors of the *Ship* on Leigh hill. He landed flat on his back in the street, only to charge back again with a mighty roar. In the dark of one early morning Gotty fell overboard while shrimping. His mate could see no sign of him and, with the boy, commenced furiously hauling in the four nets to come about and search. Gotty was in the last one—still breathing many minutes later!

Gotty's world was bounded by Harwich in the north-east and the North Foreland in the south-east; the sweep of the Thames estuary.

The English Channel was dismissed by him as being "Margit way, ain't it?". Probably it was the colourful Gotty who inspired journalist Copping to take notes of the cruise in the *Betty*, made from Leigh to Penzance, along the south coast of England, into waters and amongst people and customs strange to her crew of Gotty and the retired yacht skipper, Mr Rawson, who caused such annoyance to Arthur Copping, the "Guvnor". The *Betty's* cruise was dogged by a succession of unsatisfactory mates until they engaged Joe Cole, a Folkestone fisherman. Copping thoroughly entered into the spirit of this informal "yachting", acting as "pilot" in the Channel, from his reading of sailing directions and charts and finding congenial companionship with Gotty and Cole until, having enjoyed the delights of Devon and Cornwall, they sailed for home. The voyage provided such a fund of interest and observation that Copping was able to write an entertaining book, which he pointedly entitled *Gotty and the Guv'nor*. It was first published in 1907 and was well received, being reprinted several times. Although it was read by sailing people, it did not seem to be particularly aimed at or be sought by them at first, which is understandable in an age when cruising in small yachts was regarded as unusual and craft less than 15 tons Thames Measurement were regarded as small. There had been cruises in small yachts by noted amateurs Speed, McMullen, Knight, Kunhardt, MacGregor, Middleton and Cowper and by professional Captain Slocum, and others, who sailed their way into yachting history and into print for a small part of the yachting public. But most attention was focused on the doings of large yachts, particularly racers and fashionable yachtsmen. Few were interested in the minor adventures of an amateur of Copping's standing in the sport, cruising in a fishing bawley for his holidays. However, since then the gradual widening appreciation of small sailing craft of the past has led to a re-reading of books such as this by sailing men finding increasing enjoyment in sailing, restoring or just dreaming about these craft and the men who sailed them, particularly fishing vessels such as bawleys. *Gotty and the Guv'nor* became sought by many, but few copies were to be found, even during the 1930s. Ten years later, when I started seeking a copy, it was impossible to even borrow one from a friend. Strangely, during the week I suggested this long over-due reprint to Terence and June Dalton, a rare copy was found for me by a friend after a search lasting thirty years. Now this is to be happily changed.

Although the book is very amusing in parts, Copping is re-membered as not being a particularly jolly man, but he certainly knew how to write. All material for the book was drawn from life. The doctor to whom he refers in the first chapter was Doctor Murie, who lived locally and researched into marine life and the fisheries of the Thames mouth at the turn of the century.

In the summer following *Betty's* first cruise down Channel, Arthur Copping, Gotty and Copping's brother sailed the *Betty* across the North Sea to Belgium and Holland. That summer cruise became the subject of his next book *Gotty in Furrin Parts*, which became, if possible, even more sought than the first. It is hoped that this will be the second reprint book published in this series. Arthur Copping seems to have owned the *Betty* for two or three years. He relinquished ownership and sailing as suddenly as he commenced. Probably he found it had given him great pleasure but had exhausted its possibilities for a journalistic mind always seeking fresh experiences. She was eventually sold to a fisherman at Gravesend.

Of Ponto's later life we know little. He was mate of a shrimping bawley in 1912 and continued to live at Leigh until his death during the 1920s. That he was a central character in two widely read books did not concern him at all and he remained the same resourceful fisherman until the end.

Whilst on the cruise down Channel, Copping bought a house at Thundersley, in south Essex, intending to enjoy its large garden, yet remain within reach of London and the Thames. His subsequent travels in Europe resulted in the book *Jolly in Germany* , 1910 and a visit to Palestine in *A Journey in the Holy Land*, 1911. He visited Canada and wrote his impressions; *Canada Today and Tomorrow* and *The Golden Land—Canada*; both published in 1911. *Improved Ontario Farms* appeared in 1912 and *The Canadian Winter* a year later. *Smithers* also appeared in 1913 and *The Laundress* in 1916, before war swept Arthur Copping into its dangerous excitements and terrors. His *Souls in Khaki* and *Tommy's Triangle* (the Y.M.C.A. in war) appeared in 1917, that fateful year of the conflict. Soon after, he became the war correspondent at sea of the *Daily Chronicle*. At fifty-two years of age one might have expected him to have a relatively quiet berth on board a battleship in Scapa Flow but Copping followed the war to the frozen struggles of the North Russian Campaign. He flew over Kronsdat during its blockade by a British squadron and later studied revolutionary conditions and hardships in Leningrad and Moscow. During the period 1917-1920 he also visited Palestine as a news correspondent. After the war he continued in journalism and retained a taste for travel. During 1927-28 he was on a global tour visiting South Africa, Australia, New Zealand, several south Pacific islands and Alaska. His interest in the Salvation Army never waned and in 1928 he published *Stories of Army Trophies* based on experiences of that movement. In 1930-31 he was off on more travels, this time through Africa, visiting west, south east and central parts. At that time Arthur Copping was comfortably off and lived at "River View", Thundersley, Essex, not far from the lower Thames. He served on the local Board of Guardians and became a district councillor at a time when these things were more solemnly regarded than now. His hobbies remained gardening and carpentry. He later moved to St Leonards on Sea, Sussex, and died on 13th July 1941. He was recorded simply as "Writer"; an epitaph he would no doubt have preferred as fitting and honourable.

John Leather,
1979.

Alfred Boynton, whose local nickname was "Ponto", was skipper of Arthur Copping's bawley *Betty*. Copping changed the nickname to "Gotty" in his writings.   *A portrait by Edward Wigfull, 1912, courtesy Yachting Monthly*

I

OUR FIRST MEETING

"WHO caught the salmon?"

They were three fishermen gossiping on Leigh jetty, and it chanced that I put my question more particularly to the tall man with a square face and white trousers—the man who has a four-cornered beard on a two-cornered chin. His was a large, strong face, absolutely calm and wise.

"I did!" he replied, taking his pipe from his mouth and looking at me as though he wanted to fight.

"Couldn't 'ave arsked anybody more likely to know," commented the little man in a blue jersey.

"Got 'im fust go," agreed the fisherman wearing a bowler hat.

"You knew they were salmon?" I asked White Trousers.

"When you say 'they,' " he answered coldly, "p'raps you mean 'it.' There wasn't only one salmon caught in our boat. Then Johnny Johnson caught one, and t'other was a Southend boat—a man by the name of Brooks. Ercourse I knowed what it was! I ain't so ignerint not to know a salmon when I see one. It's dif'rent to any other fish, a salmon is."

"There ain't no dif'rence," affirmed Bowler Hat, "betwixt a salmon and a young bass."

"Ain't there!"—and the white-trousered authority turned scornfully upon his interrupter. "Did you ever see a bass with spots on 'im?"

"'Oo said I did?"

"Nobody—only you won't see a salmon without 'em."

"A bass," Blue Jersey intervened to point out, "'as got a bigger head than what a salmon's got."

"There's some people," said Bowler Hat vaguely, but with warmth, "as 'ave got big 'eads, but there ain't much inside."

"What became of the salmon?" I hastened to ask.

"Mine was e't," said White Trousers tersely. "Only if I'd known the Doctor would a liked it, same as 'e's told me since, to send up to the London Museem, 'e should a 'ad it and welcome."

"The Doctor!" jeered Blue Jersey. "And he'd a known where it come from, wouldn't 'e, and found out its birthday by looking at its

1

tail—same as 'e knowed the bottle-nosed whale was a female—when it warn't." And the speaker spat.

"It warn't a bottle-nosed," said Bowler Hat.

"It *were* a bottle-nosed," insisted Blue Jersey.

"Ain't you thinking of old Charley, what helped to tow it ashore?"

"Was the salmon nice?" I asked White Trousers.

"Not 'aving 'ad none, I can't say. The mate took it 'ome."

"The mate! But weren't you in charge of the boat?"

"That's right enough. But"—in confidential key—"the mate's mother's the owner. Nat'ral enough, 'e 'ad the salmon, and nat'ral enough, as I was a telling yer, it was e't."

A newspaper paragraph, announcing the capture of these fish, of a kind long since extinct in the London river, had identified them with Danube fry put into the water above London by the Thames Salmon Association. I asked White Trousers if he thought that could be so.

"Well, mine was a lot bigger'n the others," he testified; "eighteen inches, he was, and the others warn't no more than fourteen. It was a wonderful fine fish, mine was."

"What the gentleman was asking you," said Bowler Hat severely, "wasn't nothing about 'ow big it was, but if it mightn't be one of them little 'uns what was put in the river. To my fancy it couldn't be nothing else."

"May-be it was, and may-be it wasn't," replied White Trousers judicially. "Only, mind you, there's been a salmon took off 'ere before, and not 'alf a tidy size 'un neither. It was a twenty pound fish, or I'm tellin' a lie—as you can see fer yerself, along of its being stuffed up at the Board School. I 'ad two pound of that fish."

"And how did it taste?" I wanted to know.

"Wonderful like any other salmon," I learnt.

And then conversation drifted back to the whale.

"It was like this 'ere," White Trousers explained. "It got aground near the Nore, same as steamers do sometimes, only not so often as they might, if you understand my meanin'—seein' it's a chance for a pore fisherman to arn a pound or two fer gettin' their anchor out. And some of our chaps went off with boat-'ooks, and they jabbed away until they'd knocked the life out of it. They didn't know what to do next when they'd done that, so after a lot of talk—one bein' fer one thing, and one fer another—they took and towed it ashore jest off 'ere. They was a week gettin' the oil out, Joe Larkin's barge, what lay alongside, bein' all smothered; and by the time they'd finished, the stink was that awful you could smell it nearly as fur as Tilbury. There was a reg'lar bother, and I don't know what some people wasn't goin' ter do if the whale wasn't took away. At last they towed it off to that point there, across the Gut, and at low water they digged a big 'ole and buried it in the mud."

"That was the Doctor's idea," added Bowler Hat; "and some day he's going to 'ave the bones took up so as he can put 'em together into a nice clean skelington. A wonderful clever man, the Doctor is; and there ain't many that's got so much book larning!"

"Him having said it was a female," sneered Blue Jersey, "when us chaps know'd it warn't. 'E don't know 'alf what 'e reckons 'e do—nor a quarter. I've told 'im so. 'Doctor,' one day I says, 'd' you know my opinyin o' you as a practikle fisherman?' 'Somethin' insultin', I suppose,' says 'e. 'No,' I says, 'it ain't insultin'.' 'Well, what is it?' says 'e, 'My owner,' I says, 'gives me enough to live on,' I says, 'ter go out trawlin' fer 'im; but 'e wouldn't employ you, not if you paid 'im.' 'I thought it was somethin' insultin',' says the Doctor, and 'e bust out laughin'."

"If I was 'im," commented Bowler Hat pointedly, "I wouldn't waste the time ter talk to some people. They're too ignerint."

"Ter my mind," said White Trousers, "there's things swimmin' about the sea what no one don't know nothin' about. Fer instance, P'raps you never saw a fish with a mouse's body and two long 'orns stickin' out of 'is 'ead?"

"Nor you neither," replied Red Jersey, with undisguised scepticism.

"Stay 'ere a minuit," said White Trousers with dignity, "and I'll go and fetch it."

"That's Gotty," explained Bowler Hat confidentially, when White Trousers was out of hearing, "and there ain't another like 'im, I don't suppose, not anywhere. It isn't many can say they was under water twenty minutes and none the worse."

"And you ought to see 'im walking' the greasy pole!" testified Red Jersey. "E's got toes bent round like the claws of a crab," he added with local pride, "so 'e don't slip off where others do."

The subject of these generous eulogiums presently returned, and, in impressive silence, handed me a small, bristly, inert object, which I fingered with polite wonder. It suggested the vegetable, rather than the animal kingdom; and at the risk of seeming unsympathetic, I hinted that, in my opinion, it was no fish.

"No more I don't believe it ain't," said Gotty with composure. "But it was swimmin' in the water when I caught it, that I do know. There's those as say it's one of them nuts with seeds in what stick on sheep's backs in furrin' countries, and wery likely come off a cattle ship. But 'ow fur that's true I can't say, fer I don't know." After a moment of thoughtful reverie he added: "Did you ever see a glass walking-stick full of them teeny sweets what the nippers buy 'undred of fer a farthin'?"

I had never, unless my memory deceived me, enjoyed that privilege; and I told him so.

"There's not many," he assured me, "as 'ave. But I can show yer one, if you'd care to step round to my 'ouse. It ain't fur."

"Oh, but I really don't like to trouble you."

"Nothing ain't a trouble," came the vigorous axiom, "if yer don't make a trouble on it."

He forthwith piloted me across the railway bridge and up a narrow alley. We entered the last cottage in the row, where a short, round, happy-faced woman was thrown into apologetic confusion at a visitor finding the kitchen hung with washing. Unmoved by this domestic flutter, the great fisherman strode across that small apartment, his cap well-nigh brushing the ceiling, and, stooping, passed into a parlour beyond. Thither, having added my apologies to the lady's, I followed him.

From two supporting nails on the wall, Gotty took down the glass walking-stick stuffed with hundreds and thousands; and I rendered my tribute of exclamations.

"It was give me," said the beaming proprietor, "in one of my lucky weeks, fer the wery next day they brought me round *this*—" and he held forward to my scrutiny the large silver medal which co-operated with a watch-chain to decorate his chest. The inscription bore witness that, in fourteen consecutive years, he had been victorious on the greasy pole at Southend Regatta.

"By rights," he explained earnestly, "there should a been a pig drawd on it, but the man what made the medal said the Committee never told 'im, though from what I 'eard afterwards they *did*. Only I didn't care to make a bother."

"But why a pig!" I asked, in my ignorance resenting, on his behalf, an imputation to which he seemed to be making himself a party.

"Why—didn't you know," he exclaimed, in a tone rich with reproach, "that it's always a live pig they give fer the prize;" and the way he looked at me seemed to reflect a momentary misgiving that he was bestowing his friendship in an unworthy quarter.

I denounced myself for what was, indeed, but a passing lapse of memory; and that I secured the champion's forgiveness was manifest from the affable tone of his next remark.

"At one time they put the pig *on* the pole, so that 'im what got it out of the box 'ad it. But them times is all altered. A pig's made that funny, you see, 'e can't swim without cuttin' 'is own throat, along o' 'aving short legs and sharp feet. They cuts inter the flesh, them sharp feet does, so it was brought in croolty to animals. Not, mind yer, as there was any croolty the way I done it."

"Indeed!"

"No. As soon as ever I open the box and the porker drops inter the water, splash in I goes arter 'im; and 'e don't get no time to commit sooecide before I lay hold on 'is legs and swim 'im ashore. Only it ain't everybody that's quick enough, nor yet'd 'ave the cleverness; so the law says you mustn't put a pig on the pole—and, what's more, you'll mostly find a perliceman on the barge ter see no one don't ferget 'isself and put one there accidental."

"So you've taken fourteen pigs!" And I gazed with admiration upon a man having so honourable a record.

"Fourteen!" he protested. "More like forty! It ain't only Southend what 'as regatters," he explained, the great bushy eyebrows rising aghast at the state of my education. "There's Leigh, there's Misley—why, there's plenty o' places 'as 'em; and I mostly find time to run in on the day ter get the pig. The pig *or* a sov'rin," he added, anxious for accuracy, "fer at some places you can 'ave which you like, and that bein' all a butcher'll allow you for the pig—and sometimes make a favour of that, they do—I take the sov'rin. And a bit o' money like that comes in wonderful 'andy at times, if you'll believe me—same as when my wife's brother's missis 'ad 'er first, them living with us then like as now. It bought the cradle and charnse it, and I don't know as there wasn't somethin' over fer a frock and sich-like."

Never before was I in the society of a man who, in a series of open competitions with the world, had won a herd of swine, and in a few respectful words I ventured, not merely to congratulate him on pre-eminence, but to applaud the ease with which he maintained it.

Apparently by no means ill-pleased with the impression he had made, Gotty was nevertheless swift to take me up on the latter point:

"They don't let yer do it too easy—not till the fourth time. If you get to the end fust go it ain't counted, fer you must 'ave three tries to make sport fer the people."

"Do you walk to the end, then, four times?" for I did not quite understand.

"'Oo? Me. What, and wipe off the grease for them that 'as to foller? It ain't likely. Fust three goes I jest walks a few yards and drops over inter the water. Fourth time I goes all along the pole and grabs the flag—fer it's mostly a flag now that pigs ain't allowed."

5

"And you've never once been beaten?" I asked, in accents of warm appreciation.

"No," he answered with composure, "and what's more I've give up expectin' to. I don't look never to find the man as can walk the pole better than me—not on *this* earth," he added conscientiously, as though alive to the possibility of sensational happenings elsewhere, "I don't look to find 'im."

Triumphs of the master are, in every art, apt to excite enmity in the bosoms of jealous competitors; and thus I was moved to ask Gotty if he had ever met with foul play.

"Wunst!" he replied, and in the succeeding silence I noticed that he was breathing hard, his lips tense.

"It was at Gravesend," he said, not without emotion. "I'd bin along twice, and I'd fell off twice, same as I was tellin' yer. Then there come the third time. I got up to walk out agin, and then fall off agin, nice and comfortable; but I 'adn't 'ardly set one foot afore another when a bloke on the barge up with 'is arm and give me, oh, sech a ugly shove be'ind. Start! I was never so took unawares in my life, and it was reg'lar mercy, the way I fell, my pore neck wasn't broke. I swum ashore, I walks up the gardin, I goes up ter the table, and I says to the Committee, 'Gentlemen,' I says—though I was that upset I could 'ardly get the words out—'Gentlemen,' I says, 'beggin' your pardin', but fair's fair, and I don't 'old with murderers.' 'You go 'ome, my man,' says one of 'em, kind like, and it was easy ter see they 'adn't saw what the bloke done, and wery likely thought I'd been 'aving a drop. 'You go 'ome,' he says, 'and don't bother about that pole no more, fer you can't do it.' 'Beggin' your pardin',' I says, 'but I can; and what's more, I'll do that fust,' I says, 'if I 'ave fair play,' I says, 'and go 'ome arterwards.' 'You shall 'ave fair play,' he says. 'and look 'ere, my man,' he says, 'if you walk to the end of that pole next time I'll give yer a extry sov'rin out of my own pocket.' 'Thank yer, sir,' I says, and I didn't mind 'em laughin', fer it was easy ter see, if you understand my meanin', they didn't know 'oo they was talkin' to. Back I goes ter the barge and this time I took partic'lar care there wasn't no one be'ind to give me a shove; so I walks out and gets the flag. When I goes up to the table agin, 'Bray-vo, my man,' says the same gentleman, and arter he give me the sov'rin, it was hat round with the others, so I got nine shillin's beside."

We chatted further on kindred themes, and an early blossom of our rapidly ripening friendship was the understanding on which we parted, to wit, that on the following Thursday Gotty should take me out for a fishing cruise in the vessel under his command.

II

FISHING FOR WHITEBAIT

WHEN, at the specified hour on Thursday evening, I reappeared at the cottage, Gotty stood awaiting my arrival, cap on and in his sea-boots; and I received the hearty, yet bustling, greetings of a mariner obviously anxious to be afloat.

On the jetty we found the mate and the third hand.

"But where's that young warmint?" exclaimed the skipper, sweeping the vicinity with an astonished gaze.

"Not turned up," leisurely replied the mate.

"Ain't 'e though!" fumed Gotty. "Wait till I lay 'old of 'im! 'E don't keep time, 'e don't larn nothin', 'e don't speak respectful, 'e ain't worth 'is wittles, there you are, let alone eighteen shillin's a week. Fer all the use 'e is we might be without the boy."

"So we might," agreed the third hand.

"I'll give 'im five minutes," Gotty wrathfully continued. "If 'e don't show up afore then, we'll go without 'im—that's what we'll do. What's comin' over boys I dunno." And the perturbed skipper mopped his brow.

In the painful silence that followed, I bethought me that graceful opportunity might hereafter arise to bestow tobacco upon my new acquaintances; and, on that account desiring to supplement my existing supply, I notified an intention to visit the nearest tobacconist's. On this expedition Gotty courteously volunteered to accompany me; and ten minutes later, as he stood bargaining for the loan of a basket with the proprietress of a ginger-beer shop (for an innocent provision against sea-thirst had also suggested itself to my benevolence), I had the satisfaction of noting that the dilatoriness and general misconduct of the youngest member of his crew no longer weighed as conscious memory on his mind. Nay, when, after an absence of fully fifteen minutes, we were strolling back to the waterside, the placidity of his thoughts entered the phase of meteorological optimism.

"Well, well," came the mellow comment, as he pointed an appreciative thumb to a distant gleam of moonlight on the sea, "we'll find a bit of a draught out there, arter all."

But his composure forsook him when he learnt from the mate,

who was standing where we had left him, that the boy had not yet arrived.

"That's done it!" exploded Gotty. "Blowed if that ain't done it. Termorrow I gets another boy;" and he looked fiercely from one shipmate to the other.

"I should," said the mate, in the soft voice of sympathy.

"I *will!*" roared the skipper, and in royal wrath he strode off alone towards the head of the jetty.

When, a little later, he returned, it was to find the situation unchanged. "P'ch!" was his only remark on this occasion, and standing rigid he fixed a stern stare on black distance.

Conscious that, in the circumstances, anything like animated conversation would be in bad taste, we three exchanged a few commonplaces in hushed tones.

"Well, ain't this too bad?" the skipper presently asked us. "Jim," he added, in an injured but friendly voice, "jest go along ter the end of the road and see if you can see 'im comin'."

But ere the third hand had time to act upon his superior's order, a nimble youngster ran into view.

"We were just going without you," said Jim.

"Nearly too late, young 'un," said the mate.

"What d'yer mean by sich conduct?" bellowed the skipper.

"I don't care!" sang out the boy with light-hearted defiance; and, jumping the stairs, he raced to where our dinghy lay in touch with land and water.

We followed. The skipper, just in front of me, was labouring under great excitement. I heard his painful attempts to fashion thought into consecutive language.

Of all the—! And sech sauce, too! Who'd a'believed—! Well, I—!" Suddenly the voice rose to a roar, and across the intervening mud he inquired:

"So you don't care, don't yer?"

"No—I—*don't*," came back in a calm, deliberate treble; and I was conscious that my companion had passed into that state of mind when the tongue becomes as parchment and speech is impossible.

In oppressive silence we got into the boat. The mate and the third hand rowed, Gotty and I sitting in the stern. The boy was curled up in the bow—whistling.

We must have travelled half a mile over the dark, still water before the first word was spoken.

"You 'eard what 'e said?" Gotty asked me huskily. "'E don't care!"

8

Not well knowing what to say, I remarked that the culprit was young.

"Young!" cried Gotty, as though I had insulted him. "That don't give 'im no call ter sauce 'is betters, do it? Young! I was a deal younger'n 'im when my father fust took me ter sea. Things was very dif'rent then, let me tell yer. Youngsters was expected to be'ave theirselves—and, what's more, they was made to work. Many a time," continued the skipper, warming to his theme, "I'd be set ter splice a rope, and if I wasn't quick enough, I'd get a knock acrost the 'ands with a marlin-spike."

"You must have been a bad boy," was the grieved comment of our youngster.

"You speak when you're spoke to," thundered Gotty.

At this point the conversation was interrupted by our arrival alongside the *Breadwinner*, to which, when we had scrambled on board, the dinghy was made fast.

The next few minutes were disagreeable and humiliating to me. Gotty, the mate, and the third hand had become creatures of activity, performing mysteries by the light of the moon; and it was as though, under cloak of other activities, they were jointly and solely concerned to hunt and harass me. Try as I might, I could nowhere find standing room from which I was not promptly dispossessed, upon it proving the very place where one or other had labours to perform; and it was my miserable fate to sit on nothing that was not immediately required for another use.

"'Ere, jump down there," said Gotty, having just got me off a coil of rope that he wanted. "Then you won't be in nobody's way;" and in obedience to this behest I lowered myself into a square cavity in the body of the vessel.

This did, indeed, prove a welcome asylum, and one from which I strove, but strove in vain, to intelligently follow the labyrinthine movements of my new companions. The one matter which made a definite impression on my mind was the strange rôle which the boy filled in this little drama of the sea. His co-operation was repeatedly requested, and though to each call he responded with cheerfulness and alacrity, in no instance did the quality of the service he rendered escape criticism of a most personal and discouraging character.

The commotion and clamour of rigging and human beings melted abruptly into a picture of moon-lit peace. All sails set, we were gliding past the red light of Southend pier; the cabin having swallowed all save the chief of my companions. He had come to the stern, where, controlling the tiller by subtle movements of his big feet,

9

he applied a complacent and reflective mind to the business of lighting a short and—if one might judge by its venerable aspect—cherished clay pipe. And presently Gotty was devoting his comfortable leisure to the instruction of my lay understanding concerning the lightness of the wind, the character of vessels we were passing, and other matters pertaining to the sea.

Amid these confidences he startled me by abruptly remarking:

"Git out the b'loon fore-sel!"

But I promptly recognised this to be other than a bewildering call on my own services, for the repetition of those words in a high key of rugged authority sufficiently attested that they were addressed to another quarter.

The mate scrambled into sight, and straightway set about wrestling with a considerable heap of sailcloth.

"But where's Jim?" demanded the skipper, and he proceeded indignantly to bawl: "Ere! Jim!"

A head and shoulders came guiltily into view, and the third hand was seen to be involved with a slice of food.

"What! At it again," cried Gotty. "Bless me if 'e ain't always eatin'. Bernarners, marmerlade, cakes—'e don't mind what it is. I b'lieve 'e'd eat a baby what'd died o' the smallpox."

Without deigning any reply to criticisms so uncalled for, the third hand lent his assistance to the task that occupied the mate; and presently a wider stretch of canvas met my eyes, and, our peaceful progress resumed, I was privileged to listen anew to words of nautical wisdom.

But the crew, who had again betaken themselves below, reappeared, unsummoned, when we were abreast the lights of Shoeburyness.

"'Eave the lead!" Gotty commanded.

The hand did so.

"Seven fathom!" he announced, as he drew in the line. He threw the lead again. "Seven fathom!" Then again and still again, with these successive readings:

"Seven fathom and a half." "Eight fathom less a quarter." "Eight fathom."

"Leggo!" thundered Gotty, and there was a noisy rush of chain as the mate released the anchor.

The spirit of toil and tumult, having thus descended once more on the *Breadwinner*, tarried awhile with us.

To what precise end the commander and crew were exercising their bodies and tongues so unsparingly, I was not at the moment privileged to learn. I merely saw that they were desperately set on shoving some long netty object into the sea, while the long netty object seemed equally determined not to go. But the final victory lay with brain and muscle, though it would seem that the mutinous thing of meshes indulged at the moment of defeat in one final spasm of misbehaviour. For, immediately after the heavy splash, Gotty's voice rose in panic lamentations:

"She's fast! Foul o' the rudder, ain't she! A nice thing ter 'appen! 'Ere, Jim—the boat-'ook, quick! And wery likely broke 'er templins! Don't be all night, Jim! She's tore—I lay she's tore. Yer know, it's all that young 'un's fault! 'E must 'ave 'ung on too long at that end, istid o' lettin' go. I wish 'e wouldn't shove 'is face in so much; 'e 'inders a lot more than 'e 'elps."

"I wasn't touching it!" came the boy's shrill, indignant protest.

"Then you ought to 'a bin!" roared Gotty, manifestly blind, in his perturbation, to the finer shades of equity.

Jabbing with a boat-hook yielded no relief to a situation that filled the entire ship's company with growing excitement, and presently I beheld Gotty scramble into the dinghy, that he might get at close quarters with what was amiss.

And now I had my second experience of the astonishing swiftness with which at sea, calm succeeds storm. The net having been prevailed upon to descend to its appointed duties, the crisis was not merely ended, but obliterated. Gotty and the boy were already exchanging friendly ideas about the possibility of rain before the dawn. It was as though one should be thrilled by fire and earthquake one minute, and the next be lulled by the honeysuckle calm of rural life on a summer afternoon. Nothing remained of the recent excitement but the accelerated speed at which it had set my heart sympathetically beating.

"It warn't nothin'," Gotty took his pipe from his mouth to politely explain, when I pressed for details, "only one o' them jumps catched under the rudder. It easy 'appens with the tide runnin' anyways strong ter lu'ard. Yer see," he added, by way of revealing the full significance of recent operations in their entirety, "we're standin' now. Draggin' comes afterwards."

And gradually I pieced together a conception of how we rode there at anchor above a broad stretch of net into which the tide was sweeping unwary whitebait.

"I don't 'ardly look ter catch more than a gallon," Gotty said feelingly, by way of supplement to information of a more general character. "The net's that rotten it ain't fit ter keep crows off a row of peas; only there's a noo 'un comin', and the sooner the better. Don't it stand ter reason," he asked argumentatively, "that yer can't catch a small fish like that—and wonderful quick a whitebait is!— when there's 'oles in the net big enough fer a twenty-pound codfish ter go through!"

I made haste to assure him, for what my opinion might be worth, that his contention appeared to be logically unassailable.

His next proposition found me even more readily acquiescent.

"A couple o' howers' shut-eye wouldn't do us no 'urt, would it? What do yer say if we turn in fer a spell?"

I followed him down into the low-pitched cabin, which, in the yellow illumination of a small lamp, proved to be full of legs and heads. I wriggled into the bunk whither Gotty directed me. Peering around, I was some time in assorting that strange scene into its component parts. Knowledge covered me with confusion. For the only other bunk was occupied by the mate; and the skipper, having given his bed to me, was lying on the floor. Nor could my protests avail against his kindness.

The boy crawled into some private hole of his own, and the third hand, I learnt, was lying on deck, wrapped in the topsail.

It was a little past midnight. Gotty set the alarm to a quarter to three; and, anon, snoring proclaimed slumber.

On being disturbed by what I fondly hoped was a premature demonstration on the part of the clock, I opened my reluctant eyes to unmistakable dawn. When I reached the deck, the net had already been lifted. Its freight of seaweed and little wriggling fishes was being emptied into a tub.

"That net's wusser than I thought," lamented Gotty as he shook his head over the smallness of the catch.

The mate, the third hand, and the boy got into the dinghy, and rowed away to a belt of sand that figured mistily in the cold grey morning. With another net they "dragged" in shallow water, the boy on shore walking with one end of the supporting line, the other end being fastened to the boat, which the two men rowed. After the warmth of the cabin, this occupation repelled by its suggestion of chilly discomfort.

Seeing me yawn, Gotty prescribed a little more sleep; nor was I reluctant to resume my tenancy of his bunk.

On reawakening two hours later, I found a fire in the cabin stove, bacon fizzing in the frying-pan, a loaf of bread on the floor, and my hospitable skipper ready to put a handful of tea in the kettle.

When the crew came back there was more head shaking; for they had captured only three quarts of whitebait, six dabs, two eels, and a dog-fish.

"Are you really going to discharge that boy?" I asked Gotty privately, when, at 9 a.m., we landed at Leigh jetty.

"Well yer see," he replied confidentially, "me and 'is father plays dominoes tergether," and while he was about it he was so good as to trace back the boy's pedigree, on both the mother's and father's side, for several generations—genealogical data which yielded proof that, however pronounced the youth's maritime deficiencies might be, at least he came of well-established Leigh stock.

Casual mention of the paternal grandfather left its mark on Gotty's conscience.

"I ain't bin round ter see old Ben," he confessed, "not fer a year, if it ain't more. And not bein' able ter get about, 'e don't see nobody if they don't go and see 'im. Pore ole feller! It only shows 'ow easy we all get fergot, same as if we was dead and gorn."

Nor did these reflections fail to quicken the social instincts of their author; for he resolved upon an immediate, if tardy, call upon his ancient and invalid neighbour.

"Ain't you comin' too?" he had the further happy inspiration to suggest; and thus it happened that I was introduced to the boy's grandfather, besides becoming acquainted with salient features in the character of his great-grandfather.

III

TWO GRIM STORIES

WE found old Ben sitting on his bed in the front parlour.

"There's a man," shouted Gotty when, he having opened the door, we stood unnoticed on the threshold, "what ain't never eaten any butter," and at this unusual form of introduction I stood blankly gazing at the strange face which slowly turned to greet us.

Like parchment stretched on a skull, it was lit by one bloodshot eye, the other having manifestly closed to scenes of this world. That salted relic of the last century was, head and body, all agog and a-quiver, as with the palsy.

"Sit ye both down—sit ye down," piped the old fellow, with hospitable motion of his skinny trembling hand.

"So you've never eaten any butter?" I said.

"Eh?" he asked, eagerly advancing his poor old wobbling head.

"So you don't eat butter?" (In a louder voice.)

"No," assented the patriarch. "The sight of it's enough for me; I can't abear it. When I was a boy of seven my mother give me a bit o' buttered toast. Urch! Never no more!"

The grimace bore witness that, after eighty years, the flavour was still an unpleasant memory in his mouth.

"Once," pursued the octogenarian, "I smelt some. Urch! I was nearly took ill."

Politeness suggesting an inquiry as to the state of his health, I learnt that one side of him—cheek, arm, trunk, and leg—had gone dead and shrivelled. But a finer illustration of the subordinate position of the flesh it was never my fortune to meet. For that moribund body, as was to be abundantly revealed, held a lively spirit.

"Why, old boy," cried Gotty, in sudden amazement, "if you ain't lost some front teeth!"

"Didn't ye know—didn't ye hear about it?" squeaked the old curiosity in apologetic consternation; and the right hand started on a slow zig-zag journey to the bereaved lower jaw. "It's close on two years since it 'appened."

14

"Two year ago," affirmed Gotty, who seemed much upset by his discovery, "old Ben 'ad a set o' teeth many young wimmin 'd be proud of."

"So they used to tell me—so they used to tell me," simpered the ancient.

"How did it happen?" I asked.

"It was along o' going to a Sunday school tea," came the crestfallen explanation. "I didn't want to go, but they kept on saying I must, so the end of it was I went. I cracked a lot o' nuts, and that's what begun it."

"What sort o' nuts?" demanded Gotty indignantly.

"Bruzil nuts."

"But hadn't they any nut-crackers?" I asked.

"'They 'ad sir– they 'ad," the old man replied miserably. "But I told 'em I'd got all my teeth."

"Bruzil nuts ain't fit fer a schoolboy to crack," shouted Gotty. "You ought ter be ashamed o' yerself."

"I did ought to 'a 'ad more sense," agreed the veteran humbly. "But that's what begun it."

"Begun it!" stormed Gotty. "What else did yer crack?"

"I e't a bakin' pear," confessed the venerable fisherman, looking guiltily from one to the other.

"A bakin' pear!" exclaimed the astonished Gotty. "What in the name o' wonder made yer do that?"

"It was a big 'un, an' hard as wood, and old Bill 'Art—you know Bill 'Art?—said 'e'd give me sixpence if I e't it. So I e't it, core an' all, and nex' mornin' the fust two teeth came out."

"And now, as a punishment," I suggested, "you have to live on sops?"

Old Ben blinked at me blankly.

"Milk puddens and gruel and sich-like," translated Gotty. "Don't yer understand the gentleman's meanin'?"

"Who? Me!" expostulated old Ben. "Me eat gruel? Ercourse not! Plum pudden's more to my likin'. What I'd jest fancy now"—and a dreamy ecstasy shone in the bloodshot eye—"'ud be a dumplin'—a big dumplin'."

"'Ear 'im! Jest 'ear 'im!" said Gotty in a proud undertone. "A dumplin', and 'im gettin' on fer ninety;" and, these words reminding him that old Ben was something of an invalid, he shouted sympathetically in his ear:

"D'yer mind our smoking—the terbacca don't tickle yer throat, or nothin'?"

"Lor' bless yer, no," spluttered the hospitable old soul. "I likes it."

"You don't smoke yourself?" I asked.

"No, and never did," he replied; "and there's somethin' I can tell yer, and you'll find my words come true—I shan't take to it now."

Despite the paralysed cheek, the absence of flesh, and the bloodshot eye, old Ben puckered his countenance into an alluring smile.

"A teetotaller, too?" I queried.

"No, no. I was never what you'd call a 'eavy drinker, but I likes my three 'a'porth o' beer last thing at night."

"D'yer remember them times we 'ad," shouted Gotty "when the *Caister* went down? The silk and sich-like we brought 'ome?"

"Ercourse I do," replied the old man. "Didn't I get two sides o' bacon out of her? And lovely bacon it was!"

The poor, withered hand drifted about in a vain effort to reach Gotty's ribs.

"'Ere," he squeaked with growing geniality, "d'yer mind that brig what went ashore out 'ere? Oringes, nuts, a'monds! My! what a time we did 'ave to be sure. Wasn't they lovely oringes?"

"They was," bawled Gotty. "And I never tasted better a'monds not afore or since."

"No more didn't I," agreed the elderly authority on delicacies, "and seeing as you could 'ave pailfuls fer nothing, they was cheaper 'n the cigars my father used ter bring 'ome on dark nights."

A chuckle entered into competition with the palsy, and he made a heroic effort to wink the bloodshot eye.

"Your father was a smuggler?" I asked.

"Lor' bless yer—'e was always at it. Cigars, spirits, scent—our cellar was mostly 'alf full o' stuff. Him and a man named Joe Atkins was partners, and when there warn't no moon—Who's that?"

For the door had opened, and an elderly navvy of commanding proportions stood irresolute at the threshold.

"Mrs. Smith in?" he broke the awkward silence by asking.

"She won't be long," quavered old Ben, when Gotty had repeated the inquiry in his ear. "If you'd jest step inside, please. I know she was expectin' her cousin Charles."

"That's me," exclaimed the great healthy man; "Charles Vincent, from 'Adleigh Colerny."

"Do come in," pleaded the poor old helpless host—an invitation which, seeing the stranger still hesitate, Gotty and I stoutly supported.

"Yuss, but I don't want to be in the way, yer know," said the visitor, as, yielding under pressure, he entered, closed the door behind him, and took the chair I ventured to place at his disposal.

"You won't be in no one's way," Gotty assured him. "It's a fine day, mate, ain't it?"

"You're right," agreed the newcomer, mopping his great ruddy temples with the sleeves of his coat. "But you gentlemen ain't a-going to let me spoil your talk, now, are you?"

I assured him to the contrary, and demonstrated the fact.

"You were saying," I reminded old Ben, "your father used to go smuggling?"

"There was 'ardly a fortnight pass," the lively old wreck replied, "but he and Joe Atkins 'd be out in their whaler. There wasn't no secret about it. Lord bless yer! Everybody knowed what they was after—everybody, I mean, except them whose biz'nis it was to find out. It was along of them carryings on that my pore father came by 'is end."

"How did it happen?" I inquired; and the expression on the navvy's face—though he made a praiseworthy effort to disguise his interest—plainly asked the same question.

"They'd bin to a ship at the Nore, what they got a lot of rum out of, and my pore father, being pertic'lar fond of rum, took more than was good fer 'im. He fell overboard and was drownded."

"Couldn't he swim?" I asked.

"There wasn't many could swim better; but swimming ain't going to 'elp a man what's three parts gone."

"But you would think," said the navvy, his policy of self-efface-ment completely breaking down, "'e might 'ave kept afloat, drunk or sober, till the other bloke 'ad time to pull 'im out."

"That right enough," agreed the antique orphan, politely wob-bling his face round in the direction of his new auditor. "But Joe Atkins was another as was pertic'lar fond of rum. They was a pretty pair, that they was, and Joe Atkins was 'anging on ter the tiller 'alf asleep, and didn't notice my father was gorn not till the whaler come alongside the jetty. That oughter a' bin a lesson to many, I'm sure it ought," continued the old man, addressing himself more particularly to me. "My father was never seen no more but twenty years afterwards—I ain't tellin' yer no story—'is boots was picked up in a trawl and brought ashore."

"How do you know they were his boots?" the navvy and I asked simultaneously.

"Give me time to tell yer," quavered the oldest inhabitant.

"That's what I was a-comin' to. Nobody didn't 'ave any thought whose boots they might be, but when the cobbler come to see 'em he knew 'em at once, along o' 'aving put a pertic'lar kind o' patch on fer my father."

"How very remarkable," was my appreciative comment.

"There's many people," said Gotty earnestly, "wouldn't believe 'ow long anything will last, covered over with sand at the bottom. That 'ere blue-jacket's cap what Jim Winter found with the 'alf sovereigns in—you may depend that 'ad laid there a tidy time, fer there was somebody said caps that shape 'adn't been wore in the navy fer sixty year."

"What was the date on the money?" asked the navvy keenly.

"Jim didn't keep it long enough," Gotty explained, "ter find out. When he picked the cap out o' the trawl 'e started ter shake at and 'it it ter git the sand out, and the three 'alf sov'rins fell out on deck. Yer see, 'e didn't 'ave no thought there might be somethin' in the linin', though that's jest where a blue-jacket often will stow a bit o' money, the same as needle and thread, and sich-like. Jim only 'ad jest time ter see them coins when they'd rolled through the scuppers and gorn for ever. Swear! By all accounts 'e carried on most disgraceful; only it's enough to upset anybody, losin' a bit o' money like that,"

"No mistake," agreed the navvy.

"What extraordinary things do happen at sea!" I was moved to remark.

"Yuss," said the navvy; "But there's more hextriordinary things 'appen on shore"—an observation which I thought showed a very proper spirit in a landsman. "I could tell yer somethin'," he added, darkly, "only you wouldn't berlieve it?"

"I would try," I said humbly.

"If I was ter tell yer," he went on, almost defiantly, "that a man could get six months' 'ard labour fer a dream, you'd call me a liar, wouldn't you?"

Before I had time to clear my character from this ungenerous suspicion, old Ben intervened.

"I don't 'ear what 'e says!" he wailed, anxiously flopping his old head at Gotty and me, by way of invoking our aid to see he was not robbed by aural infirmity of such good things as might be going.

"I was just a-saying," said the navvy, thoughtfully drawing his chair close to the bed, and so getting into close communication with the veteran's serviceable ear—"no one wouldn't berlieve a man could go to quod for a dream."

18

"No—no more they would!" came the polite acquiescence, accompanied by a negative nodding of the head that was not all palsy.

"That's what 'appened to me!" continued the robust navvy.

"Did it though!" squeaked the deeply interested old invalid. "'Ow was that?"

"Why, it was like this 'ere," said the giant of clay and corduroy, fairly settling down to tell his story. "I'd been gorn to bed some time when I suddenly found out I was dead."

"Lor'!" gasped the ancient listener, his frail anatomy visibly affected by shock.

"There's no knowing," pursued the narrator, "what things you won't dream sometimes. So I woke up the missis and told her I was dead. 'Dear me,' she says, 'so you are.' Then she goes on to say as 'ow it was rather awkward, as there wasn't no money to bury me with. 'Oh, dear,' says I, 'no more there is:' and then I began to worry and worry whatever should we do about it. At last I gets an idea, so I dresses myself and goes out, and 'urries down to the yard where I worked, I goes up the wooden stairs to the office where we draws our money every Friday, and there I sees the man what was in the habit of paying us. 'Hullo!' he says, 'you're looking queer. What's up?' 'I'm dead,' I says—only you must remember what I'm telling you was only a dream."

"Right-o!" said Gotty, with a wink to me. The strain on other faculties of our infirm host had temporarily bereft him of the power of speech.

"'I'm dead,' I says," continued the navvy stolidly, "'and I want you to lend me a quid so as my old woman 'll be able to bury me.' 'Right you are,' says he, and he puts a sovereign down on the desk. 'Thank you,' says I, and I goes off with the money, taking partic'lar care, being dead, how I went downstairs, so as I shouldn't fall and drop it. That was all I kept thinking of—I mustn't drop the money, I mustn't drop the money or else my missis wouldn't be able to bury me. Then I thought to myself how easy it was to drop a sovereign, and 'ow I'd better get it changed. So having got past the Dock-gates I dropped into the 'Artichoke,' which was a house I used, and there—"

"Not the 'Arterchoke' at East India Docks!" exclaimed Gotty, in sudden excitement.

"That's it. Used to be kept by a man of the name of Woods, only it's fifteen years ago what I'm talking about."

"I know the 'Arterchoke' well!" proclaimed Gotty. "Ercourse I do!" and he relapsed into the office of a listener with greatly augmented interest.

"There was Mr. Woods behind the bar just as real as life. 'Hullo,' says Mr. Woods, 'what's the matter? You do look queer.' 'Yuss, I've been told that before,' I says. 'It's because I'm dead,' 'Well, I am sorry,' says Mr Woods, for we'd always been a bit friendly. Then I called for a screw of bacca, and puts down the sov'rin, only looking very careful all round to see no one didn't steal it. There was one cove in partic'lar, a cove with a Glengarry cap, what I didn't 'alf like the looks of, and I'd got my eye on him when Mr. Woods came and put the change on the counter. Just as I was going to take it up that bloke made a grab, and I was so frightened to think of losing the money that I turned round and landed him one as hard as I could. Then I woke up, and what d'yer think had 'appened?''

"I dunno," admitted Gotty.

"Why, blowed if I hadn't hit my old woman! All the other part of the dream hadn't been anything, only a dream; but the hitting was real. The missus had copped most of it, and my fist had gone on against the bed-post, so my hand was cut pretty bad. Well, the missus took on dreadful, and before I hardly knew what'd happened she'd run away screaming and locked the door behind her. She went off to her mother, what was a bit of an old cat; so when I broke the door open in the morning I didn't see nothing of her. I went off to work jest the same as usual, but when I come out of the yard in the dinner hour there were two coves with a bit of paper. ''Ere, Vincent,' they says to me, 'we've got a summons against you for assaulting your wife.' That was the old cat—she'd put up the missis to take out a summons."

"Did she, though!" commented Gotty, with indignant sympathy.

"When I got to the police court I didn't 'ardly know my old woman, her face was that wrapped up in bandages. She told Mr. Shiel all about it. 'We'd 'ad a few words before going to bed,' she says, and that was right enough—just a little jangle about money for the 'ousekeeping, though I'd clean forgotten all about it. 'And when I'd gone to sleep,' she says, 'he hit me a vilent blow—the coward!' That was right enough, too, though I 'adn't meant to. 'What 'ave you got to say for yourself?' says the beak pretty savage like, to me. 'It was all,' I says, 'because I'd 'ad a dream,' I says. 'Yuss,' says Mr Shiel, ''aving those sort of dreams comes of indigestion, and I'm a-going to send you to a place where you won't 'ave indigestion no more, 'cos the feeding's arranged too careful. Six months 'ard''

"Oh!"—from Gotty—" 'e didn't 'alf lay it on thick then."

"After this I found myself in Wandsworth, and a little of Wandsworth goes a long way, you take my word. I 'adn't done nothing; but they couldn't 'ave treated me more like a dog if I killed a perliceman. You dersn't 'ardly open yer mouth. The second day a warder called me, and I didn't 'ear; so he wanted to know why I 'adn't answered when he spoke first. ''Cos I didn't 'ear,' I says. 'Why don't you talk louder?' I says. Blessed if 'e didn't report me for impidence, and I got three days on bread and water. I found out after a bit it don't do to say anything, nor yet know anything in prison; and if anyone comes along and asks you what you're doing, it's best to say, 'I dunno, sir.'"

"That's a true word," murmured Gotty.

"I 'ad a visit from the parson one day, and he asks me what I was in for, and then before I could tell him he looks at a paper in his 'and and says, 'Assaulting yer wife! Oh,' he says, 'that's very wicked.' Well, I dunno why I said it, except that he'd gone and called me wicked without first finding out if I'd done it. So I says, off-hand like, 'Oh she deserved it;' and then 'e shook his 'ead, and said 'e 'oped I'd feel sorry some day, and I never saw any more of the parson except on Sundays."

"And wery likely didn't want to," commented the commander of the *Breadwinner*.

"'E could come or 'e could stay away—it didn't make no odds to me," testified the impartial ex-prisoner. "But I shan't never ferget a funny thing what 'appened when I first went there. I'd been three days without eating any of the black bread, 'cos I couldn't fancy it; and I was so hungry I was just fancying the skilly, which isn't 'alf bad stuff, and you get a good lot."

"So you do," testified Gotty. "I know, fer I've 'ad some," he added in a burst of brotherly confidence.

"Well, the warder come in and filled my can, and I took it up to drink it, when what do I see but a big black beetle floating on the top. I felt that disappointed I set up a 'owl for the warder to come back. 'What's all this row about,' he says. 'Look 'ere,' I says, "ere's a black beetle.' 'Well, don't holler,' says 'e 'or the others 'll be wanting one, and we 'aven't got enough to go round,' and with that he banged the door again and took himself off. . . . Hullo! Jane, old girl!"

And the arrival of Mrs. Smith served to remind Gotty that it was time we brought our friendly call to a conclusion.

IV

THE STRANDED MARINER

OTHER matters making their claim upon my time, a fortnight elapsed before, on revisiting Leigh, I found that misfortune had darkened the little home along the alley.

Mrs. Gotty, that round woman, gave me the ill tidings. Her husband had ceased to command the *Breadwinner*. The promoted mate now guided her helm.

"It's what had to come," said the good soul quietly. "His mother owning the boat and him grown a fine young man, with a good head-piece, they do say."

"And Gotty hasn't found another berth yet."

"No, sir, and I'm afraid he's not likely to—not before the winter. He's out every day looking for work; for it's a worry, with nothing coming in, and all the expenses getting due; and he thinks it all over in his head, that perhaps he might do this, and perhaps he might do something else. It's wonderful, sir, the things he does think of!"

Going to the staircase, she summoned her husband by his Christian name, mentioning that some one had called to see him. It might have been the vicar or a rate-collector, for any clue she gave; and I was consequently the more impressed by the homely freedom of toilet in which, when the creaking stairs had yielded their burden, he presented himself.

Bare-legged, and arrayed merely in a shirt and knickerbockers, he entered the parlour clasping a half-naked child in his arms.

He crushed my hand in his great paw, and his large face lit with hearty greeting. Gotty out of work was still the same Gotty.

The child nestled a little head of curls against his neck.

"'E does love 'is uncle, that 'e do," exclaimed the gratified fisherman, patting the grubby little cheek. "But"—turning to me with an injured air—"'e don't take no notice of me in bed. He'll crawl to 'is auntie and cuddle 'er, but 'e won't cuddle me."

"So you've left your ship, Gotty?"

"Yes," was the miserable reply; "I ran 'er aground."

"You ran her aground!"

"I'd no right to do it, I'll allow," replied the old fellow humbly, "and I never did sech a thing afore. We was comin' out of the Gut, and roundin' the bank into deep water, but I put her about jest 'alf a minute too quick, and we went on the sand. There warn't no 'arm done nor time wasted, fer the matter o' that, as it give me my charnse ter clean 'er bottom, what she wanted done wonderful bad. So arter I'd scraped off the barnicles, it wasn't two howers afore we flitted agin, and we went and got four boxes of bait, which was better 'n what most of the other borleys got that morning."

"But the owner took a serious view?"

"It was like this: when we goes aground, the owner's son—'im as was my mate, and a wery good mate too—'e gits into the punt and rows ashore, and we never see no more of 'im that day. Nat'ral like, I suppose he told 'is mother, and next day I gets a letter ter say they wouldn't want me no more after the Saturday. It was bound to 'appen sooner or later—'im a grown man now; and it ain't likely, bein' a son of the owner, 'e was always goin' to take orders from somebody else."

"What's to be done?"

"Ah, now you've arsked me somethin'. A job wants findin'—you wouldn't berlieve. Things is reg'lar chronic. I knowed there wasn't no charnse fer skipper, so I tries to git took on as mate. But there ain't no boat what wants a mate, and several waitin' ter go! So I thought, well, I won't be done—fer I can't abear walkin' the streets and nothin' to do. It gives me the fair sick. I ain't like some—'angin' about, day after day, week after week, and wouldn't say thank you if you give 'em a job. I like a bit of graft, and always did—what's more, my food don't taste comfortable if you understand my meaning', when I ain't doin' nothin'. So I tries if there was a charnse of a bit o' sand-'eavin' or unloadin' barges which is work I've bin used to, and got my own fly-tool and all. But that ain't no better—You'll find six or a dozen waitin' where there's only work fer one."

I was deeply grieved to find my old friend not merely deposed from his dignified, and presumably lucrative command, but reduced to hunt humbly for any odd job that a callous world might have to offer; and surprised and indignant to find a skipper's tenure of office so insecure, I presently found myself offering this sage counsel:

"You ought to have your own fishing smack, Gotty. Then you couldn't be dismissed, and you would pocket the owner's share as well as the skipper's;" and indeed this is a world in which nearly all the beautiful logic is uttered by theorists.

As for Gotty, he could not have smiled in a more abashed and, school-girl fashion if I had told him he ought to be the Archbishop of Canterbury.

"Do you 'appen ter know," he asked, "what a borley costs? You can't get a noo 'un—not if you 'ave it built—under three 'undred and twenty pound!"

"Well," I retorted (for your idealist is impatient of mere practical facts), "why haven't you saved some money and bought a second-hand one?"

"Because," he replied with deliberation—and preceding the remark by dramatically placing the half naked child on the floor—"because I'm a fool. There you are: I can't say fairer than that. Still!" he conscientiously added, as though anxious to deal out even-handed justice even to himself, "I *ain't* saved the money—like many more. So what's the good o' talkin'?"

Yet out of a subject apparently so barren of utility, he nevertheless did manage to extract (and I welcomed this evidence of the buoyant optimism which I had suspected as an important element in his engaging character) some faint possibility of fruitfulness.

"If you might 'appen to know anybody," he remarked, in dulcet accents, "what'd like ter own a borley, or "—his mind giving birth to a still more rosy fancy—"if you could 'andle a bit o' money yourself as you'd like ter see bring in a bit more, I could keep my eyes open fer one goin' cheap."

The dreamer and the practical man had abruptly changed places.

I assured him, promptly and sincerely, that, greatly as I should rejoice in an opportunity to engage him for skipper, I could not contemplate the necessary preliminary of becoming owner, as, among my most unlicensed aspirations, the possession of a fishing smack had never found a place, and as, moreover, I should hesitate to engage in a business to which I had been a life-long stranger.

In reply to the remarks of which I have given a bald summary, Gotty said, cheerfully enough:

"As fur as not knowin' nothin' about it goes, that don't matter at all. You don't 'ave ter know nothin' about it, not if you're the owner! I could easy look after the boat, and see that nothin' didn't go wrong."

But, let the way be never so smooth, I refused to contemplate that short-cut to opulence.

"You may think dif'rent," said far-seeing Gotty, "when you've turned it over in your mind."

Meanwhile, by way of putting time to more practical use, I asked if he had literally earned no money since leaving the bawley.

"I 'ad one bit o' luck," he testified—"a little coalboat from the 'Umber what puts 'er stuff ashore 'ere. Comes up in the night she does mostly; and luck's the right word fer it, too. There was two others gone out arter the job afore me, but I didn't know that till I see 'em asleep in their boat made fast agin the 'ead of Southend pier. They'd got tired of waitin', seemin'ly, so I didn't wake 'em up, pore dears, but took and rowed away ter the east'ard, and it wasn't much arter three when the coal-boat come along, and, being first aboard, I got the job ter 'elp unload 'er."

"Do you go out in your dinghy?"

"No, it's one I borrer. I've got a punt of my own—leastways, I'ad one, fer she don't keep the water out now, and too old for mendin'."

"So you can't do any fishing?"

"Well, I've been thinking"—Gotty scratched his head thoughtfully—"there's a place I know where you can wade out when the water's up, and catch 'em among the reeds in yer 'and. That's what I'm going to try next, and I've made a basket a purpose."

From a cupboard, with loving hands, he drew forth a large, flat basket, ingeniously faced with a net.

"If nothing else ain't no good," said the ex-skipper bravely, "there's 'awkin'. But I 'ope it won't come to 'awkin'. It's fair 'eart-breaking, 'awkin' is. I know becos I've tried."

"You've tried a good many things?"

"And p'raps you'd be surprised what brought in most money. Selling cockles in the Walworth Road is what I did best at. I catched 'em down 'ere in the morning, and sold 'em up in London nice and fresh the same evening. But all that got altered when so many costers took it up, and they buy 'em cheaper in the market than it pays you to take 'em up yourself."

"You had a regular pitch?"

"Yes—always the same spot, and lots of people wouldn't buy cockles from no one else. They got to know mine was clean and fresh and sometimes I'd turn over six and twenty shillin's—all in 'a'porths and 'alf pints. One night—jest ter show yer—I got through four quarts of winegar. That was the day I saw somethin' what gives me the cold creeps to think of—one of them awful Whitechapel murders."

"Indeed!"

"I'd bought a large feather bed and a 'anging lookin'-glass with part of the money, and after I'd took my stall to the lodgin' 'ouse, I put the bed and lookin' glass on my 'ead, and carried 'em to Fenchurch Street, where I give a perliceman sixpence ter mind 'em.

25

You see, there wasn't no train for a hower or so, and I thought I'd jest 'ave a little walk nice and comfortable. Going through Tooley Street I see a perliceman bendin' over somethin', and when I come up, that's what it was—the pore thing was quite dead, and a sight I never shall forgit. What was funny, I knew the perliceman, and 'e knew me, along o' 'im 'aving bin stationed at Southend. 'Ponto,' 'e says ter me—fer that's one of the names I'm called by—'Ponto, if you'd bin 'ere a few minutes ago, you'd 'ave seed a awful deed!' When I got 'ome to Leigh that morning I didn't want no brekfast. It's the worst turn I ever 'ad—no; I'm tellin' a lie. I fergot the railway accident what me and the missis was in!''

"When was that?

"When I was bringin' 'er 'ome from Chemsford, where she'd bin spendin' a week's 'oliday arter 'aving the fever. You never 'eard sech a bang, and the carriage we was in run 'alf up the bank. There was a colligion betwixt me and the missis, what had bin sitting oppersite one another; and arter it was all over a gentleman come up—a nice-spoken gentleman, 'e was, and wanted ter know if we was 'urt—and when I told 'im about the missis 'aving jest 'ad the fever, 'e arsked if I'd take ten pound and say no more about it. 'Wery good, sir,' I says, so they gave me the money, and I don't mind 'ow soon I git another charnse like it. Fer that ten pound come in wonderful 'andy, and we didn't 'ave no bones broken—only my missis's bonnet bein' stove in, she 'aving butted me fair in the face.''

Conversation passing to Leigh regatta, fixed for the following Saturday, I was not a little touched to find that the old champion proposed to abstain from the greasy pole competition.

"Yuss,'' he said, without spirit, "I'll stand aside fer someone else ter git it. Yer see, what with worry, and not 'aving yer meals reg'lar, some'ow I don't seem ter care about it this year. And I dessay,'' he added thoughtfully, "I ain't quite so young as I once was; and a shillin' to enter yer name and all! No; I've 'ad my innin's.''

At least I could claim a friend's privilege to put down his name, leaving him to compete or not as might be determined by his inclination on the day; and, this point settled, I proceeded to open up a new subject for thought, which chanced to be one falling within the narrower scope of my own domestic interests, to wit, the necessity under which I laboured to raise a shed in my back garden, spaces under the flooring having proved a congenial residence for a rat.

At the word "rat,'' Gotty looked, as I was no less surprised than pleased to see, ten years younger; and, upon his kindly and earnest suggestion, it was decided that, on the following afternoon, he should come over to Westcliff and lend a hand in hoisting the little wooden building.

The attitude of average British manhood towards creatures of the class I have named has ever been a subject of respectful mystification to me; and the morrow added to my experience of a baffling human enigma. Gotty came to my house in the company of a short man carrying an empty sack; and two children arriving at a Christmas party could not have worn expressions of more eager and cheerful interest.

Yet it immediately became manifest that the little man's mental complacency was seared by one sharp regret.

"I oughter 'a brought my dawg!" he told me, even while I was still a stranger to his identity, and knew not to what I owed the pleasure of his society.

"Bert Williams!" exclaimed Gotty, with an introductory jerk of his thumb. "'E arsked if 'e mightn't come and lend a 'and, seein' 'e's 'ad a deal ter do with rats. Only, that torpeder 'aving made me late, I wouldn't let 'im go 'ome fer 'is terrier. Did yer 'ear about old Salters' pickin' up the torpeder? No! Oh a reg'lar beauty, all shinin' lovely. 'E brought it ashore larst night. It wouldn't 'ave bin 'alf an hour after you was gorn. And another thing!. . . . "

Guilty of the solecism of whispering in company, Gotty leaned forward and imparted into my private ear the welcome tidings that, the mate of a shrimping bawley having fallen ill, he had been temporarily engaged in the invalid's place.

Meanwhile the little man was growing impatient, and his inquiry as to the whereabouts of the rat impelled me, without further loss of time, to lead my visitors to the back of the premises.

Their first concern was to proceed on tiptoe along each side of the shed, earnestly scrutinising its base and exchanging thoughts in an impressive undertone. Then the little man, unloosening a red kerchief from around his neck, stuffed it with precision into a hole his expert eye had detected at one end of the structure; while Gotty, working swiftly with pieces of broken flowerpot and a handful of mould, sealed up a similar aperture at the other end.

Walking and talking now with greater freedom, they set about overhauling my garden properties in search of implements suitable to their needs. A spade, a fork, a stout piece of timber, and seven bricks were placed handy for use, on one side of the shed; and, still with an eye to accessory weapons of offence, Gotty critically regarded the garden roller. But his preference proved to lie elsewhere, and he added the coal hammer and a birch broom to the varied armoury.

If in these formidable preparations I lent no active co-operation, the explanaton lay in the circumstance that, so far from desiring the rat to be killed—let alone annihilated—I personally harboured no worse wish concerning him than that he should make his home elsewhere. Nay, he had been welcome to retain the lodging of his choice (for no one could desire a more gentle mannered old rat than he had shown himself to be, on the several occasions of my seeing him come forth to eat crumbs thrown down for sparrows) were it not that, in the feminine element of my household, misgivings were based on the possibility of the pioneer rodent establishing a colony of his kind.

But a feeling of delicacy forbade me to communicate these sentiments to my two visitors, whose labours had now entered a critical stage. Having levered up a corner of the shed (and here a clothes' prop came in handy) by adroit pressure of their feet, they loomed above the resulting crevice with an upraised selection of instruments of destruction that I have enumerated.

But, to my secret relief, the rat came not forth to his doom; so that my strategists adopted the expedient of prodding for their quarry with a second clothes' prop. A negative result also attending these searching measures, muscular Gotty raised the opposite end of the shed a discreet inch or so what time his nimble associate, the fork in one hand and two bricks in the other, kept watch and ward almost simultaneously on all sides of the building. And presently, dignity yielding to doubt, the pair of hunters were upon their hands and knees, peering in disgust down each vacant space between the joists.

Having encountered Mr. Bert Williams' gaze of stony suspicion, I was in a measure relieved when, in the form of nibbled paper, Gotty in some excitement drew forth a handful of unimpeachable evidence to my *bona-fides*. However, it could no longer be doubted that this rathunt was lacking in a vital factor; and accordingly, with a painful abatement of zeal, the baulked enthusiasts occupied themselves in sheering up the shed to my requirements, free ingress of light to the arena below the floor being calculated, as I conjectured, to correct its character as a rendezvous for rats.

Later, a strange thing came to pass. My visitors were already refreshing themselves, after their labours, with afternoon tea on the lawn, when I espied the rat— all indifferent to the fact that I had company, and with the jaded air of one who, having travelled far, was glad to be home again—ambling through my snap-dragons in the direction of the shed. This tardy arrival of the game, when the hunt was all over, so scattered my wits that, without a thought for the consequences, I cried:

"There he goes!"

Instantly the little man had exchanged his tea-cup for the spade, while Gotty, in place of a biscuit, was brandishing a brick. Having thrust the broom into my hand, he took upon himself the command of the field. Posting his ally at the shrubbery into which the startled rat had retreated, he ordered me to the opposite flower-border, and himself rushed off to the strawberry bed.

So swift were the developments that I had no time for a warning shout, expressive of concern for my plants, when, by great good luck, the rat reappeared in my sphere of operations. As he ran along the border, I ran beside him along the gravel walk, and, ere there was time for reinforcements to arrive, he had found a hole in the fence, and gone safely into the next-door garden.

I turned to behold two faces aghast with the spirit of protest.

"Why didn't you 'it 'im? "Why didn't yer jab 'im with the broom?" they asked in unison.

"Because," I explained, "I did not want to hurt my flowers;" and the look on Mr. Bert Williams' face when, five minutes later, I parted from him at the front gate, clearly revealed the opinion that, though he did not mind taking the shilling, I was no sportsman.

V

OFF THE POLE

AFTER the fatigues of the chase, Gotty and I took a gentle stroll; and he gave me copious details of an affair that had made a vivid impression on his mind.

It seemed that old Salters, chancing to be looking over the side of his bawley, saw the bright torpedo approaching through the ripples at the propulsion of the tide—a sight that would have been sufficiently disconcerting to a timid person. But old Salters, a stranger to hysteria, lost no time in hitching a piece of rope around the fearsome thing, his gratification at removing a peril to shipping being strengthened by thoughts of the reward that might reasonably be expected from a grateful Navy.

At the parental command, his sons got into the dinghy and rowed their prize to Leigh.

Gotty, when he heard of the strange capture just landed at the jetty, seemed to have acted with considerable discretion.

"I didn't go anywheres nigh it," he assured me.

"It *were* loaded, don't I tell yer!" was his dignified rebuke at a word of scepticism I presently let fall. "This mornin' I see a lot o' shiny stuff on the shore—like glowworms; and young Alf Thompson says to me, 'D'yer know what that is, Ponto?' 'No,' I says, 'I don't:' and no more I didn't. 'It's what they've took out of that torpeder,' 'e says; and when I come ter look at the torpeder, what 'ad bin locked up all night in the shed, they showed me where its innards was all clent out. The way them coastguards 'ad fixed it up, a baby might 'ave played with it. That shiny stuff was the part as goes off, and I didn't mind 'ow soon the tide come up and washed it away. . . . Well, did you ever!"

Within two miles of his ancient fishing village, Gotty was nevertheless on unfamiliar ground. The broad thoroughfare of Westcliff shops had, on a sudden, hypnotised him.

Presently the awed reverie was broken:

"If any one was ter step out the grave now, 'avin' knowed this as a brickfield, they'd open their eyes, I know they would!"

He stopped before a hosier's, and gazed with the parted jaws of astonishment at a window dressed throughout with gentlemen's ties.

"I never 'ad one on only wunst," came the dreamy reminiscence. "It was my weddin' day, and my wife's sister come and 'itched it on. Talk about feelin' silly—I went about fair ashamed."

Proceeding a few more paces, he again paused, his eye enthralled by a tobacconist's barricade of dainty tins and packets.

"Don't they get 'em up smart! Not 'alf they don't;" and the glowing vision served to remind him that, some weeks before, a gentleman gave him a brightly-encased ounce like one of those. "And I ain't smoked it yet," he added impressively.

"How is that?" I asked.

"Oppertoonity's a fine thing," he replied, with a wink that deepened the mystery. "Why, it was this way. When I got 'ome and showed it to the missis, she says, 'Give it to me;' and she took it. 'I'm a-going to keep that in a safe place,' she says, 'and one day you shall 'ave it fer a surprise.' If I've arsked 'er fer that terbacca wunst, I suppose I've arsked 'er a 'undred times. But it's always 'No; you ain' a-going to 'ave it'. What she means by it I dunno."

I frivolously remarked, "Perhaps she intends to smoke it herself" —words immediately regretted; for Gotty put me to shame by supposing me serious.

"No," he said, with simple earnestness, "she don't smoke. Nor snuff," he added, with solemn enthusiasm. "Nor spirits or lickers of any sort. Only beer. Now and again she might fancy a glass of beer, but not often."

Loth to be discussing a lady behind her back, I asked if Leigh fisherman had ever caught a torpedo before.

"They may 'ave; I dunno," Gotty replied. "Only there's one what ain't loaded that nobody 'asn't caught yet, and not fer the want of tryin'! It's on the bottom off Sheernest, and, like many more, I've sometimes got the ground rope ath'art it, and 'auled in slow and careful, seein' there's a reward offered fer those as picks it up. But it always falls free! It must be nigh on eight year we've bin trying after that torpeder, and sometimes I get afraid it'll all rust away and nobody 'ave the reward."

Conversation turning to the forthcoming regatta, I found Gotty disposed, on second thoughts, to risk his reputation on the greasy pole.

When, on the day, I put in a somewhat belated appearance at the festival, there, sure enough, was the local champion in process of being rowed out to the barge.

There was a calm, with plenty of sunshine and spectators. Strange craft with brown sails had come from neighbouring anchorages to look on. Competing yachts loitered in the middle distance like a cloud of drugged butterflies. But I was looking at the figure in the boat.

In white ducks, blue jersey, and the purple sleeve cap of a pirate, the upright veteran, with his big black eyebrows and square white beard, his head so proudly poised, caused a public sensation.

"There's Gotty—there he goes!" yelled the excited juniors.

"If Ponto ain't a-going in for it again!" cried an admiring old soul, hatless and in her apron.

A group of brother-fishers bent their eyes on the dinghy with a marked absence of fervour.

"At 'is time of life!" commented one tartly.

"He's a old fool," argued another, "not to know 'e can't do what 'e could. A young 'un's game, too! It stands ter reason."

"We shall see," said a third darkly, "what we shall see."

Gotty had boarded the barge, and I saw him in cheerful conversation with members of the committee. Then he went to the vessel's stern, and, to the delight of the massed youth of Leigh, danced on one leg what time he gaily brandished its fellow in the air. Next he stepped to the bow, and waggishly shook his left fist at the small flag exhibited at the end of the greasy pole.

All this while he drank in the popular applause, his face aglow with gratification. It was his hour. Once again he stood forth to vindicate his supremacy in the arena of accustomed triumph—once more he was going to show them.

I stood on the crowded jetty jammed beside an old hawker in whose basket lay a dead rabbit. He had long gazed open-eyed, and now his thoughts found tongue.

"Crikey! That's the bloke I saw walk the pole at Southend twenty year ago. It's 'im—I'll lay me oath it's 'im. The ole sport!" And resting an open palm against his right cheek, he rapturously yelled "Bravo!"

For a little time Gotty was lost to sight, and when he reappeared his toilet had undergone a transformation. In a thin cotton shirt and old duck trousers he was ready for the water.

The throng growing irksome, I elbowed my way to the stairs, where I found an elderly fisherman willing to row me out to the flotilla of dinghies encircling the barge.

"I'd like to see Gotty win," was my attempt to open up a little conversation.

"Well, 'e ain't goin' to," curtly rejoined the fisherman, and we temporarily relapsed into a cold silence.

"Gotty always has won, hasn't he?" I said, trying again.

"That's the one what's going to win," replied the old man severely, as he pointed to a fine young fellow who, arrayed in a swimming costume, was about to open the competition. "That's Fred Burroughs, that is, and new to the game, but 'e's going to do all the winning for some years, you mark my words."

Burroughs walked three steps along the pole and calmly dived off. Then came old Gotty, who did the same. For their obvious want of effort I was prepared by the knowledge that, by a rule of the competition, success must be preceded by at least three failures.

Then came some half-dozen youngsters who, by promptly and unintentionally losing their foothold of the slippery spar, caused spasm of public pleasure.

It all was repeated twice, the number of accessory competitors, however, manifesting a tendency to shrink. Now I began to look in earnest.

Burroughs started with great deliberation, but at a third of the distance equilibrium was lost, and he went in with a heavy splash.

And now Gotty. Absolutely confident, he walked smilingly along half the length. Suddenly I saw the smile vanish. A foot had slipped. Up went his hands. The heavy old chap fell into the water with a wet thud.

Of the novices there were but two tough survivors, their efforts as hopeless as before.

Burroughs again—Burroughs making us all hold our breath in sympathy with his tense precautions. But it proved a sudden victory for the grease at the fourth step.

Gotty now stood at the bow with a new expression. No grinning or shaking of fist now. He had forgotten his audience. His mind was on his work. The thing was getting serious. He condescended to be very careful.

Half a length; some steps beyond; and then—defeat; and defeat attended by so ugly a contact with the pole that a shudder went up from the throng, and I grew anxious. But there was the old fellow gamely swimming round to the ladder, not a penny the worse.

I will not trace the contest through its further stages. Enough that, the novices but seldom appearing, the two rivals tried and failed some twenty times, each coming once within some inches of success. The the committee intervened, and the last I saw, before surrounding boats broke into a scattering medley and so spoilt the view, was Gotty in earnest altercation with the executive, manifestly preferring a claim to another try. But it was all over.

Coming ashore, the unsuccessful champion lost no time in visiting a popular rendezvous, where he danced a therapeutic hornpipe and took other successful measures against a state of teeth-chattering and arrested circulation.

When later I joined him at tea, in the little home along the alley, he proved to be bearing up with exemplary fortitude against his recent reverse.

"It's no good frettin'," he averred. "Fifteen years I got it, and I ain't got it to-day—only, mark you, I wasn't beat!"

And again, on a second serving to shrimps, "I'm a good loser, ain't I? No one can't say dif'rent."

But it came to light that, if fortune had withheld an accustomed favour, she had bestowed two that lay outside the realm of expectations.

Gotty had been a mascot to the bawley on which he was serving as the sick mate's substitute. On two nights out of four they had had the felicity to happen on a craft in difficulties on the sand; and in both cases the offer of their expert assistance had been accepted.

I gathered that, in affairs of this kind, the requisite service can be rendered by experience with unerring ease. The vessel's anchor must be so placed that, when she refloats, she will be restrained from driving further on the sand. It may well be that the unfortunate captain can, on the flood, withdraw unassisted from peril; and thus the issue for him, when obliging fishermen come hastening to the rescue, is apt to lie between sovereigns and certainty.

"There was only one other borley along of us on Wednesday night," Gotty explained, "and at fust it looked like ten pound a-piece; for she was a tidy-sized schooner. Only the captain carried on wonderful 'eadstrong. 'E didn't want no fisherman to 'elp 'im, 'e said—'e could get 'er off all right. 'Beggin' your pardin, sir,' I says, 'but there's many thought the same way, and bin sorry afterwards.' 'All right, my man,' 'e says 'when I want your opinion,' 'e says, 'I'll ask for it.' Fer a long time 'e wouldn't 'ear o' givin' us the job—not till 'e'd seed if 'e couldn't get 'er off next tide. But arter a lot more talk 'e come round a bit and said we might 'ave a pound betwixt us, but not a penny more. Only five shillin's a man! Money like that don't give yer no encouragement ter 'elp people out of trouble, do it?"

"But you agreed to his terms?"

"We couldn't do nothin' else, seein' if we'd stood by 'im 'e'd wery likely to get afloat by 'isself, and then we shouldn't get nothin', and six howers lost! But jest ter show you the dif'rence in people—the captin we come ath'art this mornin' talked all the other way, and a smaller vessel, she was, and no cargo. I couldn't 'elp feelin' sorry for the pore ole feller, fer altergether there was twelve borleys come ter do 'im good—like a lot o' 'ungry sharks all round 'im, we was! And 'im so nice spoken, and grateful like, and whatever should 'e do, 'e kep' sayin', if she went ter pieces! 'E'd fair lost 'is way, and wanted ter know if the Shoebury lights wasn't Thames 'Aven! The old chap 'adn't bin in the Estu'ry only wunst afore, and not sorry, I shouldn't wonder, if 'e never come agin. Seein' 'e was a pore man, 'e arsked if we'd mind only 'aving a pound a boat ter git im off. So, arter puttin' 'is anchor out, we all stood by 'im, and 'Enry Morgan, what's a good scholar, went aboard and thumbed over the chart with 'im, so as 'e could find 'is way up to Tilbury without gettin' into no more trouble When 'e got under way agin, we all give 'im a cheer, and the old feller come ter the side and waved 'is 'andkerchief. So, yer see," Gotty summed up, "if I ain't won the greasy pole, I've arned fifteen shillin's extry money."

And it was my privilege to afford additional consolation to the cheerful mariner. On playfully inquiring if he had yet found a bawley for me to buy, I learnt that, in a manner of speaking, he had two in his enthusiastic eye. Moreover, he took the matter in such grim earnest that I found myself conceding more serious consideration than heretofore to the romantic possibility of owning a fishing smack.

"There's two for sale at 'Arwich, and from what I 'ear there's a charnse of buyin' 'em cheap. One's fitted up with a nice large cabin, it 'aving bin used fer a pilot cutter; so"—came the astute reflection —"you could take yer friends out for a cruise now and agin, and be able ter make 'em comfortable."

"What would you call cheap?" I asked.

"Well," he ruminated, "if you got the lot—wessel, sails, and gear—fer a 'undred pound, that wouldn't be out of the way, would it?"

"No," I was fain to admit, though I pointed out that, comparatively paltry as the sum might seem, I should hesitate to apply a hundred pounds on so unfamiliar an enterprise, notwithstanding the pleasure I should take in affording a means of livelihood to a certain worthy individual.

"Well," he commented, nothing downhearted, "I won't say as we mightn't get fitted out for eighty pounds. It'd be an old borley fer that, but an old 'un 'll catch as many shrimps as what a noo 'un will.

You'd get the same money, mind yer, as what I should. Every shillin' 'arned works out fourpence fer the skipper, fourpence fer the mate, and fourpence fer the owner; only, ercourse, the owner 'as ter find the boat in noo gear, and anythin' else what she 'appens ter want. This larst year or two, shrimpin' as paid wonderful well, not 'alf it ain't.''

In the end I entrusted seven and sixpence to Gotty, so that, on his first free day, he could proceed to Harwich and gain full particulars of such suitable bargains as might be afloat.

VI

AT PETTY SESSIONS

A FORTNIGHT having run by, and still no news of Gotty or my seven and sixpence, I proceeded to Leigh in the spirit of an investigator.

As I walked up the little alley, the familiar voice welcomed me, but nowhere could I see its stalwart possessor, until the full-chested harmonics sounding again, I beheld him cautiously crawling on the nine-foot wall by which that thoroughfare is bounded on the north.

"Bird's-nesting?" I asked.

"I've lost my knife," he replied. "Fancied my little nevvy might 'ave chucked it over. No, mum" (to a woman's voice on the other side), "I don't see it. But there's 'is rubber-ball under them sunflowers."

Mrs. Gotty received me in the parlour with an exclamation of pleasure, saying she was glad to see a friend, they being in such dreadful trouble.

What! Hadn't I heard?

And from behind a teapot on the mantelshelf she took a white paper which certified, on the information of one Henry George Bilbury, that, on the previous Saturday, Gotty "did unlawfully assault and beat the said Henry George Bilbury contrary to the statute." Gotty was ordered to appear at the Petty Sessional Court-House on the following Thursday.

"Yes," said the good soul, lifting her apron to remove the first tear I had seen glistening on that happy face, "they will tantalise him, and I was there and saw how it began, though being his wife I suppose they won't let me put in a word for the old man; him being tantalised first, and not taking any notice, and then he knocked him down; and I lie awake worrying to think of him p'raps having to go to prison, and all because——"

Gotty's great form filled the doorway.

"What if I do?" he demanded, with broad-minded cheerfulness. "There's my betters gone to prison, ain't there?"

Then, dismissing this minor matter, the hospitable old fellow bestowed all his energy upon transplanting me from a draughty corner to a seat by the fire.

"But how did it happen?" I was anxious to learn.

"That?"—and Gotty's thumb indicated the summons—"Oh, me and Sparrow Fraser was talking when this 'ere Bilb'ry come and shoved 'is face in. Arsked what business I had there, 'e did, jest as if a married man with a 'ouse hadn't as much right outside the Smack as a single man living at 'ome with his father! The 'ouses was just closed, and I'd been in the Peter Boat, and coming along I met this 'ere 'Trouble'—that's what I call him, it being along of them little pink shrimps gettin' mixed with the brown 'uns. We was talking friendly, and then he come and shoved his face in. I pushed 'im away, and he framed up; then I plugged 'im, and he went down like a bullock."

"'Trouble' did?"

"No—the other man. It was 'Trouble' I was talking to when he come up. Don't you understand?"

"Not quite. What was that you said about shrimps?"

"It's when you catch a lot o' little pink 'uns along o' the browns—which is the colour, you understand, after they've been cooked, only you can easy tell the dif'rence afore they're cooked. It don't do to send 'em all mixed, so you've got to sort 'em, and that's what give me the idea to call Sparrow Fraser 'Trouble,' for it's a reg'lar trouble sorting 'em, and when 'im and me was fishin tergether he had wonderful bad luck with the pink 'uns—howers, 'e'd be, picking 'em over; so mostly when I see 'im, I'll sing out, friendly-like, 'Wot-O, Trouble!' and very likely he'll gie me back the same word, 'Hullo, Trouble!' or it might be 'Wotcheer, Ponto!' 'Im and me was talking quiet and friendly, when this man come and shoved 'is face in, which he wouldn't 'ave done if 'e 'adn't been drunk."

"Were you drunk?"

"Cert'nly not—no more drunk than what I am now. I'd 'ad a couple of three-a'porths in the Peter Boat, where I'd been sittin' in the parler—jest pleasant and comfortable, if you know my meanin'. There's the perlicemen 'll say I wasn't drunk, for I come by two on 'em along the road, and I wished 'em good night and they wished me good night."

"It's a pity," said the good wife, "you don't give up the beer altogether. P'raps you wouldn't have took offence if you hadn't had any."

"Did you ever 'ear sech talk?" he asked me, a touch of pity in his tone. Then, with judicial calm, to the partner of his bosom: "Who give the fust offence?"

"He did," replied Mrs. Gotty. "He tantalised you and you knocked him down. But it's time you kept out of these bothers, that's what I say—you getting to be an old gentleman and all."

"Did I know what I was doin', or didn't I?" pursued the cross-examiner, ignoring her last remark as irrelevant.

"You knew what you were doing," conceded Mrs. Gotty, "but I'm sorry enough you did it."

"Then if I knew what I was doin'," Gotty summed up, "what's the good of sech silly talk? These wimmin!" he added thoughtfully, but without following up that line of speculation.

"What happened," I asked, "after he came and interfered?"

"He come and arsked what business I 'ad there, so I brushed 'im on one side, quiet and gentle, and went on talking ter Sparrow. Then he came along agin and framed up."

"Put up his fists?"

"That's it."

"And what did you do then?"

"Caught 'im a smack acrost the face with the flat of my 'and."

"And then?"

"He arsked for more," explained Gotty confidentially—"reg'lar arsked for it; fer 'e come along agin all framed up. So I plugged 'im one."

"You mean you hit him a hard blow with your fist?"

"A real straight 'un, and down he went like a bullock. Then a coastguard come along and picked 'im up."

"He never hit you at all?"

"'E never got one in. I was too quick for 'im, and 'e was too drunk. There it is—now you've got it!"

"This is rather a serious affair, Gotty."

"But he gave the fust offence! That's what I shall tell 'em. Gone to a lawyer, 'e 'ave, so I 'ear; but I dessay 'e didn't tell 'im 'e gave fust offence. 'Gentlemen,' I'll say, 'did 'e come and tell you 'e interfered with me fust?' There's Rainbow Johnson and Coughing Smith and one or two more goin' ter give evidence, so I 'ear, but we shall know on the day. I ain't afraid of what nobody says so long as they speak the truth. That's what I'm going to do—I'd sooner get six months than kiss the Book fer a false oath."

"I'm sure!" said Mrs. Gotty, "if you did, I believe I'd get up and contradict you myself."

"You won't be nervous, Gotty, when you get in Court?" I asked.

"I should drop—I'm sure I should," interposed Mrs. Gotty.

"Pooh!" he exclaimed, reassuringly, "I ain't that sort. I'll stick out my neck like the old 'erons on the mud lookin' fer eels. I shan't be afraid to tell 'em what 'appened, and no lie won't go past me without my pickin' it up and throwin' it back at 'em. 'E begun it fust—that's what I've got to make 'em see. If they send me inside after that, I'll go, and go cheerful. But it ain't likely."

The situation being, however, one which left Mrs. Gotty a prey to manifest anxiety, I made bold to request permission, in the exercise of a friend's prerogative, to accompany the defendant into the judicial arena, so that, should the Court demean itself by a hostile decision, I should be at hand to meet any pecuniary exaction of which, or a period of captivity, he might be offered the choice.

At this, the dear lady's thanks were sufficiently voluble, though her husband, while obviously touched to find some sparks of fraternity still aglow in this cold world, hastened to discuss the matter in its economic aspect, and with an application of arithmetical principles that was academic in its delicate precision.

"Thank yer," he said heartily, "only look 'ere—if it's forty shillin's or seven days, that's mor'n what I'm arnin', so if you wouldn't mind bein' so good as ter give the missis five-and-twenty shillin's, I'll be able ter go inside with nothin' on my mind, and glad o' the rest; but if it don't come out so much as five-and-twenty shillin's a week, then I'd take it kindly ter 'ave the fine paid. Only don't you see, if it works out more, we'd only be throwin' money away!" in which masterly examination of the position, it will be noted, no frivolous sentiment was allowed to clog the wheels of thrift.

The allusion to money turned my thoughts in another direction, and I asked Gotty if he had paid his intended visit to Harwich.

"Oh!" he shouted, his mind suddenly flooded by a sense of uncommunicated tidings. "No, I didn't get a day ashore. But what d'yer think? There looks a chance of buying a Leigh boat cheap, the owner bein' pretty near too old ter go ter sea, what with the rheumatics and all, and when he does feel fit fer work, 'is old mate's almost shore not ter fancy 'isself well enough ter go; so one with the other, the boat nearly always lays idle, and 'e told me last week 'e thought 'e'd sell 'er. Only when I see 'im agin yesterday and said I might know somebody what'd like ter buy 'er, 'e said 'e'd changed 'is mind. 'E'll change it agin, I shouldn't wonder, but I shall wait fer 'im to speak next time."

.   .   .   .   .

In accordance with the understanding on which we parted, Gotty and I met at Southend on the following Thursday morning, and proceeded by train to the little country town where, at Petty

Sessions, he was to answer the charge of unlawfully assaulting and beating a man contrary to the statute.

It was a large, lofty room, in need of redecoration. On the broad benches sat indiscriminately applicants, prosecutors, defendants, and witnesses—sorry and seedy humanity in the main.

Every one rose when the three Justices entered. The youngest—typical eldest son of a county family, and wearing a brown tweed suit—took the chair. His colleagues were middle-aged gentlemen, who sat patiently throughout the session, interfering with no man.

Many cases preceded Gotty's. First came the anti-vaccination applicants, each stating a definite objection with emphasis, and all securing ready exemption. Then several public-house licenses were transferred from respectable persons to persons equally respectable.

Next came the rate-collector and his protesting or beseeching victims. Their arguments all met this answer from the Bench— "Judgment warrant!" One man had occupied his house only six weeks, and had regularly paid rent which, under his agreement with the landlord, included rates and taxes. But the inflexible Chairman did not care about that.

I feared for Gotty. After some unlicensed-gun cases had been heard, he was called.

The resolute, upright old fisherman strode unabashed to the little railed platform appointed for prisoners. A dapper lawyer rose to open the case for the prosecution; but Gotty got in the first word.

"Witnesses ter go out o' Court please," he remarked in a tone of command rather than suggestion.

The Chairman regarded him with stern, questioning eyes, then gave the order.

Now the lawyer told his story. The defendant came upon a group of men in the street and disturbed their Saturday night serenity by exclaiming, "Odd job lot!" which, having often heard him make the remark, I could readily believe. Then—the Court was given to understand—somebody passed this criticism on somebody else: "That man dunno 'ow to sail a boat," whereat a third party remarked, "'E's better at that biz'nis than you ever was or ever will be." Discussion on these lines waxed warm, one word leading to another; and in the confusion of voices, the trumpet tones of the defendant rose highest, making a powerful appeal to the listening ears of the prosecutor, approaching demurely along the road.

[Gotty followed this statement with rapt interest and gaze, and the smile that illuminated his massive features suggested a general corroboration.]

41

The prosecutor (the lawyer continued, in effect) went up to the defendant, and asked, with genuine concern and scrupulous politeness, "What is the matter?" at which the defendant, storming and raving, smote the courteous inquirer upon the cheek.

[The smile had gone. Gotty's lower jaw had dropped. He stared with a large disc of eyeballs.]

Peacefully, modestly, the prosecutor backed, closely followed by his brutal assailant, who rained a succession of smacks alternately on the left and right sides of the retreating and unoffending face.

[Gotty was breathing jerkily from a heaving bosom.]

And when, thus contiguous, the bullying lion and law-abiding lamb arrived across the road, the oppressor suddenly shot forth an unexpected fist and his stunned victim lay in the mud.

[Gotty's lips were moving, but his dry throat yielded nothing audible.]

Yet so far the picture was only an imperfect outline. Filling his brush with purple, the legal artist continued, in effect:

Towering beside his bleeding and unconscious handiwork, the tyrant waved his cap on high, daring any man, on pain of similar chastisement, to offer ministrations to the fallen; and among all those sturdy fisherfolk standing by (or so the story ran) none dared intervene. For this man, might it please their worships, was "the terror of the district," and all his neighbours went in fear of him. Thus, for fully ten minutes—

"Was you there?"

[Gotty had achieved speech, but only in the thin, pale voice of astonishment; and none deigned notice the departure from approved procedure.]

For fully ten minutes the insensible man lay unattended, and—
"WAS YOU THERE?"

[The paralysis of Gotty's vocal nerves had passed away, and this time the words rang bold and insistent; so that he was immediately confronted by suddenly turned faces of scandalised protest. Gotty was sternly bidden hold his peace; and after one tense moment of bewildered wrath, a great calm came over his soul. If so unthinkable an injustice were to be permitted as evidence, grossly inaccurate and one-sided, from a man who didn't see the affair, then (Gotty reasoned within himself, if I knew the language of those mobile, bushy eyebrows) of what avail to concern himself further as to the course these proceedings might take? Thenceforward, standing reposefully erect, he smiled the comfortable smile of conscious ethical superiority.]

The prosecutor generally confirmed, in the box, the opening statement of his legal champion. On the Chairman's invitation, Gotty condescended to put a few questions to the witness. There ensued this spirited piece of cross-examination:

"Was you drunk?"

"No."

"Yes, you was."

"No, I wasn't."

Yes, you was."

The Chairman (severely, to prisoner): "You mustn't contradict."

Gotty (severely, to the Chairman): "I ain't contradictin'."

Later he tried his art on one of the several witnesses for the prosecution.

"Didn't 'e frame up before I 'it 'im?"

"No."

"Yes, 'e did."

"No, 'e didn't."

"Yes, 'e did."

The Chairman (to Gotty): "Any other questions?"

Gotty (a little off-hand): "What's the good?"

When the case for the prosecution had closed, the Chairman had some difficulty in making Gotty understand that some sort of rhetorical effort was now expected from him.

Two minutes later he was explaining to an astonished Court, with much wealth of detail, how the little pink shrimps had to be sorted from the brown ones. Warming to this theme, his previous displeasure with the Bench was manifestly giving place to a more generous and friendly attitude of mind.

But the Chairman instructed him to confine his observation to the point at issue.

"Well, 'e begun it fust," said Gotty, reverting with reluctance to the unfortunate affair, "and if 'e 'adn't arsked me what business I was doing there, 'im shoving 'is face in when 'e wasn't wanted, I shouldn't 'ave pushed 'im. Then 'e framed up, and I 'it 'im."

"You admit striking him, then?" asked the lawyer triumphantly.

"Ercourse I do," replied the astonished defendant. "I 'it 'im a straight 'un, and down 'e went like a bullock."

After the fine (forty shillings) had been paid, and Gotty and I were strolling to the station, he made a confession.

"I was very sorry arterwards when I'd 'it 'im. It was a awful hard 'un—like a kick from a 'orse. It's a lesson not to act 'asty."

VII

BUYING THE BAWLEY

TWO days afterwards Gotty came to me in a state of mind bordering on delirium. It was a task of some difficulty to ascertain on what subject he poured forth such copious particulars.

This was the startling knowledge that came to me: the owner of the *Jane* had offered to sell that vessel for £50 and, on my behalf, Gotty had secured the option of purchase by paying a deposit of two and-sixpence.

"'E come ter me this mornin', and when 'e said 'e'd sell 'er fer fifty pounds I nips off 'ome and fetched one of them 'alf crowns what you give me, the missis 'aving laid 'em by in a tea cup in the chest o' drawers. She's old, we know, and bin doubled, and wants noo sails and gear, only that won't run you into more'n eighty pound altergether—inside eighty, I shouldn't wonder." ·

Thus by easy gradations did Fate and Gotty raise me to the dignity of a smack owner. For my inspection, on the following day, of the *Jane* left me willing to accept the view that, her time-worn internal appearance notwithstanding, she was a stout seaworthy craft.

Next Saturday evening I found myself, accompanied by Gotty, in a little Leigh parlour, and about to be initiated into such mysteries as might attend the acquisition of a bawley. On a sofa sat the old fisherman who had come at last to the melancholy moment of selling his boat. He told us about his rheumatism, and on cognate themes conversation continued for three-quarters of an hour.

Then at last, neither of my companions offering to take the initiative, I remarked:

"Now, with regard to buying the bawley, how do we proceed?"

"You 'ave ter brass up," Gotty explained, "'e picks up the money, and then it's all over;" and the old fisherman on the sofa nodded a sad but confirmatory head, in testimony that the ritual had been correctly stated.

I am a lover of simplicity myself; but I could not forbear to introduce into the proceedings one touch of a more prim formality than, if I could accept the foregoing testimony as conclusive, had the sanction of usage. Next minute, indeed, that little household was riven with lively bustle, consequent upon my impressive request for pen, ink and paper. For I was resolved to have a receipt, even though one had never before been given, in all the years gone by, for the purchase money of a bawley. Nay, I even went the length of having a stamp affixed, the two fishermen scarce venturing to breathe as they watched these lawyer-like proceedings.

Nor had my gluttony for ceremonial even yet wholly abated.

"Oughtn't the ship's papers to be handed over?" I asked the vendor.

"You'll find 'em in a mustard tin," he replied, "in one o' the lockers."

"I see 'em there myself," came prompt and generous confirmation from my prospective skipper, whose scrutiny of the vessel had manifestly been more intimate than my own.

When it came to paying over the money, observant Gotty thought he had detected me in a particularly discreditable manœuvre.

"This ain't right!" he protested, eyeing me aghast. "This ain't forty-nine pound seventeen shillin's and sixpence!" (for, scholar or no scholar, he is a master of currency intricacies). "This is only"— and with a scandalised and tarry finger he rapidly counted the coins over—"fourteen pound seven and six!"

But, fortunately for my credit, our companion was alive to the significance of the accompanying cheque.

When presently we took our departure from that fisherman's cottage, Gotty had the comfortable air of a mariner who has successfully traversed a difficult piece of water. But he promptly came full-tilt against a rock.

He had referred to my vessel as the *Jane*. I corrected him—the *Betty*, please.

"But that ain't 'er name!" he objected, his brow all furrows and bewilderment.

"Yes, it is," I contradicted.

For, if with lamb-like docility I had consented to own a bawley, I was inflexibly set against owning a bawley called the *Jane*; and lest this determination seem invidious, let me at once state that I should equally draw the line at owning a bawley called the *Mary Ann*. Besides, I had my personal preference in the matter of a name.

"But it's painted on the starn!" Gotty cried in despair.

"Then I'll paint it out."

"But it's on the papers! You can't alter the papers!"

"Oh yes, I can"—at which reckless and wicked assertion he was panic-stricken. His case could not have been worse had I threatened to commit manslaughter.

"You can't. You mustn't, I tell yer! You'd git sent ter prison!"

"I mean—I'll get someone else to alter them."

"That wouldn't make no dif'rence! You'd cop it jest the same—if it come out you'd put the other bloke up ter do it!"

It will be noted that, in the extremity of his perturbation to find his new owner calmly proposing such desperate illegalities, Gotty was drawing somewhat freely upon a vocabulary acquired in dealings with various grades of society.

"Where do smack owners get their papers from?" I asked.

"The coastguards!"

To the coastguards' quarters I accordingly bade him conduct me; and five minutes later we entered an office ominously hung with guns, bayonets, pistols, and other facilities for sudden human slaughter.

I communicated my sovereign will to surely the gentlest mannered little man who ever wore brass buttons. Perched on a stool before his desk, he beamed lovingly upon us through gold-rimmed spectacles, as though our visit were the crowning pleasure of his blameless life.

But when he grasped the formidable fact that I desired to change my bawley's name, he shook his little head in considerable distress, and attempted soft dissuasions. On the point, however, I was as flint. The breach of continuity in official records, the seaman's superstition of ill-luck, the embarrassment to his Majesty's Customs—I swept aside all the arguments, and gave my ultimatum: It must be.

In a flutter of courteous perplexity, he undertook to communicate with London, and ascertain whether any, and if so which, department of the Imperial Government held authority under the king and constitution to officially sanction such a purpose as the one by which I was possessed.

As we were about to take our departure, the dapper little officer anxiously entreated us to resume our seats. It seemed that the bawley's change of ownership had cast certain urgent responsibilities upon him. A full and careful record of all the salient facts had to be made in a large, morocco-bound volume. Indeed it was lucky, not to say providential, we had called.

Concerning such matters as my name, age, address, and nationality I had no difficulty in providing food for his scrupulous penmanship; but both Gotty and I were at a loss when he requested to be told our tonnage, the width of our beam, and how much we measured fore and aft.

Mildly scandalised to find an owner and skipper with blank minds on these important points, he nevertheless kindly undertook to send his agents next day on board our craft to make the measurements that would enable him to fill grievous gaps which, for the time being, must exist in State archives.

Ten days afterwards I received a communication setting forth the style of a high dignitary of the Board of Trade, and informing me that I must write to him forthwith formally asking permission to re-christen my vessel, and fully stating the reasons which induced me to prefer that request.

I did so; I made a clean bosom of it, occupying three candid and closely written pages in an attempt to make the Board of Trade understand my prejudice against the name *Jane*, and glancing on a fourth page at the grounds of my preference for the name *Betty*.

Three weeks later—and in the interval the Cabinet had met, though this may have been a mere coincidence—the Board of Trade wrote granting my prayer; and simultaneously I received new ship's papers on immaculate parchment.

If that important Government Department had deliberated long before acquiescing in the startling change I had desired them to sanction, they had seen fit, on finally taking the plunge, to indulge in a positive debauch of innovation. Not merely had the *Jane* become the *Betty*, but her former lettering of MN. (indicating Maldon as our port of hail) had given place to LO. (thenceforth to distinguish us upon the the high seas as a London boat). Nor, I blush to say, had the Board of Trade stopped there.

I had been careful to explain that Gotty was the skipper, and I merely the owner; but his Majesty's Government had insisted upon thrusting the double dignity upon me. There for the world to see was the unimpeachable testimony of parchment that I was both the proprietor and the commander of the bawley *Betty*, *alias* the LO. 96.

Meanwhile, if he had taken no part in these august matters, Gotty had not been idle. He had been working the boat. He had also, in a disappointing spell of enforced idleness, been tarring and re-fitting her. In truth, enthusiastically as he was embarking on the career of a catcher of shrimps, fate was not niggard in the hindrances she placed in his path.

His earliest trouble, and one destined to periodical recurrence, was that, for some reason that was a mystery to me (and scarcely less to him, if I might judge by the changeful variety of his explanations) he could not retain a mate. Two in succession entered our service (a retired greengrocer and a youth fresh from school) only to abruptly leave it after putting in, between them, no more than three nights' work.

On finding himself the second time without a coadjutor, Gotty came to me with knit brows and a policy to unfold.

"You can't wonder at 'em not stoppin'," he said. "There's a 'ole in the cabin floor fit ter break yer neck if anybody wasn't lookin', the torpsel's all ter pieces, the jib ain't much better, the net's so rotten it loses more than it catches, and the cabin's that dirty—well! I can't fancy my food there, and I ain't one ter be too pertikler. Now what d'yer say ter let me order a noo net, and jib, and torpsel, and one or two other things, what we must 'ave, and while we're waitin' fer 'em I'll bring 'er up on the swatch and give 'er a coat o' tar and scrape out the cabin, and get the floor board mended. Then she'll look a little more what she ought to, and we'll get a mate fast enough."

I cordially assented, and the very next night he came to me with these triumphant tidings:

"What d'yer think? I 'ardly began to over'aul 'er this mornin' when old Jerry come and arsked ter be took on as mate. 'E's older than what I thought of takin' anybody, but 'e's as active as a boy and there ain't many as knows the water better'n what ole Jerry does. You very likely might 'ave seen 'im about—a old feller with red trousers."

But on the following Saturday evening, on calling at the cottage to learn how affairs were progressing, I found that my congratulations had been premature. Old Jerry's connection with the *Betty* was already severed.

"You never see sech a techy ole feller!" Gotty explained. "'E was only along of me two days, and so techy it made me reg'lar mis'rable ter be in 'is company. I was scrapin' out the cabin most of the time, laying on my back and usin' both 'ands—and when I got 'ome the missis didn't 'ardly know me, I was that smothered. Never offered ter do a stroke 'isself, 'e didn't, but jest sat on the cabin top, grumble, grumble, grumble, all day long—and old enough ter know better, seein' e'll be seventy-three next birthday. Yer see, when I thought of taking 'im fer mate, I'd fergot about his temper, never 'aving 'ad so much of it at one time. It give me the fair sick, and I wasn't sorry on the third day when he come and said 'is wife's nevvy 'ad bought a borley, and arsked 'im ter take charge. If I can't sail comfortable, I'd sooner stay on shore; that's my nature—so I told 'im 'adn't 'e better go along of 'is wife's nevvy, seein' as that young chap might be more fond of fault-findin' than what I was. So 'e took 'isself off."

48

When, in the middle of the week, I saw Gotty again, he had already lost a fourth mate and engaged a fifth.

"After ole Jerry's temper," my skipper told me, "I didn't fancy 'aving no more like 'im, so when a young feller come and arsked ter go—'im as is a son of the chimney-sweep—I thought, the boat ready and all, I might do wuss. It wasn't the work 'e'd bin used to, you understand, but 'e says 'ow wonderful fond 'e was of the water, and always 'ad bin, and my thought was I could easy larn 'im. 'Im and me went out tergether one day, when I'd finished paintin' the cabin, and I never want no more. Once was quite enough fer me. Talk about sea-sick! I never did see anyone took so bad. I didn't think there'd be much of 'im left to bring back to his mother—and that's tellin' you the truth. Settin' the sails, mindin' the helem, haulin' up the trawl—I 'ad to do everythin'. And him down in the cabin, too! That's where I think 'e did ought to be ashamed of hisself—me having taken all that trouble scrapin' and scrubbin' and paintin', so that you could 'ave eat your dinner off the floor. Now and again, when I got a spare minute, I'd shove my 'ead down the cabin, and 'Mate,' I says, 'if you must be ill,' I says, 'do come out of the cabin,' I says. 'Come on deck ter be ill!' I hollers; but he never took no notice, so when I could fix the helem fer a spell, with no craft over the bows, I took and 'itched a twist of rope round 'im and 'auled 'im up. There he lay groanin' awful, and I thought to myself if he was so fond of the water he'd got a wonderful funny way of showin' it. At one time he carried on so painful I thought we might be goin' ter lose 'im—that's a fact, I did. But more than bein' sea-sick awful there wasn't nothin' amiss with 'im; and next mornin', when 'e come round to see me 'e was 'isself agin. But he said 'e'd 'eard of a job on shore what 'e thought'd suit 'im better than comin' along o' me, and I says to 'im, 'Very likely,' I says, 'p'raps it might.'"

The collapse of the sweep's son was, however, of the less moment as resourceful Gotty had already appointed a stonemason to the vacant office. We seemed, indeed, as I noted with some awe, steadily pushing our way through the trades.

When I ventured a dubious word in regard to qualification, my skipper was able, out of his two days' actual experience of the new mate, to silence all misgiving.

"What 'e don't know about the sea I'm larnin' 'im—and 'e was two year on 'is uncle's barge don't fergit. But talk about strength! It's a treat ter see 'im lift the trawl beam, which 'e don't think nothin' of after them big lumps of stone 'e's bin used ter carry on 'is 'ead up ladders. No more I never saw anybody what's better comperny ter sail with. When 'e ain't singin', 'e's laughin'. I tell yer! we've found a good 'un this time."

Nor, as I rejoiced to learn on visiting Leigh a week later, were these favourable impressions modified on a riper acquaintance.

As to the new mate's muscular excellence, Gotty's encomiums were even more rapturous than before.

"You could easy crack a flea on the calf of 'is leg," he assured me; though, on presently being introduced to the jovial stonemason, I abstained from any attempt to verify the statement.

His delight in his new work was soothing to an owner's heart.

"It's jist what I like," he told me, with enthusiasm.

"Why, it's more like a holiday than work. I don't care if the money is bad for the present." (And "bad," let me say, seemed a mild description of the slender revenues in which, consequent upon the daily voyages of the *Betty*, we were participating.)

"And you should jest see 'im eat!" Gotty remarked to me in private. "Great chunks of meat 'is landlady gives 'im; fer 'e's a single man; and often as not there's a tidy pickin' fer me when 'e's 'ad all 'e can carry; and don't you see, I'm careful ter give 'im a quart of shrimps, or 'alf-a-dozen plaice, or it might be a couple of roker, to take back to 'is landlady. No doubt she's glad ter get a nice bit of fresh fish like that, so she don't mind puttin' up a slice or two more meat than what 'e's likely ter want 'isself. Why! One day 'e come aboard with pretty near 'alf a leg of mutton, besides a lot of them teeny carrots; and wonderful tender they was."

Alas! If only I could close my narrative there, with matters in that idyllic harmony!

A fortnight afterwards the first jarring note was sounded in my ear.

"'E will not keep ter time!" Gotty protested earnestly, almost passionately. "Twice this week we was larst boat out, all along of 'im oversleepin' 'isself."

A week later it was all over. The skipper came round to my house with bent brows and told me the moving story.

"It come ter be more than I could stand. Late, late, late—ev'ry mornin' the same. I kep' on speakin' to 'im, but it wasn't no good. Why ! 'E never went ter bed not afore it was nearly time ter git up—everlastin' sittin' up with 'is friends, singin' and playin' the banjo. What's the result? Some mornin's so sleepy 'e could 'ardly keep 'is eyes open. And fancy anybody bein' able ter go to sleep when there might be a bit of money to 'arn! It was Thursday mornin', and jest gettin' light, when I see a coal ship agin the lower sand; so I gives 'im the tiller, and tells 'im ter stand by, and away I rows ter see if we mightn't 'ave the job ter git 'er anchor out. But it didn't turn out no good, fer the captain wouldn't 'ear of no one 'elpin' 'im. I stopped alongside talkin' more than I might do, fer our borley 'adn't turned, and my thought was 'e would take 'er through the Deep Cut and bear round nor'-west. 'What!' says the captain after a bit, 'ain't your boat comin' back for yer? Then I seed she'd gorn by the Cut and still not put about. 'Why,' I says, 'my mate must 'ave gorn ter sleep;' and off I starts ter row after 'im, the captain laughin' fit to bust 'issell. If it took me a minit it must 'ave took me a hower and a 'alf to catch 'er up, the sweat all pourin' down me and my pore arms ready ter break. There 'e was, sound and snorin', with the tiller under 'is arm and 'is 'ead restin' on it."

"That was very annoying," the scandalised owner commented "and very dangerous."

"'Wake up!' I 'ollers, when I come alongside, and as 'e didn't pay no attention, I took and prodded 'im with a oar. 'Oh,' 'e says, wakin' up sudden, 'I berlieve I've 'ad forty winks.' 'Yes,' I says 'I berlieve you 'ave,' and I thinks to myself, 'It won't be my fault, my fine feller, if you don't sleep in yer own bed next time!' For it's a funny thing, but Ned Pierpoint come to me that very afternoon and arsked me not ter forget 'im if I wanted a mate, seein' 'e was out of work."

"What trade?" I mechanically asked.

"Ned works as a carpenter, but what 'e's mostly took up with is playin' the flute in the Salvation Army. So I goes round to 'im and says, 'If you're on the jetty at 'alf past two termorrow mornin', you shall come along o' me if my mate don't turn up.' Neither did 'e turn up, so I takes Ned. But when we come ashore this afternoon, the other one was waitin' on the jetty. As black as thunder 'e looked, and 'e didn't 'alf say nothin' either. At one time I thought 'e was goin' ter frame up, and if us two 'ad started, it would 'ave bin all right! Only we've 'ad a glass tergether this evening, and 'e's come round ter see 'e couldn't expect any one to be'ave dif'rent to what I did."

A week later I was, as will be readily understood, all agog to hear how the carpenter-flautist was shaping.

"'E's all right," was my skipper's hearty report. "You couldn't want any one what's more willin', and 'e larns quick. 'E 'as a lot ter say about the Army—and teetotal, too. Never touches a drop! And I'm careful to respec' 'is feelin's. I 'aven't give 'im one swear word all the time."

We shall have you joining the Salvation Army, Gotty."

"I might do plenty o' wuss things," agreed that broadminded man.

Week succeeded week, and I had already begun to regard the mate problem as settled, when disappointing news was brought to me that the Salvationist had abruptly left our service. His departure had some relation to an apple pudding, though, being fully occupied with other matters at the time, I did not succeed in satisfactorily probing the mystery. It seemed that an overliberal helping to the pudding had (to adopt the explanation of the flautist's wife, who, as the cook, might be presumed to know) incapacitated him for work on the two following days, besides (to incline to Gotty's version of the affair) rendering him unable to send "one of 'is nippers round, jest ter give me word!"

But, if I cannot deal adequately with the crisis, I can at least state its consequence. The carpenter had gone, and been succeeded, as mate of the *Betty*, by a promising contractor's carman.

Matters were in that phase when, feeling one day somewhat run down, I resolved to try a trip on my boat as a pick-me-up.

VIII

SHRIMPING

THE blackness above was set with diamonds, but the night lacked a moon. Westcliff had long since gone to bed. Nay, an hour had passed since midnight sentinels plunged her avenues and promenade into the abrupt loss of electric light.

For a mile I was alone with the sea and the sky and the silence. But at cliff undulations where Westcliff melted into Leigh, and Nature was the only gardener, nightingales poured their various cadences into the quietude. And, pausing amid the sweet and solemn music of those birds, I heard little unseen waves softly tumbling on the shore.

Lights in the old fishing village proved strangely welcome and companionable—undignified discovery! But unless one be an armed coastguard certain vague timidities are apt to associate themselves with darkness and 1 a.m.

Gotty had laid upon me the imperative injunction to be at the jetty soon after one, and on no account later than half-past. It would be a dreadful thing, he had pointed out, if I made him lose the tide. Arriving at 1.25, I remained for twenty minutes the only living creature astir beside the water. Then I was joined by a white cat, whose humble friendliness suggested that, having arrived home too late for admittance, he had tasted loneliness and boredom in the deserted streets.

Ten minutes later something else happened. Hearing the creak of a spar, I turned to behold a cockle-boat, her brown sails all set, pass like a phantom beyond the jetty, and then creep away into invisibility.

Presently the sound of leisurely footsteps, mounting the bridge stairs, came as a reassurance that the world contained other life besides myself, the cat, and the vanished cockle-boat. I bethought me of greetings suitable to mark my sense of Gotty's gross unpunctuality. But it proved to be the new mate.

I drew his attention to the fact that, though it was past two, Gotty had not yet appeared. He accordingly went off to hammer at the door of his superior's cottage.

"If I'd thought you was waiting out 'ere all this time in the cold,"
Gotty said to me when, ten minutes later, he arrived with a
countenance aglow with good temper, "I'd 'ave been careful not to
oversleep myself—I would indeed."

The mate waded in for the dinghy, and at 2.30 we clambered on
board the *Betty*.

Gotty and the mate were in one frame of mind and I was in
another. It was still to-night with me, but already to-morrow
morning with them. They had been to bed. I had not.

So, offering no assistance in the work of hoisting anchor and sails,
I descended to the cabin, lit the lamp, spread a spare jib in the bunk
devoid of paint-pots, and straightway turned in, an overcoat and rug
serving for bedclothes.

I had put out the light. The gentle rocking of the *Betty* was full of
slumbrous suggestion. But, for the time, sleep was postponed by
uproar. Occurences on deck were photographing themselves in my
mind, through the medium of sound, with a definition that rendered
superfluous the office of the eye.

The windlass was rotating in jerks at the stern compulsion of a
handspike, as the wet anchor-chain passed complaining round with
the barrel, each released length, on coming to hand, being dropped
on deck with a din of clanking iron such as only an old sea
anchor-chain can make. I knew what Gotty and the mate were
doing, and shared in their relief when, ultimately, the anchor itself,
rusty and rebellious, came blundering up the side and toppled into
the bows.

Next they obviously got to work on the mainsail, the pair of them
hauling with entire weight of body at this rope and that, the great
sheet ascending in a succession of grunting spasms that seemed to
argue the need for more grease on the mast. Then, amid noise of
higher pitch, the topsail went to its place, and, lazily following in
their order, the jib and foresail shrieked into position; my wakeful
thoughts busy over the desirability of oiling the blocks.

All of these happenings, I say, were vividly known to me, lying
below in the wooden hollow, with every sound telephoned through
the timbers in a spirit of exaggeration. As for the footsteps, I could
almost see them. Monstrous heavily shod were Gotty and the mate.
Those sea-boots were assaulting every nerve of delicate fibre in my
quivering cranium.

But, at least, we were now under way, and a copious draught of cool
sea air, which came suddenly to fan my temples, gave assurance that
a hand was on the helm, and that, running aslant the wind, we were

heading for the open water. This experience was the more welcome as a fall in temperature justified my heavy coverings, and caused me to cancel a half-formed intention to arise and shed the overcoat.

Now the expectations of kindlier sensations soothed my thoughts, and I pictured some hours of silent sailing under the stars, with Gotty in thoughtful charge of the helm, the mate asquat beside him, and—that the sleeper below might not be disturbed—with no word spoken between them above the inflexion of a whisper.

I must, indeed, at this moment nearly have dropped off to sleep. For these rose-coloured imaginations were nothing but a dream. No prevision could have had less in common with what actually happened.

The trawl! Of course. I had forgotten the trawl. Gotty and the mate were now wrestling with the thing. I heard the splash which betokened that one of my shipmates had thrown the buoy overboard—the conspicuous piece of tarred buoyancy which, floating to leeward, afforded an alternative means of recovering the gear, should the tow-rope snap. The black wish arose in my heart—so disturbing was the thunder of boot-leather accompanying this operation of throwing over the buoy—that Gotty and the mate, while they were about it, had also thrown each other overboard.

Now they were at grips with the trawl—an ancient, strenuous struggle; the meshed monster refusing to budge; two muscular men sternly set on conquering its obstinacy. I knew the process.

Over go great armfuls of net, masses at either end of the width being simultaneously bundled across the bulwarks; and at last, when the huge bag of perforations is loosening itself as a tapering tunnel in the water, the fishermen enter upon the crowning toil of thrusting overboard the mouth of the monster, held open by rigid jaws of iron, a long beam serving for the upper lip—the monster which, that mankind may enjoy a nutritious diet, moves slowly along the sandy bottom of the sea swallowing little fishes in its ruthless maw.

A stampede of those mammoth boots visualised to my troubled brain the anxious business of making fast the ropes that towed and controlled the trawl, now at its fell work seven fathoms down.

At last, surely, by all the laws of justice, my physical self would be given opportunity to accept the chloroform of sleep. The plash of waters against the heaving hull, the sluggish creaking of the rigging—those were sounds attuned to the proper spirit of lullaby. My senses were already floating to those realms of repose and silver fancies whose airy inhabitants are shod daintily, rather than with sea-boots, when—

What was that? There was a sound in the cabin, as of something moving. Beneath closed eyes I now was wide awake, my mind busy with conjectures. Was it a mouse? Or—more probable—a rat? Neither theory was strengthened by what happened. I heard a lucifer match furtively struck. And presently another.

Obviously Gotty or the mate—bother take them both—had come down to look for something. Whatever they sought, I bitterly reflected, they might, in the name of our common humanity, have made shift to sail the old bawley for a few hours without it, rather than come disturbing me in this thoughtless fashion. Presently, on a sudden illumination being manifest through my drawn lids, I knew that the visitor had gone the selfish length of lighting the lamp. Then he fell to rummaging among paper and wood in one of the lockers. Next—could I credit my ears?—he started tinkering with the stove.

"What on earth," I exclaimed, sitting up and confronting the mate with wide-open eyes—"what on earth are you up to?" For, in moments of acute displeasure one does not always convey one's thought in polished phraseology.

"Going to give you a fire," said the mate, with the gracious cheerfulness of a man about to do a fellow-creature some substantial kindness.

"But," I gasped, "I don't want a fire," and, indeed, with the flue running up some six inches from my head, this negative attitude, all apart from the matter of disturbed repose, was a common-sense preference.

But the mate shoved a handful of paper behind the bars.

"Don't, on any account, light the fire!" I protested.

"He told me to," said the mate, carefully placing pieces of wood on the paper.

"Never mind what Gotty says," I blustered; "you obey me."

"But," said the mate, as he put coal on the wood, "we always have a fire. You see," he added, a hint of reproach in his voice, "we sometimes like to have a cup of tea."

Then, with hasty apologies, back to my pillow. Of course, of course—my night was their morning. O woe was me for lacking sufficient forethought to have sought repose in the hold.

The fire roared up the chimney, whence presently came so fierce a heat that, to avoid risk of a blistered forehead, I pulled the rug over my face. There I lay, too sleepy to realise that sleep was impossible.

Cups and plates rattled. A knife sang its way through a loaf of bread. I heard the hum of boiling water; I heard it go splashing into the teapot.

Half-way through breakfast, Gotty said to the mate:

"Well, 'e did oughter be warm enough." And the mate laughed, not, as it seemed to me, too humanely.

After Gotty had finished his repast (and swallowed, by my counting, his third cup of tea), he again varied the conversation by alluding to the poor owner.

"I suppose," said Gotty thoughtfully, "we'd better let 'im 'ave 'is sleep out."

Noises on deck had kept me awake as, trying to sleep, I lay indignant in that bunk; and it was a noise on deck which, ultimately, caused me with alacrity to arise. Gotty and the mate were hauling in the trawl. I wanted to see.

My opened eyes discovered occasion of astonishment. Visible were the paint-pots in the opposite bunk—visible also the base of the mast, stubborn pillar of wood running through the floor and penetrating the ceiling. It was no light of a lamp that revealed the cabin interior, but an illuminant more white and pure. Day had come; and, indeed, the ship's clock testified to half-past five.

I thrust my head and shoulders out into the morning—delicious experience. Bright sunshine, blue sea, little hurrying steamers with red funnels, toy barges with brown sails, tiny duplicates of the *Betty*—that is what I saw, no craft being near. Gently rocking, we were encircled by sparkling water. Kent and Essex were remote ribbons of prettiness, and Southend pier was made of thread. The joyous sunshine filled the universe. My nostrils were tickled by sweet, cool air—incense and a tonic. O ye poor millions of city sluggards, with your late nights at theatres—far from your lives is that miracle of the Estuary in early morning, when the sun is shining.

"Better put on your coat," Gotty in motherly manner interrupted his labours to advise, "else you might ketch cold coming out of that cabin"—which was wisdom.

Getting in the trawl is labour less exhausting than shooting it, because of the assistance rendered by the capstan, which, in the operation under my scrutiny, the mate turned with an iron handle.

Having got the beam on board, they hauled in the masses of dripping net, until at last they reached the bulged extremity, which dumping it on a clear area of deck, Gotty regarded with small favour. This parcel from the deep, his trained eye told him, would, when translated into Billingsgate cash, go but a short way toward buying Mrs. Gotty a new dress. I exercised my financial right to shake a disconsolate head in unison with his, though, of a truth, my own unassisted observation had scarce enabled me to judge whether we had done well or ill.

Next minute he had untied the cord, and a twitching mass of wrigglesome green-grey life had slid upon the deck.

We were out, as I knew, after the agile shrimp. But our success had manifestly lain rather in the discretion of small crabs, though, not to appal the mate by too pathetic a display of proprietorial inexperience, I abstained from drawing attention to the fact. There they crawled in variety, of several colours, some with the long legs of a spider, and each apparently concerned to show off his parts in pedestrianism. They were walking with heedless rapidity over infant soles, full-grown whitebait, little gasping cod, and other small fishes of which the names were not known to me. Also in our gleanings from below there was a half-transparent shrimpy element, which lost definiteness in a seaweed tangle.

Two pairs of expert hands immediately engaged in the business of removing the undesirables, and a lively cascade of crabs and small fish, mingling with tatters of marine vegetation, played over the bulwarks. Thus soon we were left with a reduced heap, into the texture of which quivering legs and whiskers largely entered.

A shovelful of shrimps lay before me, and I drew Gotty's attention to the fact that some of them had apparently been boiled. For a conspicuous redness distinguished these, whereas the others, individually somewhat larger, were wholly of a translucent grey.

"Them are the little pink 'uns," said Gotty, turning upon me his great sun-lit countenance, "and there ain't any that's sweeter. I don't care who says dif'rent. Only the brown 'uns are thought more of, seein' as they're bigger. That's why"—and his face took deeper lines—"the Dutch shrimps get run after so much. Them Dutch shrimps!"

The words were spoken in scorn as he tried to snap a large, yellow finger against a tarry thumb; and his accelerated breathing was audible.

"They ain't fresh," he added, growing slanderous, "nor yet got any flavour. As fer eatin' 'em"—puckering his mouth into an expression of violent disgust—"I'd sooner starve. But that's what we've got to put up with. These Dutch shrimps come and reg'lar glut the market, same as it might be ter-morrow mornin'. Then ours don't fetch not 'alf what you git another time. Larst month we'd be gettin' two shillin's and more a gallon, but with all these Dutch shrimps what's bin comin' in, it's gone down to one and three, a shillin', and"—raising his voice to an outraged pitch that caused a passing sea-gull to mend its pace—"on some days only ninepence!"

As though seeking recovered control of mind in renewed employment of his hands, Gotty applied himself in earnest silence to rummaging anew through the pile of live shrimps, abstracting further seaweed.

"It's jest the same with winkles," he presently observed, when the catch had been almost cleared of vegetable adulteration. "London flies to big winkles, same as it does to big shrimps. But those Scotch winkles ain't got near the flavour as them what we git, only ourn don't run ter the same size—but wonderful sweet they are, to them as knows a good winkle when they get it.

"And so," he summed up, in a spirit of calm despair, "when London ain't flying to Dutch shrimps, its flying to Scotch winkles."

The old fisherman's under-lip was twitching, and I made haste to engage his mind on a less painful theme.

"It's astonishing," was my sincere tribute, "how well you've sorted out the catch."

"If I couldn't pick over a few shrimps," replied Gotty, with a handsome endeavour to minimise the compliment, "I'd no business to be in charge of a borley."

Then, with concentrated thought, he put the shrimps through a further process, aiming at their better appearance. Transferring a half of the total to a circular sieve, he held it at arm's-length above the deck, what time the mate, drawing water in a bucket from over the side, gave them a succession of sluicings. And as each torrent descended, Gotty vigorously shook the sieve, so that sand and other foreign bodies might the more surely be removed.

It was a small avalanche of clean and dapper crustaceans that he finally poured into a larger sieve by his side, where they were presently joined by their brethren, also come spotless from shakings in a shower-bath.

The *Betty* had now reached a situation promising, in Gotty's mature judgment, to serve our interests, and the trawl was once more shot. Then, at a private word from his superior, the mate went below to prepare my breakfast.

Manly slices of bread, fried bacon of a peculiarly boisterous aroma, and tea of an umber strength that suggested its suitability for tanning the hide of a buffalo—that was the repast awaiting me before the roaring cabin fire, and to cope with which the healthy sea air had conjured up the necessary appetite.

Our second haul yielded two more gallons of shrimps, and several plaice of a size that secured their retention for the home larder.

After our third haul, which was rich in starfish, Gotty proceeded to subject his legitimate captives to their last ordeal.

The mate had already, on a dexterous shovel, transferred the cabin fire to a stove in the hold. This imparted its warmth to a venerable copper that the skipper had half filled with water, to which he added salt with a liberal hand. For the Leigh boats bring their shrimps ashore already boiled, and packed in baskets labelled in readiness to be put on the rail for London.

IX

CONSULTING THE SKIPPER

AT our next meeting, Gotty told me a lugubrious story of poor hauls.

"It's no matter where you go." he testified indignantly, "down by the Girdler, off Sheernest, over to Quinboro'—it don't make no difference; there ain't a shrimp to be caught. And them you *do* catch," he added almost hysterically, "don't fetch no money. Arsk any one—" he went on, "they'll all tell you the same. For, mind you if others was getting their six peds—same as what ought to be, now the weather's warmer—I'd say there was something wrong with the works. But we're all served alike. It's something chronic."

Pausing only to draw a coat sleeve across his brow, to relieve it of warm dews these thoughts had induced, Gotty burst forth anew:

"Last Toosday things did look like taking a turn, when we got twelve gallons of pink 'uns—but if they 'aven't gone and made it out on the bill only nine and a 'alf! So they 'as a pore man all ways."

"Gotty," I said, "there is something I want to tell you."

The old fellow stood confronting me with a respectful, listening countenance not wholly free from anxiety.

"I want to go for a two months' cruise in the *Betty*, if you will take me."

"Bray-vo!" exclaimed Gotty, His eyes suddenly aglow with enthusiasm. "I'm ready when you are. Anything's better than trying to catch shrimps when there ain't any."

"What do you say to going down the English Channel as far as Cornwall?"

"Jest wherever you like," he replied; and the large and airy scope of this comment, coupled with a hint of deferential aloofness in the speaker's tone, suggested a suspicion to my mind.

"Gotty," I asked point-blank, "have you ever heard of the English Channel?"

"The English Channel? Why, yes"—with guilty hesitation—"I fancy I 'ave. I've heard talk on it. But when might you be thinking of startin'?"

"Where *is* the English Channel?" I demanded ruthlessly. Gotty scratched his head.

"T'other side of 'Arwich," he ventured. "Ain't it?" he hastily added, on noting my expression.

It is not easy to convey geographical information, of however elementary a character, to one who has ever been a stranger to books and maps.

"Harwich," I began, "is in the north—"

"Nor'-east," corrected Gotty.

"Well, north-east, then. Anyway, the English Channel is in the south."

"That's my meanin'," Gotty remarked. "It's down Margit way, ain't it?"

"But you said Harwich!"

"'Arwich *or* Margit my meanin' was," he explained in an aggrieved tone. "It's down by the Forelan'," he added in a tone calmly explanatory, as though in this geography lesson he were the teacher.

"You have heard of the Foreland, then?"

"And seen it too. It's t'other side o' Margit,"

"How far have you actually been, Gotty?"

"'Ow fur? Why ain't I tellin' yer? I've bin up to 'Arwich and I've bin down to Margit. That's 'ow fur. That's 'ow fur *one* way," he added with increased dignity. "If you talk o' west'ard, there ain't many as knows the river better. 'Undreds of times I've bin up Gravesend Reach, and a tidy few peds o' brown 'uns you'll catch there—when they git up so fur, my meanin' is—and sometimes I've took a catch o' sprats up to Billingsgate when there's bin a fair wind. Only of late years we've mostly took 'em into Tilbury, where they get sent away by steamboat fer sardines, them forrinners not knowin' the dif'rence, seemin'ly."

"The English Channel," I continued, "goes south from the North Foreland; then—" and I paused to mentally review the points of the compass—"then it bends round and goes westwards, right along the south of England. And Cornwall," I added, not without a misgiving that this description was vague and inadequate, "is the end of England."

"Well, well," Gotty commented loftily, "we'll easy find the Channel if there's any sort of water in it for a craft our size."

"Gotty!" I laughed, "the English Channel is a broad, deep sea—a lot deeper and broader than the Estuary."

"'Ow many fadum in the shoalest part?" he asked keenly.

"That I can't say, and as a matter of fact I don't know what a fathom is."

"A fadum," Gotty explained, with gentle courtesy, "is six foot— there or thereabouts. The *Betty* draws five foot six, so if you can be sure of a fadum and a 'alf in this Channel wot you talk of, I'm satisfied."

"I should say the average is more likely to be twenty."

"Good enough!" exclaimed Gotty. Then a thought suddenly puckered his brow. "It ain't near New'aven, is it?" he asked earnestly.

"Newhaven is *in* the English Channel. Why do you ask?"

"Then ercourse I've 'eard of the English Channel," he burst forth with restored self-esteem. "Lor' bless yer, some o' our Leigh chaps used to go drudging off New'aven."

"Newhaven," I seized the opportunity to explain, "is only one of many English harbours in the Channel. Then there are lots of places on the other side—the French Coast."

"Not Dunkirk?" he demanded, in sudden excitement.

"Yes, Dunkirk is one of the French ports in the Channel."

"Why, now!" said Gotty, with an heroic but unsuccessful attempt to repress a tone of reproof, "if you'd said that before I should 'a understood wot you was talkin' about."

"You know Dunkirk?"

"Know it! *Know* it! I should think I did."

"I was not aware you had been to France."

"No more I ain't, but I know them as 'ave. There's a tidy few of our Leigh chaps wot 'ave been drudgin' to Dunkirk, and I've 'eard 'em say all about it. So that's where we're bound!" he added, as, complacently sitting back in his chair, he stretched forth his great chest.

"No, we shan't go to any French port."

"I dunno," Gotty the skipper replied with dignity, "but I mightn't want to put in to Dunkirk for water, or salt, or sech-like."

"But we shall be miles from the French coast," I explained, still taking opportunities, for a purpose of my own, to drive into Gotty's mind some conception of the area of water to be navigated. "We shall keep along the English coast, and there are any number of English places where we can call for supplies—Dover, Rye, Hastings, Portsmouth, the Isle of Wight—"

"I've 'eard of the Wight," Gotty exclaimed, in a manner to show how keenly he was listening. So I continued my enumeration, concerned to explore the astonishing gaps in his geographical knowledge which the interruption negatively revealed.

"Folkestone, Shoreham, Southampton, Brighton—"

"Ah"—and his absorbed face jerked in assent as he caught another familiar name. "I know Brighton—a wonderful pretty place."

"You've been there?" I naturally supposed.

"Didn't I tell yer"—with some asperity—"I 'aven't bin no furrer than Margit?"

"No farther than Margate by water. But you might have been to Brighton by train."

"By train! By *train!*" And he laughed the quiet laugh of a man who has heard a preposterous suggestion. "No, I 'aven't bin to Brighton by train," he condescended to explain, "nor nowhere else excep' London, when I used to take up cockles ter sell in the Old Kent Road; and Chelmsford, when I was courtin' my missis. And sometimes I didn't go *there* by train, but walked to save the 'a'pence, and a tidy fair stretch I made of it, for arter the first time I took pertic'ler care to go round by Rayleigh to give them gypsies a berth. Talk about rough! They'd knock down their own mother to steal the watch and chain off 'er back. They turned my pockets inside out and left me as naked as a pigeon. And you couldn't do nothin', mind yer, fer if you was to stretch out 'arf a dozen on 'em there'd be twenty more come along; and no good callin' fer 'elp, neither, fer the perlicemen took pertic'ler care never to go anywheres nigh 'em. A fair blackguard lot—that's wot they was. I do 'ear they be'ave theirselves better now, but I can't say 'ow fur that's true."

Ignoring these irrelevant reminiscences, I continued: "Poole, Portland, Exmouth, Saltash, Torquay, Plymouth—"

"Plymouth!" echoed my skipper in amazement. "But I thought that's ever so fur away. Ain't it?" he asked, in humble bewilderment.

"About three hundred miles," I replied, with studied indifference. "But of course we shall be going past Plymouth."

"'Ow fur might we be going'?" the estuary shrimper demanded, in a voice of awed curiosity.

"There and back? Well, about seven hundred miles I should say."

"Seven 'undred!" And Gotty gave a low whistle.

"Do you rather fight shy of such a voyage?" the maritime novice asked the hardened old salt.

"'Oo? Me?" came the injured protest. "Lor' bless yer 'eart, I don't mind 'ow fur we go."

Thus Gotty's co-operation was assured, and so absolutely that I now was moved to invite his criticism on some points that rather troubled my own mind.

"Do you think we shall need a pilot?" I asked.

Gotty was amused. Gotty was really tickled. But, suddenly smothering his guffaws, apparently on recalling that I was the owner, he said, "Wot did you think we might want a pilot for—to peel the pertaters?"

"No; to show us the way."

"And wot's to 'inder us showin' ourselves the way?"

"There are sand-banks in the Channel."

"They won't 'urt us," came the ready assurance, "and I'll tell yer fur why. I shall take pertic'ler care to give 'em a berth."

"There are also rocks."

"Is there? Well, we shan't go anigh 'em. I shan't take 'er too far inshore—not likely, on strange ground, too! I've got a good pair o' side lights"—pressing two interpretive fingers against his eyeballs— "no one better, thank Gawd; and if I couldn't keep her off the shore, I didn't ought to be in charge of a borley. There you are!"

"Some of the sands and rocks are a long way from shore, and some of the sands, I think, are only just covered."

"But, man alive," cried Gotty, in one of his rare lapses from the severely respectful, "we've got our lead, ain't we? And we'd see the broken water, shouldn't we? And don't you think," he added, in the tone of a mother gently reasoning with a stupid child, "if there's such things like you say to pull us up in the fairway—don't you think them we come ath'art as *knows* the ground 'ud give us word, same as I'd be the fust to do myself if I saw any one was strange to these waters. If they wouldn't," he concluded, with emphasis, "and 'ud see feller-creatures risk their lives to save themselves the trouble of openin' their mouth—well, it's a funny world!" and Gotty's countenance darkened with repulsion of the human monsters his imagination had conjured up.

"Very well, skipper; I'm satisfied. Now there's another point. Would the mate come?"

Gotty did not at once reply. With compressed lips and contracted brow, he ruminated for several tense seconds. Then came these words, spoken in a voice of conviction:

"I believe 'e might. Yus"—and from a further interval of reverie he obviously emerged with that opinion strengthened—"I believe 'e might. Though, mind yer," came the guarded qualification, "'e may stay abed, same as others I know while 'is missis washes 'is things. No one couldn't be more clean and respectable while 'e's been along o' me, that I will say; but whether 'e's only got what 'e stands up in, or whether 'e's got a change o' shiftables, well," continued Gotty, almost pathetically, "it's no use my saying, fer I don't know, I never asked 'im; and it ain't the sort o' question, if you understand my meanin', you'd be likely to ask everybody—not without you had a pertic'ler reason."

"If it were only a question of clothes," was my comment, "I don't think there need be any difficulty."

"What else *could* there be to stop 'im comin'?"

"He might not care to leave home for so long."

"Oh dear!—mightn't 'e?" replied Gotty. then with severity: "Gawd knows what's coming over mates nowadays, with not wantin' ter do this and not carin' about t'other. When I was mate there wasn't no thought of what I might like or what I mightn't. I did the work wot was expected of me, with no questions and no grumbles, and I always give satisfaction. Things"—with a dismal shake of the head—"is wery dif'rent now. Not *care* about it, mightn't 'e? Well, it beats me! It fair beats me—and that's the truth."

"Surely," I protested, "you need not pitch into the whole fraternity of mates because of something which, after all, no mate has said. It was only my suggestion. Perhaps Alfred wouldn't mind leaving home for a few weeks."

"I'm certin 'e wouldn't," came the emphatic opinion. "Alfred ain't that sort. If 'e's got the togs, Alfred 'll come—don't you make no mistake. But it's the togs what I'm afraid of. That's where I *do* come in. I've got five pair o' blue flannel drawers, what I bought off o' Ginger Jones—real 'andsome stuff, and you can't shrink 'em—my missis says you can't. They're as good as noo now, and I've 'ad 'em ten months, so that'll show you. And I've got two guernsies and one of 'em you wouldn't 'ardly know 'ad ever been worn."

Brushing these domestic matters aside, I said: "My idea is that we fish our way there and back. On a good ground we can stay for a few days, but when the fishing is poor we can move on. And, of course, whenever we've caught enough fish to sell, we can run into the nearest harbour and sell it. What do you think of that?"

"Sounds all right," said Gotty thoughtfully; "and one thing's sartin—the fishing in that 'ere Channel can't be no wuss than what it is 'ere. Talk about arning a livin'—things never was so crool. And shrimpin's bin so good these last years! That's what gits over me."

"Yes, we surely ought to do better in the Channel. What do you say to this arrangement? We each take a third share, as we do now; and in addition, I'll find the food, and give you both ten shillings a week to send to your wives."

"Anything what's agreeable to you," replied Gotty with dignity, "is agreeable to me."

"That's not the sort of answer I want. Leaving yourself out, is that a fair offer to make to the mate?"

"Certernly!" replied Gotty.

"Well," came my confession, "the thought in my mind is that a skipper ought to receive rather more than a mate. But perhaps—"

"On a shrimpin' borley," Gotty made haste to remind me, "skipper and mate share alike. That's the rule, and you can't git away from it."

"Very well. See what the mate says."

Gotty drawn in 1907 by Will Owen, the noted Edwardian illustrator, who was frequently Copping's guest on board the *Betty*
Courtesy Mrs Betty Fletcher

X

THE MATE'S MYSTERIOUS SILENCE

WHEN, ten days later, I met Gotty again, he came hurrying towards me bursting with news:

"My missis ain't took 'ardly a minute's rest since I see you last—washin', ironin', and mendin'. She's made my ducks that white I didn't know 'em, and sewed on all the buttons, she 'as! They're mostly all stowed away, drawers and all, in my old kit bag, what I 'ad when I used to go bargin', and she's clent it lovely. She's got to mend one shirt what I took off yesterday, which she washed this mornin', and then I'm ready! Only," he added, " when you give the word, I'll bring 'er up on the 'ouse, so as to lust 'er over and give 'er a coat o' tar, and paint the topmast, and the blocks, and round the colmans. We must make 'er a bit smart afore we go."

"Good; and I'd like to come aboard and help. What does the mate say?"

"The next morning after I see you I told 'im where we was going, and I told 'im what you said about the 'a'pence."

"And what did he say?"

"He didn't say nuthin'!"

"What did you understand from that?"

"As fur as that goes," Gotty thoughtfully replied, "I didn't expec' 'e would say nuthin', unless it might be 'Oh!'—like that. Alfred never is one to say much—'e thinks it all to hisself. My feelin' was 'e might want to turn it over afore he give an answer, so I never said no more, and nex' mornin' I didn't say no more, nor yet for sev'ral mornin's, not another word, my thought bein' that 'e'd begin fust. But yesterday, when 'e still didn't say nuthin', I says, to him, 'Alfred', I says 'my missis has clent my things,' I says, 'and mended 'em, I says, 'and put on the buttons,' I says. 'Oh!' he says; and as 'e didn't say no more, I waited a bit and then I says to 'im, "As your missis clent your things,' I says, 'and mended 'em and put on the buttons,' I says. 'Not yet she ain't,' Alfred says, wonderful quiet, and 'e didn't say no more, No more didn't I. But I think 'e means to come."

"He must make up his mind soon, for I want to start next week."

"Wery good," said Gotty energetically; "then I shan't go out shrimpin' no more, for that don't leave us too much time."

It was further settled that, at six o'clock on the following evening, Gotty and the mate would arrive in the dinghy at Westcliff, to take me and my luggage on board the *Betty*.

Next evening I waited on the promenade from six till seven, not a little annoyed to find the appointment broken. Returning to the front later, at the beginning of dusk, I was greeted from the water by fog-horn lungs, and looking I beheld that which filled my bosom with shame. A fisherman's rowing-boat could at no time appear other than a rough, tarry intruder among the dainty pleasure-craft of Westcliff; but the specimen sailing towards me, with Gotty riotously waving from the stern, and the mate bunched up inert before the mast, had the aspect of a conspicuous brown dilapidation. The sail was old and torn and tattered beyond the reach of caricature—like a wild array of foul rags loosely skewered together.

Yet my chagrin was tempered with gratitude. How unspeakably lucky that this marine apparition came now, in the waning light, instead of at the appointed time, when I stood with two yachting neighbours unsuspiciously awaiting its arrival.

"That sail!" I gasped, when the dinghy came alongside the stairs. "Where on earth did you get it from?"

With a not unkindly eye Gotty scanned the old mummy cloth, and then explained:

"That was give me by old Peters, seeing he didn't want it no more when 'e bought 'isself a new 'un. It was give *him* last Christmas by Grunter Morgan, what bought it second-'and off o' the little iron shop—and 'ad it nigh on three years, Grunter Morgan did. Only, old Peters said, as I 'adn't no lug to my punt, 'e wouldn't throw it away afore 'e arksed if I mightn't care to 'ave it. So I thanked 'im kindly, and it's saved a bit o' rowin' one time and another, not 'arf it ain't."

Mortification getting the better of manners, I advised Gotty to try and sell his venerable trophy to the British Museum; and, understanding the observation sufficiently to resent its spirit, he humbled me with this retort:

"It ain't a sail I like to be seen 'andling, nor wouldn't anybody, but seeing you'd 'ad so much expense in buying fust one thing and then another, my thought was I'd make do with this fer a bit, and that'd be one thing you wouldn't 'ave to put yer 'and in yer pocket for. It gits 'er along when there comes a draught o' wind, and, as fur as that goes, a brand noo 'un wouldn't do no more. That's 'ow I looked at it; and if I done wrong," added the good old fellow with proud humility, "I'm sorry. There you are. I can't say no fairer'n that."

"Gotty," I replied, "didn't you tell me these little sails are made of much cheaper stuff than the big sails?"

"That's right enough," he conceded. "Duck ain't as expensable as canvas—a new-born babe don't want to be told that—but by the time they've made the eyeholes and sewed the leach, you ain't goin' ter see much change out of a sov'rin. And a sov'rin's a sov'rin. Ain't it?" he asked.

"Haven't we another old sail that isn't made of canvas?"

"The spinniker? Why"—in amazement—"if they was made of canvas they'd cost nigh on ten pounds—a big sail like that would. And you don't want 'em made of canvas. They wouldn't be so easy to 'andle fer one thing—and there wouldn't be no sense in it. They 'aven't the same wear. There's many fine days when you don't want 'em, and it ain't likely you'd set a spinniker if it was blowing anything at all. You'd stand a charnse of 'aving yer mast carried away. A mainsel's different altergether. That's up in all weathers, and—"

"Our spinnaker," I asked, breaking in upon the stream of argument, "is pretty ragged, isn't it?"

"No more than reasonable, seeing 'ow old it is. Nothing ain't going to last for ever. I'm careful to treat it tender, and take it in when there comes anythin' of a draught. But there isn't many times when it don't rip somewheres; and then I 'ave to sit down and mend it. You can't trust yer mate—it's a 'undred to one if they do it properly. They don't larn 'em nowadays—not the same as they used—"

"By-the-bye, where is the mate?" For he was not accompanying us on our walk to my house.

Lowering his voice to a confidential key, charged with mysterious significance, Gotty replied:

"He's stayed be'ind in the boat."

"So I notice. But isn't he coming to lend a hand in getting my things on board?"

"Don't arsk me," Gotty entreated, "fer I don't know." He turned to earnestly scrutinise the vacant perspective of pavement we had traversed. The compressed lips, and involuntary little head jerks, apparently testified to a pent-up volume of private thought.

"But," I exclaimed, "I don't understand. Doesn't he know what we've brought the boat here for?"

"'E do!" was the dramatic reply. "'Alfred,' I says, 'we're a goin' up to the guv-nor's 'ouse,' I says, 'ter get 'is bits of stuff.' All 'e says was 'Oh!' and, mind yer, no one couldn't 'ave spoke more civil to 'im than what I did. It's jest like"—and Gotty hesitated for a simile to match the intensity of his disgust—"it's jest like a brick wall a-talking to yer."

"Why," I exclaimed, as a light dawned upon my bewilderment, "he is staying behind to mind the boat!"

"No 'e ain't!" came the sledge-hammer contradiction. "When I came ashore, and seeing 'im not offerin' to move, 'Alfred,' I says, 'no one won't run away with 'er,' I says."

"Oh, well! come along. We can carry the boxes without his help."

"Yus, but stay a bit!" protested Gotty, his bosom swelling with indignation. "D'you mean to tell me a mate 'asn't a right to do what 'e ought? Becaws, if that's what we're coming to—well, Gawd 'elp us."

"Oh, bother the mate! We were talking about the untidy sail that isn't made of canvas."

"Canvas! Of course it ain't!" muttered Gotty, obviously quite ready, in that warlike mood, to exchange one topic of grievance for another. "Don't I keep tellin' yer there'ud be no sense in 'aving a spinniker made of canvas? It 'ud be a lot more expensable, and—"

"Quite so—I understand. It's the spinnaker—though when I was on the boat didn't you call it by some other name?"

Gotty stopped dead, and by the light of a street lamp I perceived that he was confronting me with a visage of mingled resentment and perplexity.

"Me call a spinniker somethin' else!" he said in a hollow voice, as though striving to realise the significance of a grotesque and cruel indictment. "'Ere! what d'yer mean? *Oh!*" he suddenly cried, and in so far-reaching a voice that a little dog came hurrying out of a front garden to bark at us. "You ain't thinkin' of the bloon fore-sel, are yer?"

"That's it—the balloon fore-sail. The name had—"

I did not finish the sentence. Gotty was exercising his lungs with laughter—a demonstration of which, with a countenance of gravity assumed to mark my sense of his misbehaviour, I patiently awaited the conclusion.

"But," amid noble efforts at self-control he presently found breath to exclaim, "a bloon fore-sel ain't a spinniker!"

"Perhaps not. In fact, I suppose it isn't. Anyhow isn't our balloon fore-sail rather ragged?"

"We ain't got one," came the trenchant reply. "We 'ad one, or, I *should* say"—with a laborious anxiety for exactitude—"we 'ad

71

somethin' wot 'ad been one; but it reg'lar fell to pieces. It was that rotten a bluebottle would 'a put 'is foot through it, let alone a puff o' wind rippin' it right acrost; and the last time I went to take it in it come to rags in my 'and, same as tinder."

"Quite so. And balloon fore-sails aren't made of canvas, are they?"

Gotty started, and was on the point of eloquence. He however shut his mouth hard, drew his head a shade higher, and sampled the evening air with audible nostrils—a victory over self that compelled my admiration. Finally he suffered his mouth to open just sufficiently to let one quick explanatory word escape:

"Caliker!"

"And what do you suppose," I went on, still following my own private line of inquiry, "all three sails would cost—I mean a spinnaker, a balloon fore-sail, and a punt's lug?"

"Noo 'uns," said Gotty, growing more companionable, "'ud cost a tidy 'a'penny. You'd be surprised. It ain't only the caliker—there's all the work of making 'em."

"But how much would they cost?"

"You wouldn't get noo 'uns," he replied dismally, but with decision, "under four pound, or four pound ten."

"Very well. Will you please order them to-morrow morning, and say we want them at once."

If I had uprooted a geranium from my garden (which we were just entering), and smitten my skipper across the nose with it, he could scarcely have looked more startled.

He began a long whistle, which finished abruptly as he turned to pathetically inquire:

"D'yer mean it?"

"Of course I do. . . . Here, steady there with those sweet peas!"

For, in the attempt at some high-spirited evolutions, he had inadvertently stepped off the grass, and was blundering in soft soil amid the ominous crackling of little branches. Oh those great boots on my pansies! When I arrived to the rescue, La France fortunately had him by the coat.

Perspiring with apologies, Gotty upbraided himself in a manner vividly suggestive of a dual personality.

"There's some people," he bitterly reflected, "'as don't know 'ow to be'ave theirselves, and didn't ought to be allowed in gentleman's housen. They're too ignerint—that's what they are. . . . Silly old fool!" he added, and in a manner so minatory that I feared he might proceed to the extreme of punching himself in the eye.

XI

A SMACK-OWNER'S MIDNIGHT EXPERIENCES

IN porterage Gotty found opportunity for penance, and, as some compensation for the damage done to my blossoms, he insisted on balancing a stout oak box on his head, and carrying a piece of leather luggage in each hand; I hurrying by his side with two overcoats and a hurricane lamp.

This consignment having been received into the boat by the silent mate, Gotty and I returned for the rest of the goods, his load comprising a bag of tools, two metal basins, a deck chair, a parcel of knives, forks, and spoons, a spirit stove, three tin mugs, a looking-glass, two blankets, and a coffee-pot, so that nothing remained for me to carry but my camera and a basket of food.

Unusually bustling and pre-occupied, Gotty made but one remark on our second journey to the house:

"Fust thing in the morning," he assured me, in a tone of hearty confidence, "I'll go round and give the order. When young Tunnige comes to open the shop he'll find me waitin' outside; and when 'e knows we want 'em this week pertic'ler 'e'll put all 'is people on 'em—I know 'e will."

As the laden boat passed across the dark water, I remarked to the mate that it was a fine evening.

"Yus," he replied, with so wide a gap of silence at each end of the monosyllable that, by a natural human preference, I addressed the remainder of my observations to the skipper.

As we came alongside the *Betty*—which lay about two miles from shore, between Westcliff and Leigh—I happened to say she looked a beauty, though, indeed, in the faint light of a cloud-screened moon, she towered out of the water merely as a black figure of mystery.

"Not 'alf sech a beauty," came the hoarse whisper from Gotty, who had risen to offer me the assistance in scrambling on board, "as she'll look when she's got what there's them as knows about them and them as don't."

Those dark words were accompanied by mysterious movements of the head, from which I gathered that the proposed purchase of accessory sails was as a precious secret, not to be shared with a mere mate.

I had arranged to sleep on board the *Betty*—an intention in which, now that it came to the point, Gotty strove to shake me. Didn't I think it would be more comfortable on shore? *No.* Mightn't I feel strange and lonely like, not bein' used to the water and all? *No.*

True, during the application of these persuasions a curious sinking sensation came over me on a sudden realisation that, however much I might want to, I could not go out to post a letter or buy anything, and that I should hear no milkman in the morning. But I crushed down these feeble misgivings as unworthy to find lodgment in a British bosom.

Gotty, his feet in the dinghy, and his hands on the *Betty's* bulwarks, paused reluctant in the act of departure, and, as his head and shoulders bobbed up and down, the light from my lantern revealed a countenance of hopeless entreaty.

"I know what my missis 'll say," he dismally remarked; "that I didn't ought to 'a let you stay on board, and no more I oughtn't . . . . Look 'ere, sir, if you won't come ashore, wouldn't you like me ter stay along of yer, jest for company?"

"Don't be such a silly old ass, Gotty," I said politely. "Get along back to Leigh. Good-night, both."

The dinghy dropped away, and I heard the oars at work. Next minute the stentorian voice of the skipper was hailing me out of the darkness:

"I'll be out in the morning, soon as ever there's water in the creek—if," the voice added, in still louder key, "if it don't blow too 'ard."

"Which isn't likely!" I shouted back defiantly.

"There's times," ominous tones of thunder informed me, "when it ain't safe to put a boat out for several tides tergether. But," the laboured articulation continued, "you've got a loaf o' bread and a pot o' marmerlade, so you won't starve fer a day or two."

"Gotty!" I shouted.

"Yes, sir?" came the eager reply.

"Go—and—drown—yourself!"

The muffled sound of hearty guffaws reached me. Again there was the creak of oars; and thereafter was I alone with the night.

Now, then, was the time ripe to enjoy a treat that for several months had stood postponed. I wanted to realise that this vessel was my very own, and that, with the exception of a clay pipe on which I had just inadvertently sat, and possibly a few other trifles, all things on board also belonged to me, and in no sense or degree to any other human being. I wanted, privately, and for the sheer gratification of the thing, to bathe and wallow in the sense of proprietorship.

Of course I know that if we come back to abstract principles, this state of mind will, to many people, appear deplorable. Nay, in strict logic, it was a denial and contradiction of my own oft-reiterated political faith, and that very thought was present at the time in the background of my mind, floating, so to speak, in a haze of sub-conscious guiltiness. But it is my pen's duty to record the fact that I, nevertheless, callously persevered in the projected course of pleasure, and gave unlicenced scope to the anti-communistic me, the pro-private property me—if you will, the curmudgeon me.

Whether ownership ecstasy is common to the human race, I do not happen to know. One is very apt to suppose an experience peculiar to one's self, and then one day be surprised to find the very thing precisely stated in, say, Shakespeare, where, at first sight, it looks like an unblushing plagiarism. For myself I can at least certify that all possessions do not excite me to those pleasant feelings. I can own table linen and encyclopaedias, to give two random examples, without emotion. But my first box of bricks provoked a delicious thrill of lordly exaltation. Similarly, on the first occasion of owning a house, I had the sensation powerfully—and, indeed, prematurely— for on the autumn afternoon when the owner's spirit descended upon me, the mortgage had not been fully paid off. But I attempted an adjustment of my own and the building-society's rights by leaving the chimney-pots and roof—a liberal abatement for the balance due—outside the scope of my endearing thoughts.

Lantern in hand, I set out to explore my good ship the *Betty*, and, coming in rough contact with some spars on the deck, had early occasion to recall with increased respect some advice which, when Gotty gave it to me a few minutes before his departure, I was disposed to regard as superfluous.

"Now you be careful," he had said with severity, "as you don't fall overboard." Thenceforward I did exercise care in guarding against that contingency.

I fingered the sails, proudly reflecting that I had the supreme, indisputable right to hoist them—if only I had known how to do so. I put a proprietorial hand on the pendant ropes tangled about the mast. I touched the windlass—my windlass—and tried to recall how it was worked.

Down in the cabin I received a vivid impression of a solid and habitable freehold. I went prying into my own lockers, and found myself far richer in rusty iron properties—many of them most interesting-looking things—than I had known. In particular was I delighted with about four cubic feet of various metal objects of which I did not know the uses. At the tapering extremity of the apartment I found great heaps of my sails and nets. In one cupboard I cast a disparaging eye over part of a loaf and some dirty butter that presumably belonged to Gotty; in another, I found some fine large lamps that doubtless belonged to me.

But, if I was owner of the cabin, it was not without other occupiers. A noisy family of flies were in possession, and, not for the first time in history, the landlord was so pestered by his tenants that he attempted to expel them. Ruthless efforts to that end were, however, unavailing, and it was I who presently departed, after resolving to improve the property by putting a ventilator in the ceiling, and so securing a through draught to carry away hot and exhausted air, besides flies. For, what with the closeness of the cabin atmosphere and the exertion of chivvying the diptera, the first freshness was wearing off my ownership joys. Nay, the unstable equilibrium of my boat had come as a dismal reminder of one element of uncertainty in the projected cruise. Of recent years I had escaped sea-sickness, but my maritime experiences had been restricted to liners. Peradventure, a sailing boat would still serve me as vessels of that character did, on each occasion of my using them, in early youth.

Ventilator or no ventilator, I resolved not to sleep in the cabin on our cruise. Skipper and mate should enjoy the luxury of its two bunks. I would sleep in the hold.

Thinking to inaugurate that policy forthwith, I knelt on deck and held my lantern down into the main cavity, peering into its secrets. But no; not to-night. The place was a dirty confusion of baskets, boxes, and lumber. Moreover, it smelt rankly of brine and shrimps. To crown the matter I saw woodlice. Manifestly there must be a great clearing and cleansing and fumigating ere the hold could become a sleeping chamber. It was a fine night. I would sleep on deck.

A stubborn sprawling mass of sail was selected as bed, and, with the lamp and a book beside my head, I curled up cosily beneath blankets and an overcoat. And the thought came over me, if people were sensible they would do this sort of thing more frequently—so refreshing, healthy, and pleasant! Indeed, I felt sorry for the mass of conventional mortals imprisoned in bedrooms and still air. With ghostly clouds above, a gentle sea breeze, and the rocking of the ship, mine were ideal conditions for sleep. But, not to divorce my senses too speedily from these soft delights (for, now that I was lying down, internal uneasiness had ceased), I would first read. Like an epicure I fed my mind awhile on Robert Louis Stevenson—literature of fresh air and a healthy humanity—and fed it leisurely, with intervals of listening to the curlews calling over the water, and watching the little lights in the streak of illumination that marked the distant shore. Away towards the sea I could just discern the dim, dark form of a sister vessel, and in the opposite direction, I knew, other Leigh bawleys were anchored in a scattered line. There was a flavour of romance in the situation. But, good gracious! on looking at my watch I found it forty minutes past midnight. I must go to sleep, for laborious tasks had to be performed on the morrow. So out went the light.

Strange! The sensations of approaching sleep were wanting. For one thing, my head was uncomfortably low, and, after several experimental variations of position, I was impelled to sit up and enter upon a wrestling match with the sail, in the endeavour to bunch it into some semblance of a pillow. But it was apparently fastened somewhere, so that I had to acknowledge defeat and replace my head in its previous situation of discomfort. I went on trying very hard to go to sleep, though part of my attention was soon engaged in noting the penetrative quality of night air. Wherever there was a leak, so to speak, in my shroud of wrappings, an atmospheric current of low temperature pushed its way, and thus I was impelled, every five minutes or so, to tighten my encasement.

But anon it grew manifest that my bedclothes were unequal to their task, my body, from being merely chilly in places, having become cold all over. Reflecting that this sort of thing would never do, I arose, clutching my woolly envelope about me, and descended after all into the cabin. The aspect of the bunk bedding having, as I remembered, inspired me with little confidence, I lay down on the floor.

The superior warmth of the cabin gave me comfort, and I was already in the early phases of slumber when I was startled by thunder. And yet it was no thunder, for on a repetition of the din I distinctly heard the clank clank of a chain. So some one had come on board, and was fooling with the machinery!

"Hullo there!" I shouted, I hope in no very unsteady voice. The only reply was a still more formidable clanking of the chain. So I scrambled up, and thrust my head and shoulders through the cabin opening, desperately eager to get at close quarters with the intruder.

But I could not see him, though a man might anywhere be lurking amid those forms of uncertainty in the deck darkness.

"Who's there?" I demanded. But all was silent save the splash of water and the creak of rigging.

There are few things more calculated to heighten a sense of isolation than to find yourself all alone, yet talking to someone who, necessarily, is not there. The immediate memory of your voice jars upon your nerves, and the experience falls into the category of the creepy-crawly. I had a cold-water feeling running up and down my spine. Then a strange thing happened. The clanking of the chain was repeated, and this time the noise, without being more remote, was much reduced. It was the same sound but in a softer key.

Mystified, I withdrew into the cabin, lit the lamp, and sat on a locker to listen. In a little while, gur-r-r, gur-r-r—clank, clank—I had another long drawn-out dose of the former thunder. It was now manifest that the sound came from underneath the tapering of the cabin.

At the moment of realising what was occurring, the appropriate phrase flashed through my mind. We were—ahem!—"dragging our anchor." By Jove! a pretty state of things. However, it was, so to speak, nothing to do with me—that is to say, I did not put the anchor down nor did I feel sure what would happen to the *Betty* were I to pull the anchor up, if, indeed, I could do so. So once more I tried to go to sleep.

"Ain't that a light on Ponto's bawley?" These words presently came to me, thin and faint from travelling across the water; and at this reminder that I had failed to extinguish my lamp (which threw a glare about the hatchway) I repaired the omission. Then, perceiving a milky greyness without, I knew that day was dawning.

Going once more to the hatchway, I beheld a perspective of dim bawleys. On one that was near tiny figures were moving.

XII

OVERHAULING OUR CRAFT

IN the full daylight of five o'clock I gave up the attempt to go to sleep, and busied myself with a bathe and breakfast until, soon after eight, the row-boat returned with Gotty and the mate. Only the former responded to my greetings, and it was therefore to him I imparted my piece of sensational news.

"She's been dragging her anchor in the night."

"No she ain't," replied Gotty, with more decision than politeness. "What you 'eard was the chain droring along the bottom. I give 'er fifteen fadum, so she should ride nice and comfertable."

Gotty said we could do nothing until we had bought some paint, with which view I the more readily concurred because of a desire to see my morning's mail; so we forthwith set out for the shore.

The mate, pulling stroke, was immediately in front of me; and I fired a point-blank question into his armour of taciturnity.

"Well, mate, are you coming with us on the voyage?"

He paused from his labours, fixed me with a hostile stare, and asked, in a voice that was almost a shout:

"'Ow about money?"

"That," I replied, rather taken aback, "is a matter we have to discuss. I made a suggestion to the skipper, as a—"

"Not good enough! D' y' see, guv'nor? Not good enough!"

His style grew more pugnacious.

"Very well," I said sweetly, "perhaps we shall be able to come to an understanding. Tell me what terms you suggest."

"A share of the fishin'—that's right. All found—that's right. Then I want thirty bob a week. Or I don't go. D'yer see?"

"Very well, I'll talk it over with the skipper," for I was unable to read the secret signals that individual was sending me over the mate's shoulders. Having rested his oar across the boat, Gotty was busy with his hands, which, held flat and rigid, kept parting and joining silently on an imaginary hinge at the wrists. It suggested some one making a crocodile in wall shadows.

When the mate had withdrawn from our society, as happened so

79

soon as we landed, I asked Gotty to unriddle his previous pantomime.

"Opens 'is mouth too wide!" came the simple explanation, which was assisted by an explanatory thumb jerked over the speaker's shoulder in the direction of the retreating mate.

"You think he is asking too much money?"

"Thirty shillin's all found and a share!" Gotty's attempt, born of emotion, to run all these words into one syllable, left him almost breathless. After the impressive pause: "Too much! I should think! Why!" frowning with dignified indignation, "'e must think we're made o' money."

Something had lifted the skipper into a state of mind positively proprietorial. I, who had derived so much glee overnight from owning the bawley, could not begrudge a powerful imagination its suck at the same sugar stick. Gotty's next words hinted at the wherefore of his soul's inflation.

"Mr. Tunnige started the young woman on the mersheenin' as soon as ever she come. All 'ands 'll be on 'em till they're done, and they're to be sent round to my 'ome on Saturday for certin."

When, by appointment, and with a pound of cold meat, I returned to Leigh jetty, there stood Gotty with head more than usually erect, his boots entrenched behind a row of bright paint pots. Two were, indeed, knocked over when, on espying me, he set forth with incautious footsteps to the reunion.

Having hastily restored the sealed vessels of pigment to an upright attitude, he came to me with a self-conscious smile curiously compounded of schoolboy joy and manly restraint.

After assuring himself, by looking round, that there was no third party to overhear the communication, he leaned forward, and, with an awkward attempt to appear composed, said:

"There's a wooden case come to my 'ouse."

"Indeed ! . . . Oh yes, I know. That's all right. It's groceries and things for the voyage."

"So my missis said!" he gasped; and for the first time in my knowledge of Gotty I saw that he was blushing. "It's as big as that," he went on, his hands measuring off about a yard and a half of air—"and the weight! Come all the way from London, too, the man said what brought it."

"Yes—from the Stores."

"I ain't touched it, mind," continued my skipper piously. "Not opened it or nothin'. There it is fer you to see the same as when it come."

"Of course you haven't opened it. . . . Let us go aboard and get on with our work."

"My missis," he went on, as though speaking under hypnotic compulsion, "wouldn't 'ear of me seein' what was inside. She reg'lar druv me out o' doors."

"Why," I laughed, "open it by all means if you want to. But I thought it would be easier to unpack the case on board."

"So it would," came the eager agreement—"a lot easier."

I moved towards the stairs, and Gotty remained rooted where we had been standing.

"Ain't we going to fetch it now?" wailed the empty voice behind me.

"Surely not!" I argued. "Why take it aboard until we are ready to start? It will only be in the way."

"And all them wittles"—he spoke in measured accents, and as though addressing himself rather than me—"goin' ter wait in that parler till we go?"

"Oh, I forgot!" said I, realising in sudden consternation my inconsiderateness. "That case will be in the way. Of course we must—"

"Not at all! Not at all!" Gotty half shouted. "It ain't nowise in the way. Jest as though we'd mind, even if it was!" And this was said in so earnest a tone of kindly protest that I regarded the subject as settled. But he had not quite done with it.

"I shan't touch 'em," he asseverated solemnly. "No! I shan't go anigh 'em. An' no more won't my missis—you may be sure o' *that*."

Eager to change the subject, I inquired if the mate was coming out to help with the painting.

"'E don't seem nowise to 'urry 'isself, do 'e?" was the skipper's guarded reply, as he bent his eyebrows towards the town. "Not, mind you, as I don't know where 'e is, fer I saw 'im standin' up agin the railway when I come by. 'Alfred,' I says, 'we're goin' on board to do a bit o' paintin', and the Guv'nor,' I says, 'is comin' to lend us a 'and.' He didn't say nothin', and I didn't say no more. One thing, 'e knows we can't go without 'im, fer I give 'im the tholes. I'll tell you what I'll do," Gotty added, on a sudden inspiration—"I'll go an' fetch 'im."

In less than five minutes Gotty returned—alone, and with compressed lips.

"Isn't he coming?" I asked, and, by way of answer, the skipper showed me the rowlock pins in his hands. In a strained silence he got into the dinghy, fixed his acquisitions into their holes, carefully assisted me on board, and then, in grim silence, fell to work with his oars. I patiently waited until his thoughts should ripen into speech. Particulars of the affair came to light at last:

"Alfred,' I says, 'are yer comin' out?' 'I dunno,' 'e says. 'Or are yer goin' 'ome to 'ave yer dinner fust?' I says. 'I dunno,' 'e says. 'Oh,' says I, 'if you dunno, 'oo does? Give me them tholes, Alfred,' I says. So 'e give 'em to me, an' I come away. What's gittin over some people is more that I do know, and that's tellin' you the truth."

"The mate seems to have mutinied, in a mild sort of way. Do you understand that he throws up the job?"

"Don't I tell yer? I says, 'Give me the tholes,' and 'e give 'em to me."

"Well, that almost sounds as if you dismissed *him*."

Gotty stopped rowing, and stared at me in despair.

"Didn't I arsk 'im if 'e was comin' out?"

"Yes."

"And did 'e come?"

"No."

"Well, then, 'ow can you say I sacked 'im? 'E done it 'isself."

"Anyway"—for I was lost amid these nautical niceties—"we have no mate at the present time—that is so, is it not?"

"That's right"—and the speaker's tone suggested an improved opinion of my understanding.

"Well, Gotty, I'm very glad of it."

"Is yer, though! What for?"

"Because I think Alfred was not the right sort of mate for our cruise. On thinking it over, I would prefer to take some one who knows the English Channel."

"That's a true word!" enthusiastically exclaimed my companion, from whom I had expected opposition. "Where I've bin before I don't want nobody to show me the way. Where I *ain't* bin, I'm willin' to be took in 'and by them as 'ave. I ain't like some people—too ignerint to be larned what they don't know."

On this important point of engaging a mate of experience, I welcomed my skipper's mature judgment, ripened, as I could not doubt it was, by advice received from brethren of the sea over an evening glass of ale.

But further consideration of the matter was postponed by the fact that, having arrived on board the *Betty*, we stood face to face with the first problem in our preparations, to wit, what should we do with the copper?

82

Arthur Edward Copping, "The Guv'nor"; journalist and traveller. A portrait contemporary with his ownership of the bawley *Betty*. *Courtesy Mrs Betty Fletcher*

A shrimping bawley. The cut-away areas of the hull show the interior of foc's'le and hold. *Drawing by Colin Mudie*

Leigh Creek at half tide. Laid up bawleys lie "lusted over" on one bilge and the boats of others lie at the tide's edge. Lower down, sailing barges discharge at the Bell Wharf.

The Leigh bawley *Doris* trawling for shrimps in a calm. The mainsail is reefed for working convenience and the working jib is loosely stowed along the bowsprit. She was amongst the fastest bawleys.

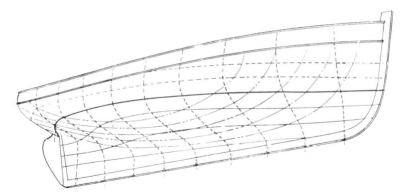

A bawley had a beamy hull but many had a fine entry at the forefoot and a clean run to a shapely transom.

Hoisting the forward trawl head and the beam on board a shrimping bawley. The "wink" is forward of the hatch and the shrimp copper is bubbling in the hold.   *Drawing by Edward Wigfull*

A bawley in Harwich harbour. The mainsail foot is triced up for vision as she prepares to anchor. The cruiser in the background is port guard ship.

WORKING SAILS REEFED UP

COMING UP TO ANCHOR

SPINNAKER AS BALLOON JIB-TOPS'L

BRAILED

WITH BALLOON FORES'L

TOPS'L OVER BRAILED MAINS'L

ANCHORED

Possible sail combinations of the bawleys' boomless rig are shown in Edward Wigfull's drawings of these versatile craft.

Copping's bawley was renamed for his daughter *Betty*, who, in this contemporary childhood photograph, preferred beaches to bawleys.

Courtesy Mrs Betty Fletcher

A bawley setting a large jib, usually known as the "bowsprit spinnaker", sometimes as the "balloon jib". The brail and rows of reef points show clearly across the mainsail. Her sails set poorly.

The answer to that question was swiftly perceived to depend on the answer to another, namely, were there any shrimps (allowing a liberal margin of meaning to the word "any") in the English Channel? As one having, at any rate, some shore knowledge of that region, I was asked for a ruling, but could merely say that I had often, at seaside resorts, seen paddlesome children pushing hand-gear through sandy shallows, and, indeed, that I had occupied some hours of my own youth in that manner, once catching as much as half a cupful of the nimble creatures in question. Gotty's eyebrows brushed this evidence aside, and then, attacking the original problem from a new standpoint, he said:

"One thing's sartin—we'll 'ave to git a noo copper when we come back, fer this one's fair 'ad it's day. I'm everlastin' plaster plaster ter keep it tergether. Mud mixed along o' salt's a good cement, we know; but that ain't goin' to 'old up a iron fireplace what's eat through with rust—not fer ever, it ain't."

"And, of course," I pointed out, "the hold would be nicer for living in without this dirty old thing"—an argument, by the way, which increased in weight the more I pondered it.

My timid effort to reconcile abolition of the copper with the retention of a possible source of revenue was not favourably received. For Gotty contented himself with an austere shake of the head when I suggested:

"Couldn't you cook them in a saucepan?"

Finally I took the plunge, and eliminated shrimping from the scope of our intentions in the Channel. Straightway, with a great shovel, Gotty attacked the copper, which capitulated on the third prod, collapsing at his feet in an avalanche of bricks, cinders, rust, mortar, and soot.

From these dusty ruins he rescued the copper proper, still whole and serviceable, and laid it respectfully on deck, where it was presently joined by iron bars, the poker, and pieces of firebrick which, because sound and shapely, the careful fisherman was reluctant to consign to oblivion. The remaining débris, lifted in copious shovelfuls, went up in the air and over the side, to dirty the sea and fill little crabs with false hope; I offering these perspiring labours the stimulus of applause. Gotty assured me I could not usefully assist, save by keeping out of the line of fire.

The zeal for clearance grows with its gratification; and once a man is fairly launched on the business of throwing things away, the spirit of riddance mounts to his brain, and he will go on. Thus, as the last shovelful of ruined copper fell into the sea, Gotty looked around for further prey. On second thoughts, away went the firebricks and iron bars. Then he made a ruthless frontal attack on the hold lumber.

Old and broken fish-trunks and shrimp baskets, decayed sieves, odds and ends of rope and net—a whole rag-shop of musty antiquities—were dragged to the light of day and sent circling into the sea, so that, with the tide running strongly past our anchored vessel, we soon had a wake of pathetic objects astern.

On the deck Gotty piled reputable trunks, baskets and sieves, the kedge anchor, a sack of coal, the pump, a box of salt, and other properties that recommended themselves to his experience as worthy of retention; and, peradventure for the first time for a quarter of a century, light and air freely penetrated the roomy recesses of the hold.

But Gotty had not done. Standing on deck, he drew water from the sea in a bucket tethered by a piece of rope, and this water he hurled at the floor of the hold. After a dozen or so deluges, he exchanged the bucket for a broom of short, stubborn bristles, and, springing down, administered a vigorous brushing to the area he had recently swilled. Then again he got to work with the bucket, assaulting the boards with copious libations.

"P'raps you wouldn't mind," he suggested, on pausing from these labours to mop his brow, "jest puttin' a few sticks on the fire, so as we can 'ave a cup o' black an' green;" and when presently we sat at leisure over our mugs of tea, I judged the moment opportune to apprise my shipmate of an intention that had been gradually maturing in my mind.

XIII

SHIPPING A NEW MATE

"GOTTY! I am going to choose the next mate."

"Is yer though!" he exclaimed, a note of admiration in his voice; and he sipped the steaming beverage with lips audibly appreciative. "Bray-vo!" he added with enthusiasm.

"Yes; I mean to choose some one that I like the look of. But of course he must know the English Channel."

"Wery good. Them I chooses don't turn out no class. Now you 'ave a go."

"Gotty," I continued, "I have seen the very man—if only he has had the experience. I saw him last week, and took a great fancy to him. I saw him yesterday, and I saw him again this morning. He is absolutely the ideal mate for us—if, by great good luck, he knows the Channel."

"Whoever might you be thinking of?" asked my skipper with a keen curiosity.

"I don't know his name, nor have I spoken to him. When I saw him first he was sitting on that seat near the jetty, but yesterday and to-day he was pottering about in a boat. He is short and plump, with a round face that is very jolly, and smiling, and good-tempered. He's about the most amiable-looking old fellow I've ever seen. You must know him. He wears a hard bowler hat."

As I was speaking, the lines on Gotty's brow had grown deeper and nearer, in sympathy with a strenuous mental effort at identification. Suddenly the furrows of perplexity vanished, and he cried:

"You mean old Rawson—what's called Treacle Tart, only that ain't 'is proper name. So it's 'im you was thinking of!"

My skipper ruminated, and, as I noted with satisfaction, he ruminated in no untranquil spirit.

"What do you think of him for a mate?" I eagerly inquired.

"As fur as that goes," Gotty replied with deliberation, "you couldn't find nobody what's bin about more. Yer see, 'e used ter go yachtin' so much. Bin all round this country, old Rawson 'ave—I know, fer 'e's told me."

"Excellent! Do you think he would come?"

"And jump at it, I shouldn't wonder. It takes 'im all 'is time to make a few 'a'pence, same as if anybody might want ter go fer a hower's row, 'im gettin' on in years, too; only, if you understand my meanin', we don't want a younger man. The 'ard graft ain't no trouble to me, but if I'd got somebody what could say where there's water, and where there ain't, and show the way into 'arbours and sech-like,—why, I'd feel more comfortable. Old Treacle Tart could do that easy—and not 'alf a tidy scholar he ain't, neither. He wouldn't 'ave no call to put 'isself out as regards work, no more than jest lend a 'and gettin' the mainsel up, or sometimes taking a turn at the helem. Yes"—reflectively—"he'll do a treat."

"And why didn't *you* think of him?" the complacent owner inquired.

"Old Treacle Tart! I never so much as give 'im a thought," the skipper made frank confession.

"Well, we've done enough work for to-day. Let's go ashore. You probably know the old boy's haunts and can fish him out. Then we can settle the matter."

"'E might be in the Peter Boat, and 'e might be in the Ship. It's jest accordin'. Wonderful fond of a bit o' company, old Treacle Tart is, though 'e don't drink. Jest a glass now and agin—that's all. And 'e don't use much terbacca—that's another thing."

Half-an-hour later Gotty drew the two coverts blank. But an inquiry put him on the true scent. Yet his brow was troubled.

"It ain't a 'ouse I care to use," he explained. "But p'raps you wouldn't mind jest goin' in to fetch 'im."

They were a genial group of mariners, and Mr. Rawson sat in the centre, a picture of cherubic amiability. It was rather awkward, but I blurted out:

"Could you spare a moment, please. I want to speak to you outside."

In a flutter of consent, the rotund little fisherman came stumping after me, a prey to polite curiosity.

"We are going for a two months' fishing cruise in the English Channel," I told him, when we had joined Gotty, "and we want some one to come as a sort of mate-pilot. Would you care about it?"

"The Guv'nor's took a fancy to yer," was supplementary information contributed from another quarter.

His beaming countenance turned from one to the other in a confusion of affability and surprise.

"Yes, why—I should be very pleased," he piped. "If you think I could be useful—well, yes, certainly—I'll come with pleasure. And how far, sir, might I ask, did you think of going?"

"A little beyond Falmouth."

"Ah, to be sure. Well, well, many's the time I've been to Falmouth. And all the harbours along the coast—there isn't one, sir, that I don't know as well as I know these waters. Wonderfully pretty places in Devonshire and Cornwall—lovely scenery, sir—as of course you are aware."

I had to confess myself a comparative stranger to Cornwall.

"Ah! you'll be delighted with it—I'm sure you will," he rattled on. "Dozens of times—I may say, scores of times—I've sailed along that coast. The gentleman whose yacht I had charge of—he was very fond of those parts, and in between the chief regattas (for we did a deal of racing, sir) he'd mostly manage to run down there for a week, or it might be a fortnight."

"I'm afraid," was my apologetic comment, "you will find our old bawley rather a rough craft after those you've been used to. And, by-the-by, Mr. Rawson"—for the misgiving came over me that my purse was over slender for the task of engaging an ex-master of a racing yacht—"on what terms would you be willing to come?"

"As to that," this most obliging old mariner hastened to assure me, "there won't be any difficulty—I'm quite sure there won't. Me and your skipper 'll just have a little talk together," he added, with a delicacy that commanded my gratitude, "and that will soon be settled. We've known one another, sir, since he was so high," indicating a Gotty of less than a yard in stature. "And now I'm sure you've a lot of things to see to, so I mustn't take up any more of your time. Good evening for the present, sir." Then to Gotty: "I'll be in the Bell at eight o'clock, if that'll suit you."

My skipper, with a hearty and sagacious nod, indicated that it would; and, still smiling, the fascinating old fellow waddled back to the genial company from which I had so unceremoniously plucked him.

The commander and the proprietor of the LO. 96 strode along the Leigh Street in a triumphant state of mind.

"He is absolutely the very man for us!" exclaimed the latter.

"It's took a load off my mind and charnse it!" agreed the former.

The question of wages was discussed in a spirit bordering on recklessness.

"There ain't much money in the firm, we know," said one, "but we didn't ought to let 'im slip through our fingers—not for a extry shillin' or two. And if there ain't no other way," he added, resolutely, "I'll 'ave five shillin's took off my money. There you are."

"If necessary," said the other, "you can offer him thirty shillings and a third share."

"If old Treacle Tart don't come fer that—well—!" and in a dazed sort of way the speaker whistled.

"And, by-the-bye, while I think of it—I shouldn't call him 'old Treacle Tart.' It doesn't sound respectful, and I'm sure he would feel more comfortable on the boat if you addressed him as Mr. Rawson, as I certainly shall."

"'Oo was goin' ter call 'im 'old Treacle Tart'? Not to 'is face, I shouldn't think o' doing so. I 'ope I know better manners than that! 'im coming ter do us good and all!"

Going to the little house up the alley, we found that Mrs. Gotty had thoughtfully prepared to reward our labours with a meat tea and lettuces. Later, at the appointed hour, we set out for the Bell.

"Most likely," thought my companion, "we'll find 'im naggin' and quarrellin' with old Daddy 'Unt. Them two are always at it—contradictin' and argufyin' like two lawyers, and the rude things they say jest to aggrivate each other you'd think they was the worst enemies out, only all the time there ain't a pair as is more fond of one another than what they are. You see, they was married at the same time and thirty year afterwards their two wives died in the same year—cureous, wasn't it!—and drored 'em tergether. They're both wonderful good scholars, and you'd be surprised at all the books they read—only I've often thought they do most of their readin' to find out somethin' what the other don't know, and then to get 'im talkin' about it so as ter show 'im up wrong."

In the act of pushing open the swing door, Gotty paused to nudge me severely with his elbow.

"What did I tell yer?" came the tremendous whisper in my ear. "Jest listen to 'em!" and indeed it was impossible not to be aware that a spirited bandying of personalities was proceeding within. Unfortunately, however, our arrival quelled the storm.

With fine old-world courtesy, Mr. Rawson had risen, pewter in hand, to wish me a "Good evening, sir," full of respectful geniality. Which of the half-dozen individuals was his foe-friend I could not at first divine, but when Gotty and I had seated ourselves in that company, uncertainty on the point was speedily removed. The interesting personage proved to be sitting by my side.

I had passed an appreciative comment on the weather, and this had been politely endorsed by Mr. Rawson, who added the supplementary suggestion that we might get a little breeze before the morning; whereupon a long, bony, claw-like hand touched my arm, and its owner, in a rasping voice, offered me this uncompromising counsel:

"Don't pay no heed to what that man says. He's misinformed about most things, sir, and I'm sorry to say the older he gets, the more ignorant he becomes."

I turned to behold a face in physiological harmony with the hand—lank and shrivelled. But there was a wealth of life in the alert, red-rimmed eyes. This thin old man and my plump Mr. Rawson made a sufficiently striking contrast, like unto a stick and a ball.

"Any way," said Mr. Rawson, complacently, "I do know the difference betwixt cement and lime;" and he cast a glance of amused triumph at my skinny neighbour.

"I've told you six times," came the old man's hot retort, "that I never looked inside the sacks, but took the lad's word. It was his mistake, not mine."

"Oh, blame it on the poor boy!" said Mr. Rawson, ruthlessly following up his advantage. "He's not here to contradict you."

"No, and I'm glad he isn't here," remarked the astute controversialist.

"Why?" asked Mr. Rawson, off his guard.

"Because he wouldn't take any good in *your* company," came the unexpected thrust, which secured laughter from the open-mouthed listeners. Ere Mr. Rawson had time to put a suitable reply into words, his nimblewitted antagonist had fortified his position by interposing a mental distraction.

"If you know so much about cement," he remarked though I had not understood Mr. Rawson to make any such claim, "perhaps you can tell us the difference between Portland cement and Roman cement."

"Portland cement is made from chalk," replied Mr. Rawson, cautiously, "and Roman cement isn't ."

Conscious that the question would have been a poser to me, I felt that this reply was highly creditable. But Daddy Hunt took a different view.

"That's what I call a dunce's answer," he declared. "Roman cement isn't made of chalk! And it isn't made of cheese, I dare say you'll tell us next. And very likely you might think of one or two other things it isn't made of."

"Well, what *is* Roman cement made of?" asked Mr. Rawson, with great presence of mind.

"But that's what I'm asking *you!*" gasped his opponent, outraged by what was, apparently, a gross breach of recognised rules.

"No, it isn't," retorted Mr. Rawson. "Your question was, What is the difference between Portland cement and Roman cement? I've said what the difference is. Now I ask you, What is Roman cement made of?"

"Limestone," replied Mr. Hunt, recognising that he stood at a disadvantage.

"Quite right," replied Mr. Rawson cheerfully, though I strongly suspected that the information just imparted to him partook of the nature of news. "But what sort of limestone?" he had the cool daring to inquire.

"Any sort," snapped old Daddy Hunt.

The machinery of hospitality being now set in motion, the thoughts of the disputants flowed for the moment in a new direction; and Gotty must have found in this digression an opportunity for private signalling. Simultaneously rising, he and Mr. Rawson mysteriously withdrew into the public thoroughfare.

An altered man, Mr. Hunt was instantly busy pouring confidences into my ear:

"If you thought of taking him with you, sir, I'm sure you won't regret it. You couldn't find a more capable man or one with more experience. I hope, sir, you'll excuse the liberty I'm taking in speaking like this, but I've known Rawson ever since we were both boys together. You *will* pardon me, sir?"

"Why," I hastened to assure him, "of course. I'm only too grateful. But I already had a very high opinion of Mr. Rawson—he is so good-tempered and obliging."

"Yes, yes. But I thought you mightn't understand. We have our little arguments together, but it don't mean anything. You see, my poor wife and his poor wife both—"

But the sentence was interrupted by the return of Mr. Rawson and Gotty.

I drew a favourable inference from the brevity of their conference. Mr. Rawson went back to his seat, his face wearing its wonted aspect of happy placidity. Gotty stepped up to me, and with a great wink that affected half his face, managed to convey a suggestion that I in turn should accompany him on an excursion into the open air.

"Well?" I asked eagerly, when we were by ourselves. After an annoying pause he replied:

"You won't 'ardly berlieve what I'm going to tell yer."

"Did you settle anything? You seemed very quick about it."

"We settled everythin'!"

"Well?"

"Now, 'ow much would you think 'e'd be likely to ask? Jest ter see, now!"

I looked at my skipper in astonishment. This reducing of the practical affairs of life to the level of a guessing competition was wholly unlike his usual direct and downright style. In my displeasure I failed at the time to perceive that his admiration of the veterans' verbal duel was taking the form of ineffective imitation.

"When you've finished playing the fool, Gotty," I remarked with severity, "perhaps you'll be good enough to tell me what occurred."

"When we come outside I says to 'im, 'Mr. Rawson,' I says, 'the Guv'nor is willin' ter give you so much and a share; and we shan't want fer grub,' I says, 'fer there's a large packin' case full o' wittles come to my house.' 'I don't want no share,' he says, 'and if I 'ave four pound a month I'll be satisfied.' 'I'll tell the Guv'nor,' I says, 'what you say.'"

So that nothing remained but to return whence we had come, and invite Mr. Rawson to seal the compact in a manner appropriate to the environment.

XIV

A LESSON IN SEAMANSHIP

WHEN next morning I met my skipper, it was easy to see that his brain had been busy in the night. He was full of what he was to do, and what perhaps I wouldn't mind doing, and what he had set Mr. Rawson to do.

Our new mate's task, considerately chosen as involving no particular strain on his elderly physique, was to scrub, tar, and paint the dinghy, to which end Gotty had drawn it high and dry; and I had the satisfaction of knowing that, even while we were talking, the worthy old mariner was thus engaged in my service, away behind the big shed, remote from the public eye.

"'E arsked me this morning did I think the Guv'nor 'd mind lettin' 'im dror ten shillin's, as it'd be a great conwenience, seein' 'e wants ter git some socks and things."

"By all means. That makes us still more sure of him. Say he can have a pound if he likes."

Gotty had thoughtfully arranged to borrow the dinghy belonging to a barge that lay beside the jetty, the skipper thereof being a man in whose largeness of heart he had confidence. A slight hitch occurred, in that neither the barge's commander nor either of his subordinates chanced to be in sight. But my ingenious companion swiftly thought out a way to surmount this difficulty—namely, by borrowing the dinghy without permission.

I ventured to remark that I thought we hardly ought to do that; at which he raised his voice in injured protest.

"'Ow can I ast 'im," he indignantly inquired, "when 'e ain't 'ere?"

Reflecting that Gotty was far better acquainted than I with the ways of that water-side world, I did not press my opposition, but scrambled into the alien craft whose oars he had already grasped.

Soon after boarding the *Betty*, I, under instructions received, got to work on the "colmans" with boiling water and soda, the broom of short bristles, and a scraping tool.

Having pottered about, apparently to little purpose, with a pail, a board, and divers other small properties, Gotty summoned me to his assistance beside the mast.

"Fust," he explained, "I want yer to lay 'old of this rope"—indicating one in the tangle—"and pull till I hollars out ter you to stop. Arterwards I want yer—*if you don't mind*," he added hastily, on a sudden recollection of manners—"to 'ave a go at this one"—indicating another and more slender rope. "Now, are yer ready? Go!"

I pulled, but as the rope did not move, I mentioned my conjecture that it was fastened somewhere.

"No, it ain't," I was informed. "Pull 'arder."

Putting therefore more energy into a further effort, I had the unspeakable gratification of beholding my companion slowly ascend, like a pantomime fairy, as he sat inert upon a piece of board.

"Don't let go!" came the anxious instruction as his boots passed above the level of my hat. Then: "Easy! Easy!" And finally a stentorian, "Whoa!" as (for I looked aloft and saw) his head bumped against the cross-trees.

Having disengaged himself, and rubbed the personal region of contact, he requested a few more inches of elevation; and then I was instructed to "make fast"—at which, realising how much depended on it, I conscientiously wound the rope round seven pins in succession. In the act of hitching it to an eighth, I looked up to see how my companion was occupying himself in his dizzy situation, but only to discover that he was gazing down at my proceedings like a man under a spell.

"That didn't ought ter come adrift, and charnse it," he observed in an awed voice, and still with fascinated eyes fixed on my multi-looped measures of safeguard.

Proceeding to act under the second head of my instructions, I found myself achieving another theatrical effect, for, as I pulled the rope down, a bucket went up, carrying paint, brushes and a hammer within reach of the elevated fisherman.

Now was I free to give renewed attention to my own task, although thereafter my activities were subject to interruption as occasion arose to modify the aerial situation of my brother decorator.

Those quiet hours of sustained application yielded vivid consequences in canary yellow on blocks and other fittings aloft, and cabbage green on the combings, the windlass, and the cabin-top below; our mutual congratulations over an evening pot of tea being marred only by the skipper's ungenerous contention that I had not stirred my tins of paint so thoroughly as he had stirred his.

Our appreciation of the extent and quality of our own work was by no means lessened when, on landing at dusk, we slipped round to see at what stage the first day's labours of our new associate had brought the decoration of the dinghy.

"Pore old feller!" was Gotty's comprehensive criticism, when we stood beside the grounded boat. "It's easy ter see 'e ain't a fust-class tradesman with 'is brush. And 'e couldn't 'ave stuck it long neither, could 'e? What a blessin' it ain't 'ard work what we want 'im for. Oh dear, oh dear! Pore old feller!"

"Well, well," I observed, I hope in not too vainglorious a spirit, "it won't look so bad when we screw on the name-plates"—brass lettering on panels of polished oak, I would have the reader to understand, I having, in weeks gone by, devoted some hours of leisure to the fashioning of these specimens of twentieth-century handicraft, the like of which, I needed no man's assurance, probably never before, during all the centuries, adorned a fisherman's rowing-boat.

The labours of the following day had an emotional prelude. Gotty came to meet me with his bosom in a tumult.

"You never saw sech beauties," was his incoherent communication. "They come 'ome larst night and I put 'em ter bed nice and dry under the stairs. Come along and see 'em."

"Who did? See what?" For I was at a loss for his meaning.

"The noo sails!"

We found Mrs. Gotty seated before the fire with the naked baby lying, frontways down, across her knees, and to be surprised with this wrigglesome lapful (so much like a skinned rabbit to my man's eye) set the good soul in a paroxysm of hot-cheeked apologetics. Having folded part of her apron over the pink trophy, she recovered composure in a sufficient measure to admit of simultaneous speech and laughter.

"Oh dear, there, now!" she remarked, "if I mightn't have known he'd be sure to fetch you. Those sails, sir—well, and I don't know what you'll think of me carrying on a-laughing like this—only, I can't help it to think of him not taking his thoughts off them since they came. They say a woman makes a fuss over a new dress, sir, but he's had them out four times, and fingering them over and talk, talk, talk of nothing else."

"Yar! yar! yar!" mocked Gotty in helpless warfare with his little round dumpling of a wife, her scorching exposure of his human weakness having, as was easy to see, wounded him to the quick. "You think yerself very clever, dontcher?" added her discomfited lord.

"No, I don't, Alf," came the smiling reply, "but I think you're a great big baby."

"Oh, do yer?" retorted Gotty, who seldom shines in polemics when his feelings are stirred.

A minute later his wife's comments had a striking confirmation, for in his delight at once more beholding the new sails he forgot the annoyance those comments had caused him.

"There ain't another borley in Leigh," he proudly declared, "with sich a nice noo rig-out as what we've got. It'll make some of 'em open their eyes, I know it will."

Indeed I had some difficulty in withdrawing him from those great masses of spotless duck and calico; but anon, out on the rocking waters, we again applied ourselves zealously to the embellishment of the *Betty*.

My own duties began with tarring the bulwarks; which done, I passed to my first experience of caulking. For when overnight Gotty had sluiced the deck, I noticed that much water passed through the boarding and dripped into the hold—which suggested unpleasant possibilities to one who contemplated using that region as a sleeping apartment and living room.

"All this dry weather's opened the seams," spake the authority, "and I dursn't give the decks a coat of tar, or when the sun strikes down on 'em you'd be fair suffocated in the 'old. We'll 'ave to git out the caulking irons and go over the bad places."

I discovered indeed that I possessed an assortment of those tools (which approximate to metal wedges, or chisels with blunt, broad edges), besides some of the all-iron hammers with which it is proper to smite them. Yet it was accessory material that more particularly engaged my attention—to wit, brown clouds of flaxen fluffiness which I readily identified as tresses cut from the head of a mermaid.

"No it ain't," said Gotty, who was in a materialistic mood. "That's tow—same as convicts make what are set to pick oakum."

You have to place a little bit over a crack, and laboriously jamb it in with your hammer and iron, and when at last you have got it out of sight you have to place another piece over the crack, and jamb that after it. This goes on until you cannot get any more in; then you are free to recommence your labours farther along the crack. Mem.: Have a care that, as you force a fresh strand in at the top, the lowest strand be not coming through below, and dropping into the hold, as happened twice in my experience, for this involves fruitless and indefinitely extended labour.

After no more than one hour and a quarter of this monotonous, noisy drudgery, I found myself envying the task of those who merely have to unloosen the stuff. After ten minutes more of it, I summoned Gotty, to say if he did not think I had done enough. Somewhat grudgingly, he took that view, but pointed out that, so far, the operation was incomplete, and that I must work a little boiling pitch along the newly-caulked seams; which I did.

At high tide my companion suddenly emerged from a condition of thoughtful silence to announce the intention of sailing into the flats "so as she'll lust over and we can scrape off the barnicles and give 'er a coat o' tar." At once the deck became a scene of hurry, bustle, and the pulling of ropes. My co-operation was identified with a succession of rapid instructions that were technical to the point of bewilderment.

When he said "Lay 'old o' that," handing me a definite rope, I knew where I was; but we were a good deal at cross purposes when his directions took such forms as "Let go yer main sheet," "Pull in yer torpsel tack," and "Look out fer that warp." However, it is wonderful how usefully one can be employed, under a master mind, without knowing what one is doing; and it came to pass that the *Betty*, no longer asleep at anchor, became full of wild life, and went careering through the water with all her sails distended.

"Lay 'old of the helem," commanded Gotty, relinquishing the restless wooden arm into my keeping as, scrambling on deck, he hurried to the bowsprit.

Since it must needs be, I took the tiller severely in hand, and promptly the muscles of my wrist were busily engaged in fighting the thing's tendency to pull itself first in one direction and then in another. Gotty, whose return I earnestly desired, had apparently found a critical hitch in the rigging, for he was occupying the precious minutes in a prolonged struggle with a rope-knot, resolute teeth assisting baffled fingers.

"Luff!" he shouted, without looking round.

"What do you mean?" asked the smack-owner.

Shove it *that* way;" and he indicated which way by thrusting a hand out behind him, and impatiently flapping it, much after the manner of a man driving away flies.

"Not so much!" he further shouted, adding rudely: "D'yer want ter jibe 'er!" though the circumstance of my not knowing what the term signified was, I think, a sufficient guarantee that my mind harboured no such desire.

By dint of keeping the tiller midway between the two points at which my work had been criticised, I managed for the moment to maintain the vessel in her anxious course of headlong irresponsibility.

But I make no disguise of the fact that my mind was oppressed by unease and misgiving. I had small liking for this blind guiding of a force over which I had no intellectual control. Nay, I found myself earnestly wishing, if the importance of undoing that knot were too great for postponement, that at least an exchange of jobs might be effected. I wondered why so obvious a piece of wisdom did not occur to my usually so sagacious skipper.

But apparently his stubborn struggle with the twisted cordage was monopolising his attention to the exclusion of all matters else. And this was the more dangerous a condition of affairs because, as I suddenly realised in dismay, two anchored bawleys lay right in our path.

As though reading my very thoughts, Gotty turned his head to remark, with impudent cheerfulness:

"Bear up."

I was astounded that he should so far forget himself; and the taunt was the harder to endure because, whatever my feelings might be, I had certainly shown no signs of breaking down.

"Bear up!" he had the audacity to repeat, and in a more outspoken manner than before.

"I am bearing up," I snapped back. "It would take more than this, let me tell you, to—"

"Bear up! Bear up!" yelled Gotty, and his face was riven with such unmistakable lines of agony, that, with a countenance to correspond, I shouted:

"What do you mean?"

"This way! This way! Shove it this way!" he cried, vigorously flapping his hand seaward. And then I understood.

Having pushed the tiller in the desired direction, and thus (as I was horrified to see) adjusted our course still straighter for the anchored bawleys and shipwreck, I bluntly intimated my willingness to relinquish an office for which I was not endowed with the requisite experience.

"Here, you come and take the helm! I've had enough."

"No," said Gotty, making no further effort to disguise the hollow nature of his attempt on the knotted rope, "you ain't doin' so bad. I'm goin' to larn yer. Stick to it. You're gettin' on all right."

The tone was that of a soft-hearted child addressing consolation to a wounded caterpillar.

There being some dregs of pride in the least exalted among us, and

97

my skipper being so obviously set on imparting tuition, I settled down, with what steadiness I could command, to suffer without complaint any complicated misadventures of which it might please fate to make me the helpless instrument.

"Aren't those two boats rather in our way?" I, however, asked; for, with the *Betty's* rapidly accelerating momentum, the anchored obstructions loomed as a very immediate danger in my imagination.

"Go betwixt 'em," was the heartless order that fell on my startled ear.

I was of course aware of a controlling relation between movements of the rudder and the course of the vessel; in other words, that I could swing the bowsprit about by moving the tiller; but the heart of my anxiety lay in the circumstance that I did not exactly know which direction of the one produced which direction of the other, nor, with everything happening so quickly, had I opportunity to make such discreet experiments as would yield me the knowledge.

Happily, however, as we neared the anchored bawleys the distance between them proved greater than I had supposed; which fact, coupled with the guidance I received from Gotty's hand, enabled us to pass the vessels without so much as grazing their hulls.

But the worst was not over. Let me rather say that so far I had but tasted peril, whereof a full meal awaited me. Half the fleet of bawleys lay anchored before us in an uninterrupted line of danger; and my infatuated skipper was allowing me—or rather, was allowing me to allow the *Betty*—to charge that line with all sails set and the breeze driving us along at a break-neck speed.

If Gotty had lost possession of himself—I reflected in a panic—that was no reason why I should not show discretion. Manifestly the only course to adopt, now that matters had reached this critical pass, was to swerve the vessel round into open water, and keep her in areas of ample room until we had pulled down, or cut down, the sails one after the other, and so suffered our momentum gradually to die down.

But before I had time to defiantly initiate that wise policy, opportunity for doing so had gone by. Bawleys lay to the right of us, and bawleys lay to the left of us. We were among the fleet, and flying into the very thick of them; and, as if these floating perils were not enough, straight ahead, just beyond the bawleys, was Leigh jetty.

I dodged, and dodged, and dodged—that is to say, the *Betty* did; for, although I was the steersman, some instinct of her own seemed to assist my convulsive handling of her helm. Yet even as we wended our swift and devious way among the bawleys, until no more than two remained to be passed, I realised how superfluous was our success, how hollow our triumph. For see! just ahead, there were the stone walls of Leigh and no dodging, no luffing, no bearing up, could possibly get us past them. Nor had we time now to get down one sail, leave alone the lot, before we must be crashing into barges and masonry. And there beside the mast stood the madman, going to certain destruction with a meaningless grin upon his face.

"Luff!" he cried. "Luff 'ard!" and merely because it really could not matter now what I did, I mechanically drove the tiller in the suggested direction, until its head bumped against the bulwarks.

Then a miracle did itself under my very nose.

The *Betty* swung round, speed fell off her like a mantle, the sails flapped noisily, and surrounding objects ceased to move. We had come to as complete a standstill as though some one had simultaneously turned off steam and put on the brake.

"Bray-vo!" shouted Gotty, clapping his hands; and when I had recovered from astonishment at finding myself still whole and hale, I began a brief harangue on the importance of preceding practical instruction in any of the arts with some explanation of general, underlying principles.

"Oh!" he laughed, "we'll make a sailorman of yer yet;" which, of course, was not the point.

XV

WE START

MY involuntary lesson in steering put me in key for further nautical instruction, and when I perceived that my expert associate after releasing the anchor, had lowered the topsail, foresail, and jib by the momentary handling of a rope or two, I had a mind to be informed of the precise methods by which those rapid transformations were accomplished.

But his response bore upon a different theme, and I noted that his brow was furrowed and his manner preoccupied. It would seem, indeed, that two matters were simultaneously exercising his mind.

"I can see yer," he said to himself what time he stared intently at the neighbouring jetty (where, following his gaze, I merely saw two men standing passively and looking in our direction). "Well, you'll 'ave to wait, that's all!" he added warmly, still in private communion with his own thoughts. "I ain't agoing to let 'er set on 'er anchor ter please nobody." Then, bitterly, to me: "There's some people so cretchety they'd make a fuss about anythin'. It don't matter," he went on in pious wrath, "'ow much you might oblige other people—that don't count fer nothing'."

"What's the matter? Who are those men?"

"Why," he protested indignantly, "them people what belong ter the barge—them people" (for my blank look revealed the need for a better clue) "what we borrered the punt off of."

I could certainly have taken exception to his use of the plural pronoun, and in the circumstances the term "borrow" seemed unduly euphemistic; but, not to pour paraffin on fire, I passed those points by, and dealt with another.

"Do you think they will mind?"

"Mind! What call 'ave they ter mind, I'd like ter know. But look at 'em—jest look at the nasty way they're standin' there! Only I ain't goin' ter let 'er come to 'urt ter please them or nobody else. Let 'em come and fetch it if they're in sech a 'urry. If not, they've got ter wait—that's all. Yer see," he continued, after looking critically to windward, and then gazing intently over the stern, "it's the worst wind there is fer Leigh, as it holds a vessel up agin the ebb, and then it ain't nothing but luck it she don't set on 'er anchor; which she couldn't do with any other wind, if you understand my meanin', fer she's ride off the tide ter the end of 'er chain. No!" he soliloquised, his brain manifestly honeycombed with anxious speculations, "I don't like the looks of it. What's more," he half shouted, his mind suddenly made up, "I won't take the risk. I'm a-goin'," came the dramatic announcement, "ter get the kedge out—I don't care 'oo's punt it is."

Drawing the dinghy alongside, he put the accessory anchor, a coil of rope, and himself, into her, and, rowing a short distance astern, he threw something overboard that made a heavy splash.

"That's the proper thing to do," on returning he remarked, in ungrudging appreciation of his own action.

"Now she can't get inter trouble. She's betwixt two anchors, and each of 'em 'olds 'er back from settin' on the other. No one couldn't find no fault with that. Ef they did," came the scalding afterthought, "they wouldn't know what they was talkin' about."

As if drawn by some appeal to a latent sense, our eyes travelled in company to the jetty, where stood the two men exactly as I had seen them before save that one had just raised his right arm by way of arresting our attention. My companion's glow of generous self-approval was quenched as by an icy blast.

Sternly calm, he got back into the dinghy, sat down on the rowing-seat with a thud, seized the oars in ruthless hands, and set out with long, strong strokes for the jetty.

Half way there he stopped rowing to shout over his shoulder:

"I don't 'ear wot you say . . "

" . . . .'Ow could I ast you," he ferociously replied to an observation that did not reach me, "when you wasn't there! . . ." "'Oo ought to? . . ."

But, the conversation being continued as Gotty rowed on to closer quarters, its development was lost to me. From watching the three energetic figures on the jetty, however, I was able to infer that a graceful, if involuntary, act of courtesy was being despoiled of all charm.

The two men got into their boat and rowed away on the falling tide, while Gotty, with the stiff carriage of a man who has vindicated his character against the tongue of slander, betook himself with leisurely footsteps homeward. Which was a reminder to me that, means of communication with the shore being for the moment wanting, I could employ my lonely leisure to no better purpose than by resuming my duties as a ship's decorator.

The white streak, the name and the lettering (all sadly in need of renewal) had, on the ground of superior scholarship, been entrusted to me; and to those matters I applied myself, with unsuitable brushes and unremitting zeal, while the receding water was giving place to mud, on which the *Betty* soon was softly reclining at an angle incompatible with my comfort.

"A wery good tradesman!"—words of commendation which, when they broke in upon my preoccupation, caused me to turn and behold Gotty restored to my society, without shoes or stockings, and with the complacent air of a man newly come from a substantial tea enjoyed by his own fireside.

In his right hand he carried a bucket of tar and tucked under his left arm was a tar brush of the variety that is nearly all handle. With these, after some preliminary scraping, he soon engaged on the exposed side of our hull, which, when later I cautiously descended barefooted to the yielding mud, I discovered in course of transformation into one huge bulge of sparkling black. Yet the praiseworthy industry achieving that result was destined to be mysteriously interrupted. Missing an answer to a question I subsequently shouted from above, I peered over the side to find both Gotty and the tar brush gone.

On scanning the vicinity I espied the truant stooping to an intimate view of a sister vessel in the region of her keel; from which examination he presently came hurrying back with such celerity as was consistent with the progress of bare feet over sharp cockle shells. It was easy to see that he was labouring under considerable excitement.

"There's two set on their anchors," he shouted, "and Laughin' Sam's copped it wonderful bad. The fluke's gorn in jest above the garbard streaks—fair buried in the skin, it is. You never see sech a sight. Pore ole Laughin' Sam! Only don't it jest show yer what I was sayin'."

His tone, indeed, revealed feelings pretty evenly divided between sympathy with the misfortune of brother fisherman and satisfaction at the proof of his own sagacity which that misfortune afforded.

"I wonder whether I didn't ought ter go and give Laughin' Sam word?" he said reflectively, clearly hesitating between altruism and tarring. His better self won. "I will! 'Im and me always was good friends—'e's not like some—and I'd like ter do 'im a turn. 'E'd be the fust ter do me a turn," he added, sentimentally, "if it layed anyways in 'is power—I know 'e would ."

Nor did good-nature stop here.

"Arter tellin' 'im, I'll go 'ome and get my fly-tool, fer there's nothin' 'andier fer diggin' a anchor out, and that's somethin' Laughin' Sam wouldn't be likely ter know, seein' 'e never did no sand 'eavin';" and the Good Samaritan departed on his mission.

I had restored "LO.96" to conspicuous visibility on the port bow ere voices caused me to look shoreward, when I saw an approaching group of fishermen, with Laughin' Sam (not, however, laughing now) anxiously leading the van, and with Gotty, a digging-tool over his shoulder, as one of the rear figures.

On the conclusion of their labours, which included the putting of a patch on the injured hull, Laughing Sam stepped across to the *Betty*, not merely to express envious approbation of our newly whitened streak, but to formally convey an emphatic assurance that my skipper was one of the right sort.

By a skilful rearrangement of weighty objects, Gotty insured that the *Betty* should list in a new direction at the following tide; and before breakfast next morning my early-rising coadjutor had completed the tarring of the hull.

In the beautification of our craft there thus remained but one small detail unaccomplished, namely, the hoisting of her colours; and this matter, as befitted its importance, we took in hand together, Gotty swarming up the rigging and affixing the brand-new crimson streamer at the apex of the topmast, while I from below saw that he placed the spindle straight.

We both appreciated a solemnity in the situation when, leaving the little piece of bunting significantly fluttering aloft, he descended to the deck.

"Now we're ready ter start on the next flood," he observed, "and if we get into any trouble where we're goin', we'll 'ave ter thank the Blessed One ter git us out of it;" and on that sentiment we shook hands. Then in silence he and I recrossed the mud.

Having made my adieux to relatives and friends, I returned to Leigh in the early evening, and proceeded to the little house along the alley. They were all there—my skipper and his spouse, the nephew, his parents, and their baby.

"Well I never did!" exclaimed Mrs. Gotty, flustered and aflush. "I don't seem to know if I'm on my head or my heels" (though, in truth, she being seated in a chair, that issue scarcely arose). "To think of mine going away for so long! And taking some of the parlour pictures with him, he is, to hang in the cabin! It will seem strange, and I do hope, sir, you'll have a pleasant time and he'll behave himself."

"Don't carry on so ridiculous!" commanded Gotty, in a tone of severity which, however, in nowise intimidated his plump little partner.

"Oh," she mocked, "you wouldn't be cross with me on your last day. And, oh, sir, I don't know what you'll say at the liberty I've taken, but we've made you up a bed in the sitting-room, so you should get a little sleep after all your hard work which I'm sure you're not used to, and going to start, mine says, at two to-morrow morning! Oh dear, oh dear, and I do hope you'll lie comfortable, sir."

Gotty's self-conscious grin as he threw open the inner door, revealed him as a confederate in this conspiracy for my comfort. In the name of kindness, that family circle had, I was shocked to see, played havoc with the orderly amenities of their parlour, for not merely had a bed displaced the arm-chair, but the table was transformed into a fully-appointed washhand stand. To make chaos more complete, a sea-chest rested upon the case of provisions, and across the sofa lay my hammock and our chart—the former made, at Gotty's thrifty suggestion, from a piece of our old mainsail; the latter, with accompanying navigation book, purchased by me in London under instructions received from Mr. Rawson.

Having returned inadequate thanks, I called my skipper's attention to a list I had that afternoon compiled of necessaries which we so far had forgotten to purchase, the articles ranging from two gallons of paraffin to a penny bottle of ink. He and I immediately sallied forth to remedy this remissness before all the shops should be closed.

Nearly two hours later, on buying half-a-dozen soup plates at a pawnbroker's, we came to the end of this task, and, if grievously burdened with small parcels, returned triumphant to the house of kindness and upheaval.

A promise to take formal farewell of certain of his neighbours lay heavy, it was now revealed, on my companion's conscience; and I learned that Mr. Rawson would be there, and that my absence would, in the circumstances, be considered a slight to the locality.

"There's bin a deal of talk one way and another about our voy'ge," I further learnt as we proceeded to the rendezvous, "and there's some as is positive we shan't catch no fish, whilst others don't see why we shouldn't. As I tell 'em, they'll know all about it when we come back."

We found them very thickly gathered together, and Mr. Rawson's benevolent countenance seemed to reveal, on our arrival, a modest sense of relief that he would no longer monopolise felicitations in which we all three had the right to share.

An energetic fiddler was in attendance, and, ere an hour had slipped by, I was amply aware with what impressive sprightliness the ancient township of Leigh is disposed, and indeed determined, to celebrate the setting forth of any of her maritime burgesses in quest of the unknown in distant and unfamiliar waters.

That my skipper's heart was touched by the good wishes showered upon him was sufficiently attested when, ten minutes before closing time, he thrust a group of brother fishermen to the right and left, and in the area thus cleared occupied himself, amid accelerated music and vociferous applause, in a spirited hornpipe embellished by high kicking of a marked degree of excellence; throughout which performance Mr. Rawson's kindly and composed countenance wore an acquiescent expression, as though he desired it to be understood that the skipper was returning thanks for self and crew.

When, a little later, the genial company separated in the roadway, Mr. Rawson went his way and we went ours, with mutual reiterated reminders that we were to meet three hours later to go aboard and set sail.

I had, so far as sensations went, but put my head on the pillow when a brutal thud fell upon the parlour door, and in a voice that I recognised there came the intimation:

"Get up! It's gorn two."

Giving myself no time even to analyse the sense of injustice that weighed upon my spirits, I groped through a perfunctory toilet and was presently busy assisting Gotty load the goods on a borrowed trolley—an operation not unattended by hitches which, if partly arising from the darkness of the night and the poor character of our lamp, were in some measure attributable, I could not but feel, to the precipitancy of my companion's movements. Soon we wheeled our way to the abode of Mr. Rawson, whom we found faithfully awaiting us in his front garden, drowsily asquat a large white bundle; and after he had saluted me with sleepy cordiality, and added his possessions to the trolley's burden, we pushed on to the water-side, where, assisted by the owner of the vehicle, we were not long in transferring our goods to the newly decorated dinghy, whose gunwale I conjectured to be perilously near the water's edge when three human beings added their weight to that of the cargo.

Before Gotty had pulled half-a-dozen strokes, I unintentionally gave his nerves a shock.

"I suppose we've got everything," I chanced to remark.

"Ain't we?" he cried, abruptly, arresting his oars. "What 'ave we fergot?"

"I say, I *suppose* we've got everything."

"I 'ope so"—and I heard him anxiously groping among the contents of the boat. "Yus," presently came the reassuring report, "'ere's the noo sails;" and then, in a tone of still more grateful relief, "'Ere's the case of wittles. You give me quite a turn," he added reproachfully, as he resumed labours which soon brought us skilfully alongside the *Betty*.

Gotty and the mate were soon busy hoisting the sails, and judging that, having regard to the darkness, my co-operation would be more likely to retard than advance their labours, I descended into the cabin, and, having lit the lamp, set about lighting the fire.

As I knelt within close range of the welcome warmth and realised we were slowly moving through the water at the beginning of our long journey, Gotty put his head in at the opening, and, in a voice of persuasion not without its tinge of melancholy, said:

"Was yer thinkin' of makin' a cup of black and green? I don't know as it mightn't freshen us all up."

I intimated that so excellent an idea should be promptly acted upon if he would fill the kettle, I being uncertain where the cask of water was stowed.

Ten minutes later I engineered three mugs of steaming tea on to the deck.

"It's fust class!" Gotty paused from absorption of the liquor to declare; and indeed the spirits of the entire ship's company rose under the tonic influence.

In the resulting gossip, I happened to remark:

"Aren't we likely in a high wind to get the pictures broken?"

"There!" exclaimed Gotty in a startled tone of distress; "if I 'aven't bin and left 'em be'ind! Dear! Oh, dear! What d'yer think of that, now?"

"Well, well," was the consolatory comment of Mr. Rawson, "they'd have been a bit in the way, wouldn't they?"

"But the idea of me not remembrin'," continued Gotty, in a tone that showed how bitterly he was disappointed in himself, "arter takin' them off of the wall and laying 'em on my beddin', so as I couldn't ferget 'em. Why!" with a shout of consternation as he rose in confusion to his feet, "I've forgotten the beddin' as well. That *is* all right! Picshers, matris, blankets, piller, quilt—if I 'aven't bin and left the blessed lot under the kitchin table!"

Then the panic spread to Mr. Rawson.

"Why, bless me!" he cried, letting go of the tiller, "I've left mine behind, too! Tut, tut! could anything be more provoking?"

The kindly old fellow, indeed, under the stress of this misfortune, had suddenly grown positively petulant.

"I put them just inside the doorway," he complained, "so they shouldn't get damp on the grass, and meaning to go back and fetch them when you came. Then—how very annoying—I forgot all about it."

The lights of Southend pier showed faintly far astern, and day had dawned sufficiently to reveal the fellow-sufferers as, dumbfounded by the dismal coincidence, they stood regarding one another with grey faces.

When I suggested that we should go back for the omitted baggage they shook their heads, and entered into explanations concerning the ebbing of the water. But I think it was pride, not tide, that deterred them.

XVI

FIRST DAY AT SEA

WHEN I returned to the deck, after rinsing the mugs and teapot, and restoring them to the locker, day had fully come in a morning glory of dainty greys and blues, and we were gliding towards an horizon that sparkled with silver sunlight.

In certain comfortable moods one is apt to notice incidents unconsciously, and not become alive to their significance until, later, the memory record is, as it were, accidentally discovered. Thus at the time, under the soft influence of that fair scene, I was not aware—or, rather, I was not aware of being aware—that a conversation which had proceeded between mate and skipper in my absence, abruptly terminated at my approach. Yet in what immediately followed, the appeal to my senses was emphatic enough. I was to receive a delightful surprise.

"Of course, sir," said Mr. Rawson, with the winning smile which, from the outset of our acquaintance, had excited my esteem, "we ought to just call in at Harwich before going south. We're both agreed that's no more than proper."

"Well, yer see—" was the beginning of an observation from Gotty that had no continuation. For, in my eager assent to a proposal that necessarily had for me so strong an attraction, I was guilty of the rudeness of interrupting the commander of the vessel.

"Excellent!" I exclaimed. "And it will be such a surprise to my daughter and the friends she's with. It did occur to me, of course; but I was afraid it would be too far out of our course."

"As fur as that goes," said Gotty, "'Arwich ain't any way. If there comes a bit of wind, we'd be there this arternoon, easy. Then comin' away, we could take a slant right acrost ter the Forlan'."

"By-the-bye," I said to Mr. Rawson, because he appeared the ringleader in this benevolent conspiracy, "it isn't exactly Harwich where they're staying, but Felixstoweferry."

"Harwich is one side of the river," the kindly old mate explained, "and Felixstowe's the other, only, you see, sir, we must go to

Harwich because of the harbour. The ferry would take you over."

"Or I could easy row you acrost," observed my skipper stoutly.

Thus agreeable deviation from original plans being thus determined on, Gotty, after engaging in a careful survey of the heavens submitted to Mr. Rawson a suggestion of which, by reason of the technical language in which it was couched, I derived merely a general knowledge that it involved some delicate point of seamanship.

"Yes," assented the helmsman, "I think you might;" whereupon, with a glad countenance, the skipper swiftly betook himself to the cabin.

Thence he presently emerged hauling a vast quantity of whiteness, which he attached to ropes and a long pole, so that in a little while it was stretched out sideways from the bow as the spinnaker of his idolatry.

"Now she feels it," he exclaimed, regarding the snowy sheet with the eye of infatuation. "Yer see"—to me, in an earnest aside—"it's a leftin' sail what reg'lar carries her through the water."

Strangely enough, the old mate was even more profoundly affected by this dazzling wing that the *Betty* had spread forth into the sunshine.

"Why, I declare," he cried, in a beaming ecstasy, "with the new mainsail and all, we are quite in yachting trim;" and he squared his shoulders, and scanned the surrounding sea with an intentness of mien betokening a determination, come what might, to discharge the duties of his office with unflinching zeal.

"When I was in charge of the *Pelican*," he presently recalled, "we came along here—well, it might be a mile and a half to the nor'-east—on just such a morning as this, and I well remember the time, sir, for we had taken three cups on the south coast that year—no, I'm telling a story; it was two cups and one gold medal—and after lying off Southend for a few days, so that my gentleman could run up to one of the race meetings—I think it was Ascot, but I won't be sure (he was a great patroniser of the turf, sir, and had some fine horses of his own, at one time)—well, we were bound for Burnham that morning, and in all the years I was yachting I don't remember such a week at we had there. Nothing could keep near us—nothing! We ran away from all the others, sir;" and, as though these stirring memories prompted the action, he turned aside to draw the mainsail more taut.

Gotty, who had been listening with the parted lips of awe, had no comment ready; so, feeling that Mr. Rawson should receive some verbal indication of our sympathetic interest, I ventured to ask:

"Did you steer?"

"Yes, yes!" replied the veteran, and in a tone gently apprising me that the remark I had let fall could be attributable only to inexperience. "The skipper of a yacht always had the helm in a race. My gentleman was most particular about that, and one day when I was called away to go to a funeral, he had her scratched for a race, rather than any one else should take my place. Most likely you wouldn't believe—"

But I did not learn what was the particular matter with which my powers of credulity might not be able to cope. For at that moment Gotty broke forth with exclamations highly irrelevant to the subject under consideration:

"Don't Dan Porter look ter be fast? I *know* 'e is! Ain't 'e?"

Following the course of his anxious eyes, I saw, some way ahead of us, a bawley neither sailing nor at anchor, but with her mainsail sluggishly flapping.

Mr. Rawson gave the vessel his careful attention, and then delivered the verdict:

"She's fast. Dear me! The second time this week." "Pore ole Dan!" muttered Gotty, and he proceeded to explain for my benefit: "Out 'ere fish-trawlin' pretty near every mornin,' 'e is, and no one only old Dan dursn't put 'is gear overboard anywheres nigh 'ere, on account of the wrecks laying so thick on the bottom. But old Dan's wonderful well acquainted with the ground, and often as not 'e brings in a nice lot fish—not 'alf, 'e don't—fer it's a funny thing, but where you find wrecks there you're sure to find soles and plaice. They seem to 'arbour 'em."

Hand to mouth, and in a sympathetic voice of loud and lofty pitch, Gotty inquired across the intervening water:

"Are yer copped it bad, mate?"

A figure came to the side of the other vessel—a portly figure with a face which, it was easy to infer, was normally of a benevolent character, but which at the moment was crimson and choleric; and Mr. Porter bellowed in pain and reply:

"This is comin' ter be a nice d— place ter fish in! I believe the d— wrecks lay side by side in a d— long row, I'm d—d if I don't!"

"'E ain't quite 'isself, old Dan ain't!" said Gotty, drawing back much scandalised (though, I think, less on his own behalf than on mine). "Only," he added apologetically, "you can't 'ardly wonder at the pore feller takin' it so much to 'eart, when it's very likely two pound gorn—and fust 'aul, too!"

Then—as though realising that he was not absolved from sympathy with suffering because of the sufferer's language, however deplorable that might be—he once more gave his voice the requisite elevation, and asked:

"Is she much tore?"

"Gorings clean gone and the uppers ripped right acrost!" came the technical, if tempestuous, reply of the irate Mr. Porter; and disgustfully he held up handfuls of his injured property. "Never no more!" he shouted, savagely shaking his head.

"That's always what 'e'll say," Gotty informed me with an austere wink. "Every time's goin' ter be the finish, but then 'e thinks it over and over in 'is own mind till 'e gets 'isself ter believe it wouldn't 'ave 'appened if 'e'd bin more careful; and 'e comes back fishin' 'ere as 'appy as a lark, 'is mate says, and a baby couldn't be more civil-spoken till 'e gets fast agin, and then 'is company ain't fit fer nobody. You see, 'e trusts 'isself more than most, and it makes 'im reg'lar mad to get took in by 'is own thoughtlessness."

Mr. Daniel Porter had by this time gone below—peradventure to enlarge his mate's acquaintance with the English language—and soon we had left that little scene of human emotion remotely astern.

For, as my companions noticed before I did, the wind was freshening. Nay, it was not long before my cautious skipper was taking in the spinnaker with a swift activity suggestive of athletics.

Ripples took the place of a flat sea, and ripples in turn were succeeded by waves, so that the *Betty* heaved herself about in a confusion of grey water, and the sails and the rigging complained of stretching and strain. If I became silent and thoughtful, the spirits of my companions rose with the wind. Gotty broke into song (something about a bold young sailor leaving his mother with a hey, hey, hey, and a ho, ho, ho); while Mr. Rawson devoted to the tiller a positively enthusiastic earnestness. Also—when the bold sailor had, at the sixth verse, gone to sea and got out of the way—he favoured me with some more of his recollections.

"It's just like being on the *Pelican*, sir, and when I look round I almost expect to see my gentleman back again. Ah! he was a nice man, and so open-handed with his money! Besides spirits and bottled beer, there was always plenty of claret and port wine and sherry on board. Oh! he'd have no stint on his yacht. And cigars and cigarettes—boxes of them! I've never tasted such game pies since— sent down from London, they were, with a lot of other beautiful food; though we'd got a good cook on board."

"Is that gentleman dead?" I asked, the thought being, I admit to my shame, born of the wish; for, to tell the simple truth, those

pantry references had heightened unpleasant sensations from which
I had been free when the sea was smooth. Moreover, on moral and
ethical grounds, as I told myself, I did not approve of Mr. Rawson's
paragon of prodigality.

"Yes, sir, he died twenty years ago. Poor fellow, he had a lot of
trouble towards the end. It broke his heart, I think, when the yacht
went, and then everything else was sold. I did hear he had been
living up to £3000 a year on an income of £800. Ah! he was too
generous, too open-handed—that was his downfall."

"I should call him a thief," I said, pursuing my posthumous
enemy into the very grave—to such lengths of tactlessness and bad
taste will the premonitions of seasickness drive a certain class of
mind.

"No one don't know 'ow bad they is, nor yet 'ow good, till they get
the charnse of showing it," said Gotty, who was offensively smoking
shag tobacco in a foul clay pipe.

Pelican reminiscences being stayed for the time being, I sat me in
my deck chair and yielded to a feeling of drowsiness, from which
presently I was partly roused by Mr. Rawson's almost motherly
endeavour to interest me in a pair of cormorants perched upon a
beacon. Gotty, equally unaware that I wished to sleep, deemed it his
duty to give me details of two sunken ships whose masts, protruding
prominently out of the water, I should not otherwise have noticed.
But observing me gape thrice amid his moving narratives concerning
these ill-fated vessels, he politely admitted my need of the repose of
which overnight I had been robbed, and so, leaving me undisturbed
in my chair, withdrew to talk in subdued tones, and as between
sailorman and sailorman, with the old mate.

Though to all outward seeming I slumbered, my senses remained
alert to what was passing, and indeed I occasionally opened a
humble eye on the proceedings of my pair of mariners. On a chance
allusion to compasses, Mr. Rawson (in a spirit of precaution for
which I felt grateful) requested Gotty to fetch the *Betty's* so that he
might satisfy himself as to its reliability.

"It's a great big 'un in a box," explained Gotty, who, I knew, was
not a little proud of the instrument, which was part of the bawley's
outfit when we purchased her.

He brought it on deck and removed the box-lid, which proved to
be in two pieces.

"But the card don't move!" was Mr. Rawson's horrified exclamation, when in vain he had varied the position of the box.

"I dessay it's a bit stiff," the skipper hastily explained, and, having lifted the glass cover, he lent the assistance of his thumb to polar influence. Yet if, under this persuasion, the dial consented to rotate, it must have manifested a disconcerting impartiality at a stopping place; for the old mate indignantly exclaimed:

"First it points east, and now it's due south! A pretty state of things—no compass! And suppose we ran into a fog, or night came on before we made a harbour. This ought to have been seen to before we started."

"I never so much as give it a thought," was Gotty's abject explanation.

"Then you ought to," snapped the old yachtsman; and Gotty made no reply. But I noticed (for the incident had opened my eyes in more senses than one) that, hanging his head dejectedly, the skipper was fidgeting with the instrument. Finding the dial was easy to remove, he removed it.

Then exclamations of surprise broke simultaneously from my shipmates.

"Why if it ain't 'alf full of water!" was Gotty's supplementary comment.

"And been there for years, by the look of it!" quoth Mr. Rawson scornfully. "You've never used that compass!"

"I never 'ad no call to—not to steer by, my meanin' is; but I've many a time took it out ter look at it. Only the other day I was showin' it ter the Guv'nor. 'Ain't we got a lovely compass?' I say, and 'e says 'yus.' Only I never knowed it was 'alf full of water, or I'd 'ave poured it out sharp, fer I know a compass didn't ought ter 'ave water in it." Obviously the regrettable omission was now rectified, for I heard the intrusive fluid splashing on the deck. Gotty resumed, more cheerfully:

"I dessay it'll work all right now. There you are!"

For manifestly he had replaced the disc, and was now watching it behave more in harmony with science. "That's north, ain't it? Now go agin. There you are! It's gorn back. Nothin' ain't the matter with that compass, I tell yer."

"When we get to Harwich," said Mr. Rawson severely, "I shall take it round, first thing, to my friend Goldsmith, and get him to test it."

"Well, that'd make sure, wouldn't it?" said Gotty humbly.

"Pull your jib sheet in a bit," said Mr. Rawson; and Gotty went forward to do so. Then I must have fallen asleep. For I awoke to hear Gotty say:

"I fancy it must 'ave been fergot. But I'll 'ave another try, fer it may be under all them swiss milks. My! Ain't there a lot. Here it is, ain't it? But it don't 'ardly look like sugar. Pscht!"—it was the sound of lips rejecting a disappointing flavour—"It's soda! Hullo! More soap! What's this? Razins! This feels like sugar—no, its currents, and not 'alf a tidy lot. Soap agin! What-ho! Terbacca! And don't it smell all right! Why, if this ain't *another* lot o' soap! What's 'e want it all for?"

"I'm sure I don't know," replied Mr. Rawson, in the manner of a man too prudent to waste his time over baffling mysteries. "What's in that bottle?"

"I dunno. P'raps you can tell by the label."

"Lime juice!"

"Oh! Sour stuff, ain't it?"

"Yes. Do you see any tea?"

"No—nor yet sugar. But there seems a tidy lot of most everything else. 'Ere's another sort o' oatmeal. 'Ere's another eight pound o' them biscuits! More corfee! And good night! if there isn't some more swiss milks!"

"Perhaps the sugar is in this big tin."

"Oh, I ain't looked in there, 'ave I? And the chap what put on the lid didn't mean nobody should look inside, seemin'ly."

"Here prise it open with my knife."

"Now, you've got ter come. Ah! That's shifted it. Hullo: Treacle! I told the Guv'nor I was wonderful fond o' treacle. 'E said he liked marmerlade best. But I 'aven't seen no marmerlade. That's funny! Stay a bit. There's a tin down here bigger'n what this one is. Lend us yer knife agin. Hullo, what did I tell yer? Marmerlade!"

As this was getting personal, I deemed the moment opportune for revealing myself as awake, which I did by sitting up and timidly surveying the still-heaving sea.

"Bin 'aving a little shut-eye, ain't yer?" said my skipper, in a kindly voice. "We've opened the case," he added, not without a note of apology. "It's a 'andsome lot o' wittles and no mistake. But I don't see no sugar, nor yet tea."

Feeling a better sailor for my sleep, I personally overhauled the stores, and found that the skipper's misgivings were ill-founded. But one item of the order I did miss, to wit, a piece of bacon destined for breakfast rashers, and I chanced to mention the circumstance.

"That's all right, sir," said Mr. Rawson heartily. "I told him to boil as much as would go in the saucepan, and put the rest in soak to get the salt out."

"Indeed. And now, Mr. Rawson"—for I wished to change the

subject—"you must be tired of steering. Suppose you give the tiller to the skipper."

"Certainly not," said Mr. Rawson, with decision. "This is no trouble to me. If he'll just look after the sails when I tell him, we'll manage all right."

I glanced at Gotty and Gotty glanced at me. But neither of us spoke.

XVII

MATE OR MASTER?

HAVING gazed from afar at Walton-on-the-Naze and Clacton, we glided and tossed on towards Harwich, my private uneasiness having reached no worse phase than that which gave me a lively preference for dry biscuits over boiled bacon.

The business of finding a berth amid the varied shipping in the river Stour was one in which the wind and the minds of my shipmates acted as three independent and conflicting forces.

While Mr. Rawson was manoeuvring the helm with the intention of running to the left and berthing beside some yachts (of whose sprightly trim he had already expressed warm approval), Gotty's supervision of the sails was controlled by a desire to run to the right and berth with other Leigh bawleys away behind the coal hulks. This confusion of purpose, on becoming manifest to the two parties concerned, gave occasion to a somewhat heated dialogue in which the dignity of the sensitive skipper rather bruised itself against the rock-like will of the good-tempered mate. And meanwhile the wind, instead of temporarily ceasing its activity to give time for human agreement on the question at issue, continued to propel the *Betty* up river at so considerable a speed that, as each disputant made haste to inform the other, the opportunity for carrying out either policy had already gone by.

"Well, we've got ter do somethin', I suppose!" shouted Gotty, in perturbation tinged with irony. "Now then—shall I drop 'ere? Nothing ain't amiss with this ground, is there?"

"All right—let go," assented Mr. Rawson stiffly. "We can't better this now. She'll lay all right here."

Down, accordingly, went the anchor; and I may say that, had I presumed to offer my lay opinion on the point, I should from the outset have favoured this position, for here we were in open water, and well removed from the multitude of vessels that lined the shore on both sides of us.

All the canvas was lowered, and my crew had just completed, in painful silence, the task of lashing the mainsail to the spar, when we espied a boat, which contained a man in a peaked cap, rowing vigorously in our direction

No sooner had Gotty seen the small craft than he turned to me, and, in the tone of a man who despaired of the world and almost all its inhabitants, exclaimed:

"Now, there's somebody else not satisfied, seemin'ly. I tell yer, it don't matter what yer do, it's shore to be all wrong ter some one's fancy. Now I wonder what this pore feller's got on 'is mind;" and, with a countenance unsoftened by any sign of welcome, he set himself calmly to await the visitor's arrival.

"Now then," came a gruff voice from the rowing boat, as it drew alongside, "you've got to clear out of this."

"Oh!" replied Gotty, his tone conveying a delicate sense of amusement. "'Oo says so?"

"The harbour-master!" was the stranger's ruthless retort; and, like a policeman dealing with a hansom cab, he proceeded very deliberately to copy our number into a pocket-book.

"We ain't interferin' with nobody!" protested Gotty. Then raising his voice in argumentative expostulation: "What 'arm are we doin'?"

"You ought to know better," observed the official, not deigning to answer this further question. "Laying right in the fairway like this!"

"Well, we ain't sech a big wessel that we take up *all* the water," was Gotty's searching comment.

"Come, come," said Mr. Rawson, waddling forward with importance. "Do I understand, sir"—with a courteous inclination towards the official—"that the harbour-master objects to my berthing here?"

"Yes," replied the representative of authority, whose mollified manner testified to the greater esteem in which he intuitively held the elder of my companions. "You see, he's very particular to keep the river open for the steamboats, and you are lying right in their course. In case you don't know the new rules," the man in the peak cap graciously added, as he took a paper from his pocket, "I'd better give you a copy."

"I am much obliged to you, sir," said Mr. Rawson cordially, as he leaned forward to accept the leaflet; "we will shift our anchorage at once."

"Yes," added Gotty cheerfully, "as soon as ever I've took the Guv'nor ashore we'll drop acrost to them old bunkers."

(I privately signified to him that I was in no hurry. "H'sh," he whispered, with a confidential wink; "you be quiet.")

117

"You've got to move at once," the official snapped. "Those are the orders."

"So we will move at wunst," retorted Gotty hotly. "But I must put the Guv'nor ashore fust, mustn't I? The idea!" And having bestowed a frown of disapproval on the official (apparently by way of signifying that he was surprised at him) he set about drawing our dinghy alongside.

The other boat, following the course that we must take, had secured some yards start of us. But Gotty, after a quick look over his shoulder to measure the intervening distance, rolled up the sleeves of his jersey with significant deliberation, and set off in swift pursuit, with the view, as at first I supposed, of exchanging further speech with his adversary, but, as it proved, merely to pass the other dinghy in cold silence, and so humiliate its occupant by an exhibition of superior oarsmanship.

It behoved that Gotty should return with all reasonable despatch to the *Betty*, and thus opportunity served for but briefest mention of a matter on which, it seemed, he was no less anxious to talk with me than I to talk with him.

"The old feller is agoin' it—no mistake," observed my companion ere we parted at the stairs. "I ain't nobody, you ain't nobody, and 'e's everybody. There you are! Ercourse we know 'e's come ter do us good and where we're going 'e's acquainted with, and we was never there afore; so I don't take no notice, nor no offence, 'im bein' a ole man and all. But 'e didn't ought ter carry on so masterful, nor yet make 'isself so busy."

"No," I heartily agreed, "that will have to be stopped. But you get back now, or there'll be trouble with the harbour-master."

I told him that I should probably return that night, which seemed a reasonable conjecture; but I calculated without a knowledge of the sportive spirit in which the people of those parts have settled their topographical nomenclature.

Having journeyed across the confluence of the rivers Stour and Orwell (and, let me parenthetically observe, I was relieved by a view the little steamer afforded of our bawley sheering to a new anchorage), I looked in vain for the house-boats and boat-houses with which, as was known to me, my holiday party were associated. I had come to Felixstowe shore and I had come by the ferry, yet I certainly had not come to Felixstoweferry. On that point all the people I consulted were agreed. What was even more bewildering, none knew in which direction Felixstoweferry lay, some being indeed sceptical as to the existence of a place so named. One old gentleman went out of his way to explain that, although most persons spoke of it as Felixstowe, the locality in which we stood was, strictly speaking, Walton, which was the easier to remember, as there was another place of the same name a few miles south.

Ultimately I found a singularly well-informed railway official, who pointed out the Felixstoweferry was not in Felixstowe at all, but at Bawdsey Haven, a few miles to the north. As to how to get there, he advised taking the train as far as it would go, and then asking again.

Acting dubiously on this counsel, I, in due course, alighted at the railway terminus, where it was my good fortune to fall in with a flyman who, though the name "Felixstoweferry" was fresh to him, was full of knowledge concerning "the" Ferry at Woodbridge Haven (which, by-the-bye, as he was careful to explain, was several miles from Woodbridge); and he betrayed an alert disposition to drive me thither. True, we joined issue as to what would be an appropriate payment for the service; but that hitch being smoothed away he conveyed me, through winding country roads and a sandy causeway by the sea, to the floating pleasure parties into whose midst I proposed to project myself.

I hope it may be the good fortune of these pages to meet the eyes of that flyman, and of the persons I consulted at the ferry pier on the shore that is opposite Harwich: for I desire to inform them that, at seven o'clock, I was telegraphing from a picturesque building, situated within a stone's-throw of where the fly had set me down, and over the door of which, painted in bold letters, was the inscription, "Felixstoweferry Post-office."

The telegram was addressed, "Fishing boat *Betty* LO96, Harwich Harbour," and ran as follows: "Please trawl off Harwich to-morrow morning and come in with catch to Woodbridge Haven;" and when the next day's sunlight was fading, and still in vain I watched the shimmering waters of that peaceful inlet, I arrived at the frame of mind inevitable to one who has promised his friends a box of fresh fish and finds himself without opportunity to receive their thanks.

At eight o'clock I set out on foot to re-discover my railway terminus, and arrived at the distant ferry pier two hours later. The steamboat had ceased running, but I found a waterman to row me over.

Identifying my property among the flotilla of fishermen's dinghies clustered about the stairs, I waited until, some half-hour later, Gotty strode upon the scene. My first words, demanding an explanation, collided with his words, offering one.

"The young feller didn't bring it aboard not afore this mornin',

119

and 'e said it come last night, only they didn't know where she was layin', and there was ninepence ter pay! Couldn't 'ave give theirselves the trouble to arsk, seemin'ly, fer I was agin 'ere till past twelve o'clock, up and down, back'ards and for'ards, not knowin' when you mightn't come, you 'avin' said you'd most likely be back larst night."

I hastened to apologetically commiserate with this victim of post-office remissness; but none the less I desired to be informed why, when the telegram did come to hand, there had been so complete a failure to realise the desire therein expressed.

"Well, jest see 'ow it's bin blowin'!" protested Gotty, and peradventure a landsman must necessarily have accepted this explanation had it not been undermined by a supplementary one, put forward with the opposite intention: "The other boats 'ad bin gorn four howers afore we got the telergram."

This served to remind me that, while exploring the shingly slopes of Woodbridge Haven during the early afternoon, I had descried a bawley trawling in the blue distance, and indeed had pointed her out to my admiring friends as unmistakably the LO.96, busy over their tomorrow's breakfast.

I desired Gotty, in such language as seemed appropriate at the moment, to tell me how it came about that, while one boat was held in harbour by the wind, identical craft were riding the high seas in pursuit of the purpose for which they existed; and I furthermore requested his attention to this additional point, namely, was not the *Betty* capable of sailing a few miles, and catching a few fish, without the escort, support, and countenance of an entire fishing fleet?

A human note entered into the voluble and perturbed explanations that these inquiries called forth:

"I told 'im so! I told 'im we oughter go, seein' you'd sent the telergram on purpose and very likely told your friends we'd be bringin' 'em a mess of fish and all. But 'e said no—it was too late ter start now, and when 'e was on the *Bellycan* 'e always got 'is orders the night afore. It's everlastin' about the *Bellycan*, and what they 'ad to eat, and 'ow wonderful clever 'e was at racin' quicker than what anybody else could. Only I told 'im, I says, 'Mr. Rawson, you mustn't think this 'ere bawley's a yacht,' I says, 'fer she ain't. The Guv'nor's come out ter see a bit of fishin',' I says, 'and 'e'll think it wery strange,' I says, 'if we can't get 'im a pair of soles and one or two plaice, and p'raps a roker,' I says, 'ter give to 'is friends.' But the old feller's that obstinate, 'e won't never allow 'isself to be told by them as knows best. Another thing, with the weather so blowy, 'e says, there wouldn't be no charnse o' gettin' into that 'aven what you spoke about; and that's where I 'ad ter let 'im know best, fer I never was there myself."

"Now look here, Gotty," I said. "This sort of thing has gone far enough. You are the skipper, and you must not be overruled by Mr. Rawson. You must be gentle but firm, and make him see that the decision in these matters rests with you."

"Ercourse I'm the skipper!" cried Gotty, with a sudden access of dignity rather suggesting that he had been overlooking the fact himself. "But why," he asked indignantly, "can't 'e see that, and treat me accordin'? It ain't my place ter be always for'ard. The idea! And 'im sayin' this must be this, and that must be that, and me not allowed a word in anythin'. I never 'eard of sech a thing!"

"Well, you must assert your authority more!"

"'Ow can I," he replied, in the raised voice of wrath, "when 'e don't let me? You wouldn't 'ave me catch 'im a clout acrost the 'ead, would yer? Him an old man gettin' on fer seventy!"

And, his lawless imagination having tentatively fastened upon me the responsibility for this aspiration, his looks clearly showed that he was scandalised and repelled by my inhumanity.

"No, no! Certainly not! What I mean is that when necessary, quietly show him that you are the master."

"Now, didn't you tell me most partic'lar," Gotty replied, in a tone of frank expostulation, "that I was ter give way to 'im, and arsk 'is advice, and make 'im feel comfortable, and"—for a retentive memory was busy recalling all the scattered scraps of counsel which, in my first joy at securing the elderly mariner's co-operation, I had imparted—"and see 'e didn't want fer wittles, and never ter call 'im Ole Treacle Tart? Didn't you say," continued the accuser, "that you'd found a better mate than what all the other ones was put tergether, and you didn't know 'ow we could get where we was goin' if we 'adn't got 'im? And now, when I've done all that," he added, getting a trifle entangled in his own eloquence, though I could pretend to no uncertainty concerning the barb-wire line of his argument, "it's all wrong, seemin'ly, and I oughter do somethin' dif'rent. There ain't no pleasin' nobody!"

Though to be thus ruthlessly trailed along the path of my miscalculations made me a fitting object for all the sympathy I had at disposal, a tribute of pity was nevertheless compelled on observing that, having scaled this height of bitter pessimism, the commander of my fishing smack was panting and perspiring with feeling.

So, obeying the impulse of a contrite heart, I pleaded guilty to

121

each sharp count in the indictment, and then besought my companion to lay aside any ill-judged suggestions I might have let fall in hours gone by, and so smooth the way of our two heads to jointly consider what, in the difficult situation that had arisen, was best to be done.

Mollified by my more reasonable attitude, he conceded a fuller measure of sociability; and we proceeded with dispassionate affability to discuss the complex psychological problem presented by the presence of selfwilled, elderly, and good-tempered Mr. Rawson. Nor was it long before we were agreed that, following a little show of quiet firmness on the part of the skipper, fortified by the moral support of the owner's authority, our shipmate would readily subside into his subordinate position, and thenceforth restrict his initiative within the limits we were anxious to impose on its exercise.

This conversation, continued as Gotty rowed me to the *Betty's* new anchorage, brought one piece of new knowledge to my astonished mind. We had agreed as to the old fellow's good-hearted and urbane qualities, and I chanced to say:

"I was very pleased with his thoughtfulness in proposing that I should come here to see my daughter and friends."

"'Oo did?" Gotty stopped rowing to incoherently inquire.

"Of course," I hastily added, "I must thank you, too, for he wouldn't have known they were here if you hadn't told him."

"I never told 'im nothin' o' the sort!" was the bewildered and bewildering comment.

"You must have! How could he have known?"

"No more 'e didn't know! Me tell 'im! Me! Don't yer think I know better than go and tittle-tattle about your private consarns what you may see fit ter tell me? You ain't shorely got so bad an erpinion o' me as all that!"

"But how in the world did he know, then?"

"'E didn't know, don't I tell yer—not afore you told 'im yerself. Why now!"—a memory illuminating his mind with its retrospective significance—"I thought it was a funny thing the quick way you took 'im up; 'im and me 'aving jest bin talkin', and I says to 'im (fer I didn't 'ave no thought of your people bein' 'ere and you might want ter come and see 'em), 'Mr. Rawson,' I says, 'We didn't oughter go to 'Arwich, seein' the Guv'nor ain't told us to!' But 'e said you wouldn't make no bother where we went; and 'e was that set on it along o' 'is two nephews living 'ere, what 'e wanted ter see, and 'is ole friend Golesmith. But I was tellin' 'im you'd think it strange of us to 'ave our own fancy to go 'ere and go there; and

then you come along, and at the fust word there you was all fer goin';
so I kep' my mouth shut arter that,"

And thus I was made acquainted with a strange coincidence, and
one counting heavily for disillusionment.

Yet if this discovery served in a notable degree to ripen my
knowledge of Mr. Rawson, that process was destined to receive an
even more potent stimulus ere we had been two minutes on board
the *Betty*.

"'E's turned in and snorin' fit ter wake the dead," testified Gotty
on returning from a visit to the cabin; "and 'e's bin and gorn and
wrapped 'isself up in your two overcoats and one o' your blankits!"

XVIII

TWO NIGHTS IN A HAMMOCK

NEXT morning I was fain to admit that my first night in a hammock had not been an experience of unalloyed pleasure—a circumstance for which the inadequacy of my coverings was only partly accountable. A factor making even more powerfully for discomfort was the lopsided fashion in which, by reason of our inept manipulation of improvised lashings, the canvas receptacle had persisted in hanging. In nautical language, the thing had an ugly list to starboard, so that had I not introduced much discretion into the disposal of my limbs I must needs have rolled out on to the floor below.

For the rest, it had been wholly congenial to lie beneath an unscreened canopy of stars; for I had insisted upon the dubious Gotty slinging my hammock across the hold opening, correctly assuming that the combings would afford adequate shelter against chilly breezes.

"Now do 'ave my bunk ternight," the generous skipper (reverting to an offer he had vainly made overnight) interrupted my morning toilet to urge. "I can easy sleep on the floor, without takin' no 'urt, and you'd be more warm and comfortable."

Having assured him that, when we had made the readjustment of cords necessary to secure an even balance, my easy repose would be assured, I asked:

"How did *you* sleep?"—a point, indeed, on which I had misgivings.

"I did lay a bit 'ard," he confessed, raising a sympathetic left hand to gently rub the extremity of his right shoulder; "but I was warm enough arter I fetched the old jib to lay over me;" and I mentally marked down cabin beds and bedding as among the articles to be purchased at the earliest convenient opportunity.

Over a sturdy breakfast of fried eggs and cheese (for which the night air of Harwich had armed me with a zest) I met Mr. Rawson, who had awakened to the world's affairs with a composed conscience and the fresh shiny complexion of one who has slept long and soundly.

124

Before the meal was over, I had committed a grievous error in tactics.

"Well," I remarked in a tone studiously casual, "we'll sail round to Woodbridge Haven this morning."

"Right you are!" Gotty postponed a gulp of coffee to instantly observe.

"Begging your pardon, sir," said Mr. Rawson, with a shade of severity on his amiable face, "but you are forgetting to-day is Sunday."

As a matter of fact I had not lost touch with the calendar to that extent, but I had been placing one method of travel in a category with others. Obviously, however, on such a point, free latitude must be allowed to the opinion of others.

"If you would rather not sail on Sunday, Mr. Rawson, of course that settles it."

"I should most certainly object," he replied—"in fact, I could not consent to such a thing. We have all the week for getting about in; there can't be any need to work on Sunday. No, I intend to spend the day quietly, reading the newspaper, and then this evening I daresay I shall go to church. Unless," he added thoughtfully, "I might drop in to the Duke's Head to pass an hour or two with my friend Goldsmith"—a revelation of broad-minded impartiality concerning occupation for a Sabbath evening which at least placed the old fellow remote from any suspicion of hypocrisy.

"Very well," I said, we will go to Woodbridge Haven to-morrow, after catching some fish to take to my friends."

"Wind and weather permitting," supplemented Mr. Rawson, in the mellow voice of philosophy. "'We will,' as I used to say to my gentleman, 'if we can.' But we none of us ever know, do we, sir, what the morrow may bring forth?"

Not feeling called upon, or indeed qualified to dispute this axiom, I contented myself with a general statement, uttered in a voice of some confidence, that I dared say the weather would be all right.

"It looks reg'lar set in fer fair, don't it?" was Gotty's cheerful interjection.

"You never know!" observed Mr. Rawson. "I well remember—"; and before the skipper and I knew where we were, so to speak, we were involved in further reminiscences of a vessel whose equipment and exploits had no power to excite our enthusiasm.

That afternoon yielded me a pleasant walk to Dovercourt with Gotty, and, as far as our shipmate was concerned, evening brought us the knowledge that, in the strange competition of choice which

125

held his mind in so delicate a balance, the Duke's Head had won.

An adjustment of hammock lashings, and the utilisation of warm clothing taken from my trunk, gave me the promise of a night of more comfortable suspension, though the realisation of my early hopes was cruelly prevented by the untoward putting of a foot through a decayed portion of the canvas; which resulting aperture so speedily resolved itself into a perilous slit, that I made haste to transfer my weight to a situation less soft, but more secure, on the flooring.

Next day proving all it should be, my companions had anchor and sails up ere I concluded my interrupted slumbers, and in a little while—with Mr. Rawson again on fixed-point duty at the helm—the *Betty* rocked forward over smooth and slumbrous waves, with her trawl collecting samples of creatures that live in the sea.

A first haul placed us in possession of a pretty plateful of soles, slips, and plaice, with a young conger thrown in to give variety; and, although Mr. Rawson viewed the proceeding with manifest disfavour the skipper returned our gear to the deep, that Providence might have an opportunity for further favours.

This second haul, when the time came for turning the windlass, proved to contain an item which set all our hearts a-quake.

"Heavins! Ain't it a weight!" perspiring Gotty had exclaimed, while exerting the lion's share of the effort involved. "It's never all fish, shorely? No!" he quickly added, "I can see it ain't. Ps'ch!"—in token of deep offence to his nostrils.

Peering over the side with a cautious curiosity, I drew back on catching sight (with appeal to another sense) of the bulging extremity of a bulky shape encased in canvas.

Mr. Rawson also looked, and saw, and drew back.

From that moment we were three men, with grave faces, speaking seldom, briefly, and in voices barely above a whisper.

At first I was thinking of the option that still was ours—to unloosen the end of the trawl and so return that dark object to the sea, our minds innocent of prying, the sack still holding its secret. I wondered what was the course of custom.

"The tackle?" asked Gotty, and Mr. Rawson assented with a nod. A pulley in the rigging was then utilised to assist in hauling the trawl-end, with its repellent burden, to the deck.

We all gathered to windward of the thing, which exuded black water. Gotty drew a big clasp knife from his trouser pocket, and cut the lashings at the head of the sacking.

We looked upon a dark, compact mass of something for which we had no name. The skipper cautiously removed a handful, which, having subjected it to a close scrutiny, he threw into the sea. Then he took out another handful and threw that also into the sea. Silently continuing this process, he was presently digging into the mystery with both hands, finally groping elbow-deep to the bottom of the sack.

I had watched with growing relief, and the tension was ended, and our mistaken melancholy banished, when the investigator put his thoughts into speech.

"It ain't nothin' only the sweepin's out of a steamer—cinders and soot and sech-like—put in a ole sack ter be out o' the way, and then thrown overboard, most likely arter they come out of 'arbour. But don't it reg'lar 'oller? That's often the way when anything's laid under the mud at the bottom. Comin' up inter the fresh air fetches out all the smell. Ps'ch!"—and he lifted the half-emptied sack in strong hands, and tumbled it over into the water.

The legitimate captures, which had been flopping unheeded among the seaweed and crabs, now received the skipper's attention, gasping juveniles being restored to their element, and indignant adults added to those which had earlier come to hand.

Our prow was pointing to that part of the land which coastguard houses and a flagstaff identified as Woodbridge Haven. I imparted to Mr. Rawson such particulars of the entrance as, on my recent visit to the place, I had been able to glean. The inlet, I explained, was narrow and shallow; and my attempt to describe the course of the channel was buttressed by a suggestion that it would be wise to employ a local pilot. But the desire to be useful missed its gratification. Ripe nautical experience bent a polite but deaf ear to these counsels of the landsman.

"I dare say, sir, we'll manage all right," was Mr. Rawson's cheerful but only comment, which he accompanied by a quite superfluous smile of indulgent toleration; so that I was sorry, as the saying is, that I had spoken.

Nor could I thereafter sit apart in dignified silence nursing a secret hope that he would steer the *Betty* to destruction amid the perils of which he would not allow me to warn him; for, as sole owner of the uninsured craft in question, I could find no spiteful solace in that thought.

As we sped on towards an ominous line of broken water, Gotty sighted a buoy, and straightway my experts were at loggerheads as to what might be its precise significance.

Still on we went; and now a rowing boat was visible newly come out from the harbour—which circumstance I noted with the greater satisfaction as it promised confirmation under one head of my unheeded counsels.

"That'd be one of them pilots what you spoke of!" exclaimed Gotty, who, at the time I mentioned the matter, had given no sign of attention.

"No doubt," I said briefly.

Mr. Rawson, with a composed and genial countenance, ignored the little boat.

It drew nearer. That we were the target for which its occupant was steering could no longer be doubted. Presently he was hailing us.

It was left to Mr. Rawson to reply, and his request to know the stranger's business drew from the pilot an offer to take us into the haven, if it were our wish to go there. Still the initiative was left to Mr. Rawson.

"Well, sir," he asked, with sprightly indifference, "shall we get him to take us in?"

"Do we need a pilot?" I asked coldly.

"That, sir," he beamingly made answer, "is for *you* to say."

As a matter of fact, I had a very definite preference in the matter, for, little as I might desire to be shipwrecked anywhere, I was eagerly hostile to the idea of such disaster happening under my daughter's eyes.

"I wonder how much he would charge," was my thrifty comment.

Raising his voice, the old mate bluntly asked the question, and the man in the boat mentioned a fee of five shillings.

Not knowing if piloting were one of the professions in which timely demur of the patron induces graceful concession by the artist, I was guilty of the suggestion that we should offer him three and sixpence.

Mr. Rawson did so, and it was as though the words had exercised a magnetic control over the tiller of the pilot-boat, for she altered her course, and was now returning whence she had come. I hastily gave Mr. Rawson other words wherewith to reverse the current.

"All right! Five shillings then!" promptly restored the dinghy's course to one which, a minute later, gave us the company of the stranger—a tall, broad fellow in a brown wide-awake—on board the *Betty*.

Mr. Rawson—and this is, in fact, the point to which I have been leading up—still held the tiller.

"Here!" said the pilot, touching him lightly on the shoulder, and preparing to succeed to the helm, "I'll take that."

"No, you won't," replied Mr. Rawson, refusing to budge.

"Yes, yes," persisted the other impatiently. "I must come there."

We were racing on, and, just ahead, the sea was rolling over the bar in snowy billows.

"I tell you, I know my place," protested the old mate. "I've had a pilot on board before to-day. You show the way; I'll keep the wood."

I knew that Mr. Rawson's will was of tolerably tough texture, but this standing on a point of etiquette amid the very breakers improved my knowledge in that direction.

Gotty stood regarding his nominal subordinate with the dropped jaw of keen disfavour.

The pilot, directing a swift look ahead, surrendered.

"All right!" he assented between clenched teeth. "But be careful You do what I tell you . . . . Ease her?"

Next minute, the direction having been ignored, he was shouting with wrathful urgency: "Ease her! Ease her, you old fool!"

"What!" cried Mr. Rawson, anxiously pointing to where the waves lashed one another into spray. "Take her through *that*?"

It certainly looked the worst of the water.

"Yes, yes," stormed the man who knew. "I know what I'm doing."

"Oh very well!" Mr. Rawson huffily replied, with the air of a man who washes his hands of responsibility; and he made the tiller adjustment which carried us, pitching and tossing, through the watery tumult.

Almost from second to second the pilot rapped out other instructions, which met with no further opposition from the helmsman, and a minute later our devious course had carried us into the narrow, sheltered waters of the haven, where, within hail of my friends' boat-house and house-boats we dropped anchor.

There we remained for a week. All that while the wind persisted in coming from the south. Mr. Rawson smiled upon my impatient wish to defy its opposition. Nor could I defy his. For Gotty agreed that a northerly element in the wind was essential to our further progress.

XIX

THE BATTLE OF FOLKESTONE

EARLY one morning we set sail from Woodbridge Haven; yet not so early but I had found opportunity to slip ashore for a private word with the pilot. Thus was I able, on his high authority, to inform my shipmates that, with the wind as it was, we could easily bang our way before nightfall to Folkestone, which I had previously mentioned to the skipper as, probably, our next destination.

"Now look here, sir," said Mr. Rawson, with his indulgent smile, "if you'll just be advised by me, we certainly won't go to Folkestone. Anywhere else you might have a fancy to call at, I'll be only too pleased to try and meet your wishes; but Folkestone harbour is dry at low water, so it would never do for us. When I had charge of the *Pelican*, sir, that was a place we were always careful to avoid."

Sooner or later a battle with the self-willed old man was inevitable, and I could hope for no more favourable issue than one concerning a port with which I happened to be well acquainted. In any case (for I am a human being) his last argument must needs have goaded me to war.

"You will seldom see less than fifty fishing boats at Folkestone," I said. "If they can use the harbour, I suppose we can. I am going to Folkestone to see some friends, and call for letters."

"Yes, sir," replied Mr. Rawson, in his most winning manner, "but you don't quite understand. The Folkestone boats are fitted with supports—legs, we call them—to keep them upright when the tide is out. We have no legs, and that makes all the difference. As for seeing your friends and getting your letters, that will be quite easy. We'll go to Dover, where there's a splendid harbour, and you can run into Folkestone by train. It only takes a few minutes."

"It certainly is a short journey by rail," I admitted, "but, on the whole, Mr. Rawson, I would prefer to go by water. We can list over in Folkestone harbour, as we do at Leigh. At one time, people tell me," I added, "the Leigh boats had legs, but they proved to be unnecessary."

Thus, by great good luck, my ignorance of nautical matters had been redeemed by just the few little facts that enabled me to deal with the autocrat's arguments. And behold! his face bore witness to discomfiture, and he was silent.

To our brief debate Gotty had been a listener, and I interpreted his facial rigidity as cloaking an alert disposition to offer the support of an ally should the backward state of my maritime education give advantage to the adversary. But I had not read his mind aright.

"There was some of 'em talking at the Ferry Boat what knows Folkestin'," he ponderously remarked, "and by their account the bottom's all stones, so, if there comes anything of a swell, a little wessel stands a charnse to 'ave 'er side stove in. Only, if she's got legs—well, that's what they told *me*!" he added in confusion, nonplussed by my furtive efforts to frown him into silence.

"Ah! that most likely would be the case," Mr. Rawson chimed in, with restored amiability. "When a boat's held upright on her keel, you see, sir, she can stand the jarring; and no doubt the Folkestone boats are stronger built than ours."

"Nonsense!" I was rude enough to exclaim. "Really, Gotty, I'm surprised at you listening to a lot of silly taproom gossip"—at which the titular commander of my vessel, still dead to all diplomatic niceties in the situation, obviously was deeply wounded. "There's a lot of lovely mud at Folkestone," I added, meaning no disrespect to that delightful place, and, indeed, drawing my bow somewhat at a venture. For, to add to my annoyance, this attack from a friendly quarter, which had so revived the enemy I had laid low, was one I knew not how to parry. For anything I definitely remembered to the contrary, there might even be force in what Gotty had said. Indeed, the very name Folkestone seemed to hint at something of the kind. But the die was cast. I had pitted my will—my obstinacy, if you like—against Mr. Rawson's; and I was ready to run risks.

So I told the pair of them, with the firmness of finality, that we were going to Folkestone; "and," I briskly added, "I should like you to get there as soon as possible, please."

"Very well, sir," said Mr. Rawson, with a smile of all-embracing kindliness that might easily have been mistaken for a benediction.

When, a little later, I had Gotty to myself in the cabin, I lost no time in shaking my fist in his face, and pointing out, *sotto voce*, that he was a silly old ass.

"Wot's the matter *now*!" he gasped, and in manner to show how demoralising to his nerves had been the recent controversy.

I descended to particulars.

"You come complaining to me about Mr. Rawson being so masterful, and overruling everybody, and taking charge—"

"And so 'e do!" Gotty broke in warmly. "Shorely you can see that fer yerself!"

"Of course I can. But can't you see we must make a stand against that sort of thing? So, having arranged to go to Folkestone, I refused to let him upset my plans. Then you must needs come and try to spoil everything."

"I never tried to spoil nothin'!" he retorted indignantly. "You wouldn't take no notice o' what I said, knowin' better yerself, seemin'ly. And p'raps you might. Only that's what they tell me—the 'arbour's all stones."

"Well, and what if it is? We're not afraid of a few stones, are we?"

I looked at my pupil almost in despair, feeling that nothing short of a coal hammer would convey a sense of the subtle principles of diplomacy through that tough cranium.

"Do you think," I went on in random haste—for this private conference must not be much longer prolonged or we should have the old helmsman drawing his inferences—"do you think there would have been any of this nonsense about Folkestone if his old friend Goldsmith lived there? Can't we easily anchor outside the harbour if it isn't advisable to go inside? And don't you see we'll never manage him if I pull one way and you pull another?"

One of those shots—I know not which—hit the target. On a sudden the light of understanding shone in that large face. Perplexity had given place to fraternity.

"Right-O! Now I see wot yer drivin' at. As fur as that goes, if we didn't want ter lust over, we could lash 'er agin the wall; or if there mightn't be a berth, we could set alongside some boat what's got legs. Yus! I didn't know no more'n the dead wot you was after, seein' as you 'adn't give me word. 'E don't 'old with goin' ter Folkestone; so that's set you ter go there. And wery proper, too!"

It was not the happiest way of stating the case, as my affirmative wish certainly did not arise from Mr. Rawson's negative one; but the definition (even without the knowing nods and sagacious winks accompanying it) was sufficiently approximate to reveal a mind in tune with the delicate mutual obligations which our hapless situation involved.

"I'll go and tell 'im," he whispered, with the overprecipitancy of the newly converted, "'Mr. Rawson,' I'll say, 'a few stones needn't 'inder us from goin' ter Folkstin'.' No, I won't!" he greatly relieved me by adding, "fer then 'e might fancy you and me 'ad bin talkin'"—and Gotty's face testified to a greater resentment of that possible suspicion than, as it seemed to me, the facts justified.

This secret debate having proceeded amid clouds of steam from the kettle, we now, in carrying mugs and a pot of tea on deck, suggested an innocent domestic explanation of our absence. In an interval of happy truce with our rotund and benevolent-looking foe, I poured out his portion of the refreshment, and Gotty put in the sugar; themes of easy conversation presenting themselves in the attractive aspect of the Essex coast, our gratifying rate of progress and the wind's tendency to increase in force.

But it was only a truce. Having rinsed the crockery in a pail, and restored both to their appointed situations, Gotty reappeared on deck with, as it seemed to me, War writ large on his expressive countenance. Nor on this occasion did I misread the tokens.

He straightway set about a conscientious attempt to impose upon the course of events the stamp of his mental spirit.

He mentioned an intention to lower the topsail. Instantly Mr. Rawson bade him do no such thing. Thus, by no means for the first time, they were at issue on a question of seamanship. But now the development constituted a wholesome novelty.

"Carryin' the torpsel in this wind," persisted Gotty, with a stately composure full of promise, "is too much strain on the stays."

"How am I to keep her on this course," Mr. Rawson demanded to be told, "without the topsail to steer her with?"

"Easy enough," Gotty explained; and he took three cheerful steps to the mast.

It was a dramatic moment. My hopes rose high as I gazed with admiration at the man who, a resolute hand already on the appropriate rope, was about to vindicate his authority as skipper, and thereby release us from galling thraldom to one who had encroached so comprehensively on the rights of that office.

But I have not yet told all.

"Very well!" cried Mr. Rawson, scrambling to his feet and hastily evacuating the stern. "I've done! You can take the tiller!"

The very thing, of course, that Gotty desired to do. But how often, in sharp crises, will a man's impulse prove a traitor to his interests! At my skipper's feet lay the crown of victory. But instead of adorning his resolute brows therewith, he made the woeful mistake of unravelling it as a scourge for his back.

"All right, Mr. Rawson, you needn't be so 'asty," was his limp and lamentable response, as, with fatal irresolution, he released his hold of the rope.

The incident was over. Mr. Rawson, swift to accept those soft words, had already returned to the helm; and the topsail remained aloft.

Alas! Gotty's dash for freedom had but tightened our fetters. In attempting to depose Mr. Rawson from the position of captain, he had, as it were made him an admiral.

My crestfallen ally had betaken himself below, to deaden his feelings by chopping firewood; and the venerable helmsman reigned with benign aplomb over the fortunes of our craft, gazing contentedly about him as though embracing all the visible universe within the scope of his benevolent approbation. That sight speedily palling upon me, I withdrew into the low-pitched privacy of my hold, ostensibly to read, but in fact to ruminate. Out of the grey texture of my thoughts there arose the stern resolve to persist in insisting on Folkestone; to go there, happen what might, and let wily hindrances be interposed never so thickly in my path; to stubbornly, pitilessly, tame the old man to that one act of obedience.

Let me say at once—not to keep the reader in unhealthy suspense —that we did get to Folkestone. But the stages of our progress thither, and the manner of our arrival, are forbidding memories.

On the first day he took us all the way back up the Thames estuary, and we anchored for the night in Sheerness harbour. On the following day, at about noon, we arrived at Ramsgate. Next morning we pushed on to Dover, and abode there for twenty hours.

In a word, when there wasn't too much wind, there was too much calm. The tides also were in the conspiracy to hold us back from Folkestone.

If among my readers there be any landsmen who think they could persuade an experienced mariner, aged seventy, that the elements would permit him to prosecute a voyage more expeditiously than he has a mind to, I hope they will experiment. I have convinced myself of the limit to my own powers in that direction.

Gotty's attitude, when I appealed to him, struck me as almost cowardly.

"I must allow 'im ter know best," he remarked, with an air of magnanimity which, in all the circumstances, seemed a little gratuitous. "You brought 'im ter show us the way, and I never come so fur south afore. But ain't them chalk clifts jest all right? I call 'em reg'lar 'andsome!"

And, indeed, as the sunny panorama of the Kent coast slowly unwound its beauties to his untravelled eye, his applause was enthusiastic and sustained. Nor was I one whit less exalted by the sparkling wonder of it all; and, indeed, I question if this world provides a keener joy than to the man who, on good terms with his pipe and his conscience, finds himself a-rocking on the blue sea, beneath the boundless immensity of open sky. The words for it are sweet air, appetite, contentment, and—I had almost said—freedom. That brings me back to the leek in our jar of honey—to the leak, if you will, the metaphor being graciously indifferent to orthography.

As we set sail from Dover, on the fourth day out from Woodbridge Haven, I found myself directing a covert, lynx-like gaze at the countenance of our Cromwellian helmsman. Day after day he essayed his arguments, various and artful, but I had been politely unalterable. Now he was past Shakespeare's cliff, entering the sheltered waters of East Wear Bay, and steering straight for the visible portals of defeat. Never had I seen that remarkable old man looking more cherubic.

Purringly I wondered, had he secretly retained a last shot in his locker? No. For it was not a shot—only a little squib of a thing, and quite below the level of his great powers. We arrived outside Folkestone harbour at a time when, it being low water, only a crab or a seagull could go in.

"Never mind," I told them. "We'll drop anchor here and wait for the tide;" and, it being the mate's business to drop the anchor, Gotty dropped it. And we did wait there. And the tide did come up. And we did go in. But I think Gotty's voice will always break with emotion when he tells people how.

Afloat you can see little of Folkestone harbour, so narrow is its mouth, until you are in the act of entering thereat. Such was our situation, a pier-head frowning down on either side of the *Betty*, when we discovered, not thirty yards ahead of us, the advancing prow of a barge about to sail out of the haven. Simultaneous exit and entrance, with vessels of any size, being obviously unwarranted by the dimensions of the place, it followed (the sunny morning ensuring plenty of promenaders on pier and jetty) that we were assisting in a spectacle that instantly engaged public interest. The avoidance of disastrous collision (not that we should have hurt the barge) manifestly depended on the fishing boat describing a graceful curve to either the right or the left of its far less mobile *vis-à-vis*.

Nor, brief as the space of time in which all this happened, did we lack guidance. A peaked-cap official on the main pier-head was shouting to us to go to the right, and placing his meaning beyond the possibility of misunderstanding by energetically waving his hand in that direction. A man at the bow of the barge was vociferously bawling an identical instruction, and also indulging in hand-waving to correspond. Two jerseyed figures on the jetty, and a civilian on the stone pier, were busying themselves to a like purpose; and, to complete the semicircle of uniform counsel, an old fisherman on a Folkestone smack was shouting and semaphoring as vigorously as anybody.

"Got to go ter starboard," cried Gotty from the bow, as he likewise flapped a demonstrative hand. "To the right! To the right!" I, standing by the cabin-opening, turned to explain to the helmsman, as I mechanically waved in unison with all the others. In those few instants, indeed, the air rang with the words: "To the right! Go to the right!"

I have but to mention one little supplementary circumstance, and my account of the incident is complete. Mr. Rawson went to the left.

When the shouts of expostulation had died down to murmurings, accompanied by indignantly pointing fingers, I turned to Mr. Rawson with the inquiry:

"What on earth did you do that for? We were told to go to the right!"

"I heard what they said," he cooed, with a composure so absolute that for a moment I wondered if I had been grievously misjudging him, and if he were merely a dull old lunatic. "I knew, sir," he added, with sprightly assurance, "what I was doing. We gave the barge plenty of room. I don't think there is any one here who could teach me much."

I felt quite sure there wasn't. Nay, it seemed questionable if all Europe and America contained the gifted instructor who could puncture that armour of complacency with any new knowledge.

For my part, I seemed to want air. And Gotty's case was much the same, if I might judge by the gurglings and broken explanations with which, after tying up the mainsail, he accompanied the labour of lashing the *Betty* to a little wooden pier. By a sign and a nod we arranged to forthwith go ashore. I told Mr. Rawson we probably should not be gone long.

"That's all right, sir," came the graceful, not to say indulgent, response. "I dare say you'll like to have a run round and see your friends. I'll have a pipe of tobacco and a look at that book you lent me. He needn't come back till it's time to put the 'taters on."

"If," I said to Gotty, when we were out of earshot of the old man, "if anything had gone wrong just now, we should have had to pay. Every one told him to go to the right."

"Ercourse we oughter 'a gorn on 'er weather. I never see sech ignerince! You mustn't go ter lew'ard of a barge when she ain't got 'er leeb'ard down. Any one what's used ter the water oughter know that much."

The old fellow's voice was husky with the humiliation of it all.

136

XX

FREEDOM

IT happened somewhat awkwardly that, while prosecuting these adventures on the unfamiliar sea, Gotty's city-bred owner should be preparing for later adventures on the still less familiar land. A letter waiting at Folkestone apprised me that, legal preliminaries being nearly accomplished, I might at any moment be sent for to complete the acquisition of the little Essex homestead on which, as a lifelong Londoner gone back to the land, I proposed to produce fruit, vegetables, honey, and other marketable commodities. Temporary stability of address being thus desirable, I resolved to linger awhile at the pleasant port to which, so much against Mr. Rawson's wish, we had come.

Yet, as I pointed out to Gotty, there was no reason why we should not do some fishing, particularly as, since leaving Woodbridge Haven, we had been too much taken up with Mr. Rawson to shoot our trawl. Accordingly early next morning we went out with the Folkestone boats to try our luck in Dungeness Bay. Nor could this be construed as an act of poaching or presumption.

"When you was gorn ter see your friends last night," Gotty explained, "I got talkin' ter some of these Folkestin' chaps, and not 'alf bad company they ain't, neither, only fust it reg'lar puzzled me ter make out what they was sayin', they talk so funny. There was some on 'em give me word ter come out to the west'ard this mornin', along o' them. I asked if there was any fastnesses, and they said nothin' wouldn't pull us up if we kep' inside five fadums, and don't go ter the west'ard of some housen what we'll see. If you 'aul jest along the shore, by all accounts, that's where you're most likely ter get the big 'uns."

Acting in accordance with this friendly counsel, we fished within hail of several Folkestone luggers, Gotty basing favourable anticipations on the cloudy state of sea.

"When the water's clear," he observed feelingly, "you might jest as well keep the trawl aboard. The fish see the beam comin' along the bottom, that's what I berlieve, and it gives 'em time ter get away.

But when the water's thick you do stand a charnse to 'arn a shillin'—that's if there's any fish to be caught;" on which point, as I knew, his mind was a prey to frequent and dismal misgivings.

The end of the net, when at last the time came for our united efforts to lift it over the side, was bulging with flapping whiteness, so that the owner's bosom swelled with gratification, even if his skipper did shake a dissatisfied head and allude, in a spirit of criticism, to the size of our captives.

Nor have I ever seen Gotty other than discontented with our hauls, a circumstance, however, which I am less disposed to identify with the pessimism it seems to reveal than with the optimism I am convinced it reflects. It is not so much that the hauls of his laborious achievement are so poor as that the hauls of his buoyant imagination are so rich. A codfish looks a sprat to the man expecting whales.

Certainly the owner and skipper never saw eye to eye when the confusion of wet life and glistening prettiness lay strewn upon the deck. Often it was only a doubtful nine pen'orth to him, but always an aquarium of wonders to me.

The haul under consideration introduced us to four pairs of soles and half a box of plaice, some individually of a size outside the scope of any man's appetite. It introduced us to something else—another rumpus with Mr. Rawson.

Gotty was tying up the trawl end, and with a cheerfulness of demeanour suggesting that he was already taking mental stock of our next draught of fishes, when the old helmsman, coldly and pointedly, asked him what he was doing.

"Shorely we're goin' ter put 'er in jest once more?" came in persuasive accents from the skipper, as he looked from Mr. Rawson to me.

"Certainly," I agreed.

"Oh, no," said Mr. Rawson, "we've done very well for one day. There's quite as many as we can eat, sir, even if," he added significantly, "you pick out the best for your friends. It's time we went back now, or we shan't be able to get in the harbour."

As far as it went, I admitted, that statement was correct enough. "But," I found courage to point out, "I want to catch some more fish so that we shall have some to sell in the market."

For, on the previous afternoon, had not Gotty and I watched the auctions, and been greatly impressed by the prices prime was fetching? "O dear me!" Gotty had murmured in my ear, "one pound two fer that little lot! You wouldn't only get eight shillin's at our place." So of course we wanted to catch some fish for market.

But at my commercial confession, Mr. Rawson's temper (I regret having to record the blemish) got a little out of hand.

"It isn't what I looked for," he snapped, "nor what I'm used to"—which I took to mean that the owner of the *Pelican* never forgot himself in that way. But then, he was a gentleman, whereas I (will sceptical friends please note), besides being a farmer, am a fisherman.

"As for missing the tide," I pointed out, "that doesn't matter. We can do what the Folkestone boats do—anchor outside the harbour and wait."

"I've had about enough of this," muttered Mr. Rawson, not without wrath, as he went forward to assist in shoving the gear overboard.

Two hours later, on pulling up the trawl absolutely empty, we realised that it had been moving along the bottom upside-down—under which humiliating misfortune neither Gotty nor I bore up with anything like the fortitude displayed by Mr. Rawson.

Trawling no more, we returned to Folkestone, anchoring outside the harbour; and Gotty and I went ashore in the dinghy. Having purchased beds, bedding, and oilcloth, we called upon some friends of mine, the visit yielding an incident which, if it seemed of no great consequence at the moment, was destined to a sensational sequel on the morrow.

A buoyant, not to say boyish, school-girl was all aflame to accompany us when next we went a-trawling; and the owner, for reasons he judged sufficient, met that request with a reluctant shake of the head. But the high-spirited petitioner was not so easily to be baulked of her desire, and so turned to the skipper with a torrent of enthusiastic appeal. Soft-hearted Gotty soon capitulated.

"I tell yer what we'll do, Missy. You can't be along of us fishin', but when we come in ter-morrow arternoon we'll lay to outside, and I'll row ashore and fetch you. Then we'll take you fer 'alf-an-hour's sail afore we come in;" at which the delighted young lady, breaking into song, careered away to spread the news.

"Now, don't you forget," I warned Gotty.

"It ain't likely," he replied with dignity. Nor did he forget. But what he did do—or, rather, what someone else did—will be told in due sequence. Meanwhile I have to state what happened when Gotty and I, later in the evening, went line-fishing off Copt Point.

The first thing that happened, by the way, was that we could not get back to the *Betty,* certain of the youth of Folkestone harbour having—as my companion indignantly discovered, after much vain searching and shouting—utilised our dinghy for a trip to the pier extension. To make matters worse, when a pair of plausible youngsters came rowing back with her, she was, as Gotty's quick eye readily detected, deficient in the spade and sardine tin he had brought ashore with the intention—though perspiring efforts in that direction had not been crowned with success—of digging worms for bait.

The manner in which my skipper took this loss speedily attracted all the boys within hearing; and a minute later I beheld him as the centre of an attentive juvenile congregation, to whom he discoursed on theft, dwelling more particularly on the moral—or perhaps I ought to say, the immoral—aspects of his subject. Lapse of time yielding no promise of practical outcome, I broke in with the mundane offer of sixpence for the boy who, not being himself the guilty party, should place us anew in possession of our property; at which the youngsters departed like unto a company of rooks scattered by a gun. There ensued an interval only sufficient for Gotty to purchase three pennyworth of worms from an old man who, to judge by the number in his can, must have had something of a genius for digging them. Then the boys came helter-skelter back, one carrying the spade, and another the sardine tin, while four others noisily proclaimed their superior title, based on complicated explanations, to receive the sixpence. With a rough attempt at justice, I rewarded the boy who brought the spade—a boy with a record, by his own account, singularly free from blemish—and soon we were rowing away from a controversy that bid fair to end in bloodshed.

Proceeding later to the Point, but a few hundred yards from where the *Betty* rocked at anchor, we lost no time in dropping our lines in the water, Gotty immediately pulling his up with two wrigglesome whiting affixed thereto. A fisherman to the marrow, he was all a-thrill at this early success, though, alive to the importance of quietude in our deadly business, he strove manfully to muffle his feelings. For half-an-hour or more we remained absorbed in our work, the jubilant skipper catching two to my one, and every few minutes adding to the community of whiting flapping at our feet.

As we sat gently swaying in the deepening darkness, with the inky mystery of rocks and cliff just ahead, and nothing visible of the harbour, far to the right, but tiny twinkling lights—as, I say, we were thus peacefully engaged in that solemn silence, our ears, on a sudden, were troubled by a piteous wailing, with the like of which, in all my experience of machinery, menageries, and the domestic cat, I had hitherto escaped acquaintance. The din passed into a variety of appalling cadences—each the abject appeal of dull misery.

There came a holy silence.

Then again my hearing was assailed by that dolorous clamour, so like the frightened howling of a lost soul.

"What is it?" I asked Gotty, who, with turned head, was a figure of listening rigidity.

Yet a third time had that voice of gloomy sorrow afflicted us with its miserable moaning ere my companion, in the sudden light of knowledge, found tongue:

"It's that steamboat comin' what 'e don't like. So 'e's blowin' the fog-'orn fer us to come back."

That our outfit for the voyage included an eighteen-penny instrument of the kind, I knew. But this was my first acquaintance with the music of which it was capable.

Gotty was amused; I was annoyed. Having friends at Folkestone, it was wounding to my pride that the voice of illusory fear, pitched in so high a key of pathos, should arise from my vessel.

"It ain't as if," said Gotty, grasping his oars to row to the rescue, "we wasn't careful to arsk where we could lay clear of all craft. And nobody couldn't say they can't see that light on our stay—a fine night and all! Pore ole feller! We give 'im the charnse ter go ashore, or come along of us, didn't we? But no; 'e would stay aboard And now it's give 'im the jumps, seemin'ly."

As, when we arrived alongside, Mr. Rawson took upon himself to reprimand us, I soon found myself chopping logic with him.

"Well," I asked, "and suppose the steamboat had run into you, what then?"

"Why," he cried indignantly, "I might have been drowned."

"Quite so, but how could we have prevented the bawley being run down?"

"I never said you could prevent it," snapped the old man.

"Very well," I observed, growing indignant in turn, "then we might have been drowned too. Surely," I added, "it would be better for you to be drowned alone than for us to be drowned with you;" and, indeed, when one came to look the situation squarely in the face, his action in blowing the fog-horn, if not downright selfish, was carrying a love for company to an extravagant length.

"Oh! That's the way you look at it, is it!" were the wrathful words with which Mr. Rawson closed the conversation.

Our relations with the old man, it will be gathered, were strained. The snap occurred on the following afternoon.

All the morning we had been trawling in Dungeness Bay, and at one o'clock, with a box of numerous small flat fish, we turned our prow towards Folkestone. Having performed some share of the toil, and it being a day of glorious sunshine, I had not long participated in a substantial dinner when the luxurious thought possessed me to go and recline on my new spring bed, and pass a composed half-hour with a favourite author. The intellectual portion of this programme, however, missed its full accomplishment, the *Betty's* gentle undulations speedily lulling me into a profound and grateful slumber, from which I emerged to find myself amid physical factors of mystery. The lashed and lowered mainsail loomed as a canopy over the hold opening, and the vessel was dead still.

Scrambling out, I made the astounding discovery that, all sails down, we were in harbour, and berthed beside the little wooden pier. And so recently as dinner time I had reminded Gotty of his promise to the enterprising school-girl!

Standing at the stern, he answered my heated inquiry by rolling two despairing eyes heavenward, shaking a helpless head, and pointing to the cabin. There I found Mr. Rawson, and the upshot of our five minutes' animated conversation was that he tendered his resignation and I accepted it.

To have our fish put up to public auction, what time we modestly stood watching the competitive zeal of the purchasing public, was a minor pleasure which, in view of the larger one now opening to our mental horizon, Gotty and I were content to forego; and so he took the prosaic short-cut of fetching a coster, who offered us three and twopence for our captives, which he carried away on the understanding (fully acceptable to Gotty's business instincts, which were necessarily identified with more experience than I could lay claim to) that he would pay the money when he returned the box.

The transaction was destined to develop an untoward feature, whereof, however, a knowledge did not reach me until later in the afternoon, and after I had spent a fraternal and valedictory half-hour with Mr. Rawson, whose gloomy misgivings as to what might befall us, now that we should lack his experienced guidance, were in a measure qualified by the fact that, to lessen the encumbrances he would have on the train, he was proposing to entrust his cherished sea-boots to our care.

Having seen the old man off, I sought for Gotty in a quarter where a recent experience encouraged me to believe he might be found. Nor was this anticipation disappointed, though I was indeed ill-prepared for the scene of tense animation into which, on pushing open the swing doors, I thrust an intrusive head.

There towered Gotty, his brow furrowed by a concern and

142

perplexity manifestly shared by our coster patron standing by his side, the aproned figure beyond the bar and some eight or ten fishermen grouped around.

"Jest step inside fer a minute," cried Gotty, in a voice that was all excitement, "and see what you can make of it. My Guv'nor, what I was tellin' you about," he added, in an introductory aside. "'E put the money down 'ere," indicating, as I gradually understood, the precise spot on which the coster had deposited payment for our fish. "I see 'im count it out—three shillin's and tuppence. You see 'im too, didn't yer?"—turning about for confirmation that came promptly from a row of nodding heads. "Then 'e stepped o' one side, and when I went ter pick up the money, there was a shillin' gorn. Talk about funny—well, I dunno what ter think about it. There you are."

Amid voices of sympathy and corroboration, the publican was anxiously explaining to me that, as he did not like a thing of the kind to happen in his house, he had carefully and thrice raked through the sawdust on the floor, but to no purpose. The coster's distress was sufficient testimony to his innocence; and on learning of several witnesses to the occurrence who had since departed, I privately inferred that the thief, if theft had been committed, was no longer in our midst.

"Whether I've bin done down," observed Gotty, who was perspiring under stress of the mystery, "or whether it's jest gorn"— and he waved his hand in vacant air, in comprehensive suggestion of all occult channels through which a shilling might have taken its departure, "I can't tell yer."

If I could not solve the enigma, which had already, it seemed, engaged the attention of that company for more than an hour, I could at least abbreviate its sequel—to which course I was the more strongly impelled as I desired my skipper's company elsewhere.

"Oh well," I said, "the shilling is gone, so we won't bother any more about it. After all, what does it matter?"

"There you are! What did I tell yer!" exclaimed Gotty, turning with eager enthusiasm from one to the other. "That's the Guv'nor all over. 'E don't make a trouble of nothin':" whereupon three elderly Folkestone fishermen, as though recognising an owner after their own hearts, raised their mugs, and, with solemn ceremony, drank my health in their own beer.

Peradventure the punctilious reader will opine that modesty should have deterred me from recording that incident. Not at all. To be able, here and there, to reveal the author in his real character, sweetens the labour of writing a book.

XXI

FOUR NEW MATES

MATELESS at moorings, Gotty and I revelled in our freedom, though during several succeeding days we had cause to remember the price at which we had purchased it. Finding a successor to Mr. Rawson proved, indeed, a protracted and troublesome task.

Early we thought we had found our man. Several friendly fishermen testified to his seamanship, and knowledge of the Channel, while his docile demeanour recommended him strongly to our approval; so that I had already gone the length of formally engaging him for a month, dating from the morrow, when a kindly old gentleman, who had heard of our intention, came privily at dusk to sound an appalling note of warning in my ear. I knew that the Imperial Parliament had concerned itself with verminous persons, but never before had I heard of a man whose condition was such that a duly elected municipal body had, in the name of the public, subjected him to a thorough cleansing and fumigation.

Whether the old gentleman had uttered the envenomed words of personal enmity, or conferred upon two strangers almost as great a kindness as one mortal can confer upon another, I was at a loss to decide. The same doubt divided the mind of my skipper, who, when I gave him the sensational news, was aghast.

"'Oppers is bad enough, but—!" he exclaimed with eloquent incompleteness. "Why, whatever would my missis say? She's pore, we know, but wonderful clean."

Anxious but discreet inquiries having convinced us that my elderly visitor was no slanderer, nothing remained but to break the contract as best we might—a task of the greater delicacy as it might well be that the individual in question had, since the ordeal referred to, maintained the satisfactory condition in which it had left him.

Not being fully agreed whether, in the circumstances that had arisen, action lay with the owner or the skipper, we undertook the ugly job in combination.

"Look 'ere, mate, you ain't got proper shiftables ter come along with us," Gotty told him; and I added a small pecuniary solatium.

The next mate we happened upon was certified free from so

monstrous a blemish, besides being strongly recommended on other grounds. Though warned that this young man, who had a conspicuous squint, was very quiet and unobtrusive, we were ill prepared for the abundant revelation of those characteristics afforded by his first full day in our service. Engaged overnight, he arrived on board just as we had breakfast prepared; and, having participated in that repast, he asked if I would lend him something to read. After devoting a silent hour to the monthly magazine I placed at his disposal, he went for a walk. From this constitutional he returned in the nick of time for dinner, at the conclusion of which meal he once more withdrew from our society, into he did not again intrude until we had spread the cloth for tea. Arising from the refreshment, he diffidently expressed a disposition to sleep on shore until such time as we might resume our voyage.

"Right you are mate," said Gotty, eyeing our acquisition thoughtfully. "Only we're agoin' out fishin' termorrow, so be shore you come aboard by seven, afore we go aground."

"Talk about a rum 'un!" commented my skipper, as he watched the interesting figure of our mild-mannered mate. "Why, 'e ain't lifted a finger all day. When 'e arsked fer a book ter read this mornin', I couldn't 'ardly believe my own ears, me 'aving started to wash up the cups and saucers jest to show 'im the way, seein' 'e was strange to the boat. Then 'e see me mend the net, and mop down, and let go the lashin's; fer it wasn't only one eye what was readin' the book, t'other followin' me all round like a cat. And never offered ter lend a 'and or nothin'! What does 'e think we took 'im fer, I wonder—not to be a orniment shorely, with them eyes and great patches on 'is trousis."

Next morning, on awakening at eight o'clock, I found the *Betty* still in harbour and aground. Gotty took the situation calmly.

"Jack Frost ain't turned up," he explained, "and very likely, more than gettin' 'old of a bit o' grub, 'e never 'ad no thought ter stand by us. Yet I dunno," he added, at the recollection of a circumstance in antagonism to that theory. "I fancy 'e brought some clothes aboard, too;" and having visited the cabin, he reappeared carefully holding two garments at arm's length.

These, as though with some vague idea of airing them, he deposited on the cabin top.

We were soon busying ourselves over the preparation of breakfast, and no sooner were the eggs cooked and the coffee made than, on looking up, we beheld the mate apologetically gazing down at us from the little wooden pier.

"Ain't you rather late?" asked Gotty, as he began an attack on the round of toast I had handed him.

"I was down here at seven," said the mate in a voice of mild defence.

"Oh!" replied the skipper, his mouth in no condition for argument.

"I did call out," continued the young man, without animation, "but there was no one about, so I went away again."

"Oh!" the skipper again remarked; and we continued our breakfast in silence, the young man remaining impassive on the pier. Several minutes went by, I bethinking myself how best we could terminate our contract with a mate so palpably deficient in useful human qualities. Ways and means lay nearer to hand than I realised.

Having finished his second egg, Gotty arose, and, after carefully brushing the crumbs from his beard and chest, stepped to the cabin top. Thoughtfully raising the two alien articles of attire—a pair of trousers and a waistcoat—he hurled them in quick succession, and with a faultless aim, at the owner, who, on recovering from the double shock, picked up his property and silently stole away. Neither spoke a word or uttered a sound. The form of dismissal, indeed, was one which, in its simplicity and directness, belonged to the region of drama.

"I've 'ad quite enough of '*im*," Gotty observed, as he resumed his seat with a view to treacle on a buttered roll. "Why! I've bin up since 'arf-past six, and 'e never come anywheres near."

As that afternoon we sat deploring the state of unprofitable inactivity in which, because we had no mate, it was our fate to abide, I jokingly offered my services in that capacity.

"Well! you'd do all right," exclaimed Gotty, and with such solemn heartiness that I resolved, for one trip, to realise in earnest what was proposed in jest.

Acting on the advice of three young fishermen who manned a Folkestone lugger, and who had already given us proof of a friendly disposition, we went out next morning and fished, with four other boats, in East Wear Bay. Within the indicated limits free from rocks and wrecks, we made a succession of hauls in a light wind; and were gratified by the capture of several large soles, three good-sized brill, two weevers, a rock crab, and many plaice of medium dimensions.

Gotty, in constant touch with rudder, sails, and trawl, was a creature of vigorous activity, perpetually running to and fro, and so zealously applying himself to his multifarious tasks that his features

A bawley broad reaching in a strong wind. The small jib is set up to a traveller which is run half way along the bowsprit to preserve sail balance.

The entrance to the fishing harbour of Folkestone, Kent, where the *Betty* had an adventurous approach.

The fishing quarter of Folkestone, circa 1907.

At Folkestone Copping shipped Joe Cole, a hand from the local fishing luggers, such as this one leaving Dover.

The *Betty* entered the narrow, tidal harbour of Rye, Sussex and collided with a local smack.

Merchant sail was still active when the *Betty* ventured down Channel. She passed many vessels such as this brigantine, creeping along under all sail in light airs, probably laden with coal.

In West Bay the *Betty* trawled in company with big smacks from Plymouth and Brixham.

At Looe the *Betty* put to sea to fish in company with the fleets of Cornish luggers.

Looe, Cornwall, looking upstream. Circa 1907.

The *Betty* visited the Cornish port of Fowey, crowded with shipping awaiting turn to load China clay at the quays.

streamed with perspiration. My responsibilities were practically limited to turning the winch, assisting to shake the net free of seaweed, and haul it aboard, and lending a hand to sort the catch.

During a final haul the freshening wind put white caps on the waves, so that the business of running into the little crowded harbour was not one to be lightly thought of. Nor did I lightly think of it; though Gotty assured me I need not worry; and that we should come to no harm if I did what he told me.

As we approached the harbour entrance, he posted me at the mast, with instructions to gradually release two indicated ropes when he gave the word. Thereby, I knew, would the mainsail be lowered; though in what order, and at what rate, I was to release the ropes were points on which I fain would have had tuition. But my instructor's attention was too intently fixed on his immediate cares as helmsman to appreciate these vacancies in the pupil's mind.

What happened was this: we were running like an express train for the gap between the piers and Gotty shouted, "Lower away!" immediately adding, in correction of my first promptings: "Not that one. Look sharp!" So I grabbed the other rope, and had not released it more than half-a-dozen feet or so, when he cried: "T'other one! T'other one!" So I turned my attention to the rope I had proposed to deal with at the outset. I released it a few feet. "Lower!" he shouted. I released it a few more feet. "Lower!" he yelled. I released it still a few feet more. "Lower!" he howled. Even again I suffered a corresponding length to run through my hands. "Lower! Lower!" once more came the agonised instruction. "Let it all out!" Gotty thundered. I did. I let go of the rope altogether, to make quite sure this time.

At the moment I merely knew that my hat was knocked off and that I nearly went sprawling. Next minute I learnt that the descending gaff had narrowly escaped Gotty's cranium, that the mainsail was hanging over in the water, and that spectators on the stone pier were giving unmistakable proof of being amused.

"That ain't nothin'," presently my skipper was remarking in reassuring accents. "If there was never no worse trouble than that it'd be all right. Lor' bless yer, gettin' the sail wet don't signify. You ain't done so wonderful bad, let me tell yer, fer a beginner."

Never before had I so fully appreciated the services of a clever youngster, known by the name of the Bullfinch, who had fallen into the way of coming on board the *Betty*, notably on the occasions of our entering the harbour, to make himself generally useful.

Critically examining our catch, this alert youth said we had not done so well as we might, though better than some, and he went on to point out that Gotty's separation into prime and offal was, in some details, inconsistent with Folkestone usage. When the Bullfinch had emptied our boxes and rearranged the fish properly (Gotty reverentially watching the expert manipulator), our young guide and counsellor asked which of us proposed to act as salesman in the market. We modestly explained that, though somewhat at a loss how to get in touch with those personages, we thought of entrusting our interests to one of the auctioneers.

"But you're allowed to sell your own fish," the Bullfinch explained.

Freely admitting my own incapacity for the task, I asked Gotty if he would like to essay it. Smiling bashfully, he said he thought he would rather not.

"I'll sell them for you if you like," volunteered our youthful ally; and that was agreed to. Gotty shouldering the boxes, we set out for the market; and presently, standing demurely in the throng, we watched the Bullfinch as, our wares strewn on the pavement at his feet, he competed for the attention of purchasers, his confident treble sounding in such contrast to the deeper voices of the auctioneers that some spasms of unthinking laughter arose in the crowded little market. Nothing discouraged, the self-reliant youth persisted in his business-like clamour, shrilly reiterating each bid he received until it was superseded by a superiority of sixpence. Finally the parcel was knocked down for eight shillings; so that after paying a commission to the Bullfinch, and handing a moiety of the balance to Gotty, I put three and sixpence in my pocket with the comfortable feeling that I had, as the saying goes, earned it by the sweat of my brow.

But that morning's fishing had another consequence besides adding to our financial resources. It confirmed me in a resolution that had been gradually taking shape in my mind. The mental seed, if I may so express myself, had been sown by masterful Mr. Rawson, and it had germinated on a careful study of our chart and navigation-book. I determined to pilot the *Betty* to Cornwall and back, should Gotty prove willing to trust himself in my hands. He did.

"And why shouldn't yer?" he exclaimed, his fervent acquiescence taking an interrogative form. "We ain't likely to find a better scholar than what you are. It don't matter what book it is—I'd back you agin any one for readin' it; and no trouble, seemin'ly. And good 'and-writin', too—so I 'ear from them as see what you've writ in the noospapers. It's my misforchin' that I never 'ad no schoolin'—only two days; and the fust day they set me to chop firewood, and next day to carry coals. ''Ere,' says my father when 'e come to fetch me away. 'I know a better school than what that is,' and 'e sent me ter work—to 'elp arn wittles fer my little brothers and sisters. Yus," he added, reverting to what, after all, was the subject under consideration, "if you can't prick a chart I'd like ter know 'oo can."

Yet it happened that, by the very phrase in which he expressed so gratifying a confidence in my latent capacity as a navigator, Gotty induced a disconcerting doubt on that point to arise in my own mind. Pricking a chart I vaguely identified with some process analogous, so far as the implement employed was concerned, to eating periwinkles. It had always conjured up a mental picture of a man in a reefer coat leaning over a great sheet of paper, and making a long series of minute perforations thereon—though what guiding principles controlled his action, and what practical object he had in view, I was at a loss to understand.

"Why," cried my companion, when I gave him some hint of this intellectual darkness, "you don't do it with a pin. Pricking the chart only means you find 'ow ter go where you want to without gettin' aground nowheres, or comin' ath'art a rock what's jest under water only you can't see it."

That uncertainty removed, we once more turned our attention to the everlasting Mate Problem, agreeing that a willing seaman, equal to all deck drudgery, would fulfil our requirements, and that if he knew nothing of the Channel, and was innocent of scholarship, so much the better.

In Stephen Cole we next day found a man with all these qualifications, and I engaged him for a month on his own terms— twenty-five shillings a week and his food.

XXII

IN A COLLISION

AT midday we resumed our voyage in a calm so absolute that the long oars were needed to force our sluggish way round the pier extension. Then, our sails hanging useless, we lay on that sea of glass, not indeed stationary, for the tide's gentle influence bore us westward broadside on, though progress was only to be perceived on re-glancing, in the leisurely lapse of time, at the sunny coast-line, when features of Sandgate and Hythe were seen to have slipped to the east by small degrees.

A breeze springing up anon, drifting gave place to sailing, and the new vitality with which the bawley plunged forward on her course had a corresponding influence on the spirits of her crew.

We were in Cole's world, and thus it was fitting that he should take the helm. Of robust physique and middle-aged, he wore ear-rings, and had a bronzed Italian look, for all that he was Folkestone born and bred. His taciturnity—arising, as we realised on a fuller acquaintance, from a modesty nearly related to diffidence —yielded under the elation of finding himself at the post of responsibility, with two deferential shipmates outside the pale of his local knowledge.

As we approached Dungeness—dreary stretch of shingle with a lofty lighthouse—Cole told us how thickly the bay was strewn with wrecks and anchors, and how many lost trawls lay rotting in their clutches.

"We've come by sixty-three fastenings," he grimly explained. "The *Northfleet* lays in a line with that tower, there's a large yacht astern, and over here three old anchors are set in a triangle. They've been there as long as any one remembers—three Dutch men-of-war, so I've heard people say, that lay off here to make a swoop on Dymchurch, but a gale came on and they had to run for it, with no time to pick up their anchors."

"It's jest like our place," Gotty deplored, as he shook his head over the widespread perils by which an honest fisherman's life was beset. "That's the wake of a wreck, ain't it?" he added in some excitement, as he pointed to where uniform ripples gave place to water of oily irregularity.

"Yes," said Cole, "that's an old brig;" and they explained to me how, on tidal pressure meeting the obstruction of a submerged wreck, the resulting upward impulse of the water makes its impression, in calm weather, on the surface.

Sailing by the headland, we were within pistol shot of the lifeboat conspicuously strutted in readiness to take the water by gravitation.

Barely eight miles now separated us from the haven I had chosen for the night—Rye harbour; and, keenly enjoying a glorious evening, we sped on in constant view of a beach whereof the monotony was only broken where half-submerged nets and posts formed some automatic apparatus for catching fish. In the gloaming we had a glimpse of the cliffs of Fairlight, dimly purple.

Meanwhile the amateur pilot had been consulting his book and chart, though with no very urgent sense of responsibility. The new mate's practical experience extending to Rye, there was no need at present for printed knowledge.

My book made it abundantly clear that, what with shallows, currents, and the narrow dimensions of the Channel, the task of entering Rye harbour was not to be lightly essayed; and thus I had judged that Cole did wisely when, on coming abreast that inlet at nightfall, he put the *Betty* about, to wait for high water before running in.

"We must git out our side lights," Gotty somewhat tardily remembered; and he and I descended into the cabin to haul those beacons from their locker, and get them ready for service. He tackled the green lantern, while I dirtied my finger with the red, our task being the more difficult because, as I discovered in some dismay, the oil-holders were misfits, and, owing to mutual antiquity, the cogs were powerless to move the wicks.

"We must look sharp," said Gotty when, his omnipotent clasp-knife having seen us through the latter trouble, he triumphantly reached finality by burnishing the glass with his thumb, "for I jest see two wessels comin' up, and most likely they'll be turnin' with us, seein' they can't go in till there's water."

So it proved. Having assisted to lash the lanterns into their appointed receptacles on the rigging, I gazed at the coloured eyes, as it seemed, of two monsters swinging around and about us.

"They're Rye smacks," Cole explained. "It always beats me how big craft like that get in and out of their little harbour."

In comparison with the great length and width of those Rye boats, with their towering masts and enormous areas of brown canvas, the *Betty* seemed a mere little tub of a thing.

151

That the small stranger excited the curiosity of the Rye fishermen was attested by the near views of her which, by adroit helm manipulation, they were at pains to secure; nor did we lack proof of an altruistic element in their interest. Shouts arose from one of the smacks—thick melodious Sussex throating which, when Cole supplied an interpretation, proved to be an intimation that, for a vessel our size, there was already plenty of water over the bar. He did not, however, act upon the hint he translated, nor was I other than pleased to note his preference for tarrying outside yet a little while longer, to make additionally sure of our subsequent security in going in. But I did not appreciate the full extent of his sagacity until, on one of the smacks shaping her course for the harbour (as the pale starlight sufficed to show us she was doing) Cole handled his tiller to a like purpose, so that we fell in line behind her, with the advantage of a sure guide to the path of safety and deep water.

Our entrance into the harbour mouth was full of interest to a pilot bent on his own education. This was my first opportunity to test book knowledge in the light of reality; and I was not a little uplifted in spirit, on an absorbing study of lights and other features of the place, to find they so exactly answered to what I was instructed they would be.

As for Gotty, not having read the book, he was astonished by the strength of the current running past the pier-head.

Having thus accounted for the thoughts that occupied both our minds, I would have the reader picture us as standing somewhere near the middle of the vessel. With regard to Cole, he, of course, was astern, steering.

On oath in a court of law I could return nothing but unsatisfactory answers to the question whether at that time I heard shouting. Perhaps I heard it in the semi-conscious way of a person who, his attention being on other matters, gives no heed to the experience of his ears.

And now I have to deal with the sensations and happenings that were crowded into a mere second of time. I heard the shouting, and realised that it arose from the smack in front of us, but the impulse of wondering what the demonstration might signify was, as it were, interrupted at its inception on a realisation that some panic sense of urgency had communicated itself from Gotty to Cole or from Cole to Gotty, unless indeed—for I cannot feel sure on that point—it had afflicted both simultaneously.

Let me now pass on to what occurred in the next second. Strongly predisposed to believe that something wondrous untoward was happening, or pending, but with a mind wholly blank as to what that something might be, I looked ahead, whereupon a momentous piece of knowledge smote my brain without explaining itself. As that statement is open to the same criticism, let me say that the known and ample interval between our vessel and the other had been eliminated as by a horrid piece of conjuring. I saw the fact, but so incapable was my intellect of deducing its cause that mine was the dumbfounded attitude appropriate to one confronting an arrested law of nature.

"She's fast!" were words, feverishly spoken by Gotty's voice, that illumined my understanding. The Rye boat had grounded in Rye harbour. All her sails still bellied out, she had nevertheless come to a dead stop right in our path. A dire peril had arisen from the perfection of our measures to ensure safety. By a sardonic reversal of all probability, the habitué had done the very thing that the stranger was following her to avoid doing.

In the fraction of time to which all these explanatory words apply, we were careering forward under full canvas at the propulsion of a steady breeze and a strong current. The space between the tip of our bowsprit and the smack's stern, looming massive and mountainous before us, would be about a yard and a half.

Unlike pens, eyes, and tillers, the human mind, in its performances, is practically, if not entirely, independent of time. In the retrospect I find that my own mind was particularly busy during the early phase of the period, so infinitely brief, that the *Betty* occupied in covering that yard and a half of intervening space. The sounds of activity and excitement that came from behind were a sufficient suggestion that our rudder had gone, or was going, round. Yet obviously this operation came too late to avert disaster. I knew that the *Betty* was about to butt full-tilt against that towering mass of brown solidity.

We are so apt to picture ourselves confronting unexpected peril with distraught minds and upraised arms and hair, that I may be forgiven for revealing the contrary condition, on that occasion, of one whom nobody could mistake for a hero. Two emotions held dominion in my mind—a sense of the inevitable, and curiosity. I knew that nothing I could do would affect the situation, and so I did nothing. For the rest, never having seen a collision before, I was keenly interested. Nay a feeling of chastened gratification was identified with a dim apprehension of the fact that I was on the point, not merely of witnessing one of those spectacles, but of witnessing it from, as it were, a seat in the front row. Impressions left by descriptions of collisions, and photographs of vessels that had taken part in them, prepared me to expect that the *Betty's* crushed bow would be associated with cavities in splintered woodwork and perhaps a submerging inrush of water. A swimmer, it was doubtless natural there should be no apprehension of drowning, even on behalf of the mate, who was no swimmer; but what strikes me as strange is that I should have been untroubled by any recollection that the *Betty* was uninsured and that I was her owner.

To the thoughts that occupied my mind, in what seemed so leisurely a fashion, as the *Betty* was charging the smack, I have to make one curious little addition. Realising that my pipe had gone out, I had already started my hand pocket-wards in quest of matches, when our vessel reached the other.

I had made no provision—a foolhardy omission—for steadying myself when the bump came. Nor do I remember the bump. That memory must have been destroyed by experiences immediately succeeding. At first the most vivid impression was of the noisy and protracted splitting of wood, as though a falling church spire were ploughing its way through a barricade of egg boxes. Then, like a tangled shower of interminable eels, cordage was descending about us so copiously and continuously that I stretched a protecting arm over my head, though, as some shuddering thuds informed me, the avalanche included items of far greater avoirdupois importance than mere ropes.

These experiences were followed by a realisation that our stern had swung round, and that, broadside to the stream, we were drifting by the still motionless smack. Please understand that the spirit of philosophical contemplation in which I had awaited the collision did not survive its occurrence. To say truth, we were three sufficiently distraught figures as, not yet knowing what had happened, we blundered aimlessly about the limp wreckage by which our deck was strewn. Poor old Gotty uttered lamentations in a broken voice. The mate was fumbling and staring and seemed to have lost his tongue. I was whining for information as to the extent of the damage.

"I dunno," Gotty gasped. "Topmast's down—broke in two pieces. Look 'ere!" and he lifted the fractured end of a length of wood sufficiently bulky, on falling from so considerable an elevation, to have brained an elephant. "No, you never!" he shouted with great controversial warmth, in reply to an observation that came from the smack.

"We *did* holler to you!" reiterated the Rye fisherman, in a voice that quavered with emotion.

"Not till we were right ath'art you, you didn't!" Gotty sprang to the side and howled back in angry denial: "What's best to be done?" he turned to the mate and inquired. "Better drop the anchor, 'adn't we, and see what's the damage?"

Cole, without pausing to discuss the point, floundered aft and released the chain. The next minute I—even I—perceived that a grievous error had been committed. There we lay tied and helpless, scarce more than a vessel's length from the smack, whose bowsprit was pointing straight for us. At any moment the rising tide might float her, and under that towering array of sails she would bear down upon us with a weighty momentum that our poor little craft must prove powerless to withstand.

"Git it up! Git it up sharp!" cried Gotty, when I called his attention to our peril. He leapt to the tiller, and, having lashed it to one side, set about extracting a long oar from the wreckage on our deck. Cole meanwhile was desperately groping for a handspike. At last he found one, and got to work on the windlass.

"'Urry up, fer Gawd's sake!" urged Gotty, as he laboured at the oar to swing our stern round.

"If you don't clear out, you'll cop it a blank sight worse!" thundered a voice from the smack. "You've no business to come in here at all without a pilot."

The speaker had but paused momentarily from participation in labours, involving much struggling and shouting, in which the crew of the smack were seeking to safeguard their own interests. Their dinghy was carrying a tow-rope to a lantern-bearer who came running to the rescue along the footway of a dam; and, I should mention, it was a cross current caused by the heavy fall of water over that dam which made Gotty's task so formidable.

Failing to find the second handspike, I sought to assist Cole with the broken handle of an oar, for the sound of his toil was ominously lacking in rhythm and vitality. Nor, as my unsuitable instrument kept jamming, did I materially expedite the operation. It was mightily disconcerting, on looking up from our feverish fumbling, to note the great brown menace looming down upon us.

From Gotty's querulous reproaches, it might have been inferred that he thought we were doing the job slowly on purpose. The nerves of all three, it must be confessed, were unstrung.

At last the *Betty* swung round, with the anchor up. Yet, her sailing gear all collapsed, she proved so unresponsive to the helm that Gotty, in a tone of rugged urgency, bade Cole get into the dinghy and tow her.

In his precipitancy Cole rowed the dinghy stern foremost; but that way served, and in a few minutes we had moved away from the still stationary smack.

Arriving at the jetties, we—at the suggestion of a mild official who, in the name of harbour dues, came to claim 1s. 6d.—berthed beside a group of smacks. Gotty was for the sixth time telling the story of our woes to sympathisers who came in rowing boats for the news, when our great brown-sailed enemy went gliding by.

"Don't tell lies!" roared the voice we had heard before. "We *did* holler out to you."

"No, you never," Gotty bellowed back, "not afore it was too late."

A rankling memory for me was the old Rye fisherman's impertinent suggestion that we ought to carry a pilot; and, stooping to a tardy *tu quoque*, I raised my voice to advise our deep-throated foe that, when next he entered his own harbour, *he* should carry one of those useful auxiliaries.

On overhauling the *Betty*, Gotty discovered that the only serious damage was the snapping of our topmast. Yet I found that neither he nor the mate had any inclination for supper.

"I couldn't fancy anythin'," deplored the skipper. "I reg'lar feel all of a tremble."

"Not for me, thank you, sir," moaned the mate. "It's made me feel sick. I tell you, my heart was in my mouth all the time. I wouldn't go through that again for fifty pounds."

"Oh," I laughed, setting them a healthy example with biscuits and cheese, "I wouldn't have missed it for a hundred. Sit down and don't be a couple of silly duffers;" and the end of it was that we joined in a hearty repast, and afterwards played dominoes.

Next morning we discovered that none of the Rye shipbuilders had a topmast of our size, and that to have one made would involve a considerable expenditure of time, not to mention money. So (the careful Guv'nor having his bag of tools on board) we bought ten shillings' worth of fir tree, and set about making our own topmast. It took all morning to scrape off the bark, and the rest of the day we devoted to chiselling out the necessary holes, grooves, and recesses, and fixing the fittings thereto.

During the last three hours I toiled alone, my shipmates having withdrawn for rest and refreshment to a neighbouring ale-house.

Thus the owner, whom the Board of Trade certified as skipper, had now served as mate, been appointed pilot, and given proof of his powers as a shipwright. For it was an excellent topmast, though I say it who perhaps should not.

XXIII

LOST IN A FOG

TO save time, trouble, and lawyers' fees, I sat as judge and jury to settle the question of liability raised by the collision; and the finding of the court was that there had been no proper look-out on the damaged vessel, whose crew, it was held, were under the stronger necessity to be vigilant as—in order to profit by the experience of the defendants, without rendering any payment for the service—they deliberately came skulking into harbour at the tail of the other craft.

Thus when, at eleven o'clock next morning, we had spliced our broken ropes, hoisted the new topmast, and re-rigged the *Betty*, I knew of no reason, the tide having just turned, why we should not straightway set sail. Gotty's plea for delay—based on our need of water and bread, and the honourable obligation under which we lay to return a borrowed scraping-iron—was easy to brush aside. Gliding down the water-way, we hailed a lad in a boat, and gave him sixpence to take back the tool with our compliments.

A calm prevailing, we engineered a safe exit to the open sea with Gotty and I labouring at the *Betty's* long oars, and the mate towing her in the dinghy—perspiring toil in that September sunshine. Thereafter we floated softly to the west, gazing with approbation at the southern margin of our native land.

A gentle breeze coming to our assistance anon, at teatime we dropped anchor outside the unfinished harbour walls of Hastings, and Gotty and I rowed ashore for supplies.

Our coming was awaited by a group of robust lads who, when we grated on the beach, were unanimous in pleading for permission to mind our boat. It was a prayer to which my skipper, with a lively sense of the superfluous, was wont to return an unhesitating reply in the negative. In doing so on this occasion he somewhat enlarged upon aspects of the matter that presented themselves to his mind.

"We don't want none o' you young warmints pullin' our punt ter pieces. So don't you go anywheres nigh 'er d'yer see? She's a lot more likely to come to 'urt with some of you aboard than what she would be without yer. So you jest leave 'er be."

Uttering "Boo!" and other hostile comments, the youth of

157

Hastings retired to a discreet distance, whence with unfeeling laughter they watched Gotty's efforts, which were not immediately crowned with success, to tether our boat to a stone: we having lost our punt's anchor when fishing off Copt Point.

Gotty shouldering our cask, we set off for the fisherman's well, of which I retained from childhood the recollection that it was inscribed with the admonition, "Waste not, want not." Several minutes were occupied in journeying thither, filling our beaker, and returning; and the sight that met our gaze when we reached the summit of the beach caused us to take long strides down the broad slope and yielding shingle. Our dinghy, adrift from the stone, had already reached the wall, against which she was in imminent peril of receiving injury; and the youngsters were asquat in a long row, feasting their eyes on the spectacle.

So it was arranged that Gotty should remain in the boat while I went into the town for bread, apples, and bait. Difficulty arose under the third head of my responsibilities. Following many vain applications, made at a venture, I was referred to a bronzed and bearded individual who, given the advantage of a university education, would, I should think, have made a successful company promotor. He produced a handkerchief of dead worms which, he explained, were a halfpenny each, that being what they cost him. Having done business to the extent of fivepence with the unscrupulous old longshoreman, I returned to Gotty, whom I found— apparently as the outcome of further dealings with the juveniles— full of gloomy misgivings concerning Hastings' future.

After catching an eel, I turned in, leaving Gotty the option of staying at anchor off Hastings till daylight, or moving westward on the turn of the tide. For note how simple, in certain situations, are the duties of a pilot. Having told them to give the shore a berth, to keep the Beachy Head flashlight over their starboard bow, and on no account to run into any other craft, I sought my couch with the comfortable knowledge that, if those simple directions were followed, my shipmates could sail for hours without needing any further assistance from me.

At 2 a.m. the pilot was sitting up in bed absolutely nonplussed by the sounds and sensations to which he had just awakened. That we were moving, and moving in the lightest winds, was attested by the free, languorous swaying and pitching of the vessel. But what, in the name of bewilderment, was that roar of breaking water? The only conjecture that my brain could yield was one vaguely identifying the noise with some waterfall or cataract of which both I and the compilers of my navigation-book were unaccountably ignorant. Yet the spasmodic character of the splashing, and the quality of perspective in the sound—as of one watery upheaval near and others further away—gave denial to that hypothesis.

On scrambling to the hold opening I looked upon a scene in which peace and tumult were marvellously associated. In a clear, calm night, with a full moon, the surrounding sea shone to a remote distance as a rippled plane of silver, save where—here, there, and beyond—it uprose in fountains of commotion, and ink-black portions of some great living creature protruded for a moment in the sparkling confusion of water.

The bawley was sailing through a shoal of porpoises, and all those great splashings, in the splendour of that lonely sea, held some property in a sublime enchantment. Gotty had turned in, and I found the mate, a silent, still figure at the helm, under the spell of that glorious scene. He spoke in an awed whisper of the mighty blow-fish.

At daybreak we found ourselves still to the east of Beachy Head, and it was not long before, wind being wanting, we anchored to avoid being set back by the tide, Gotty utilising some portion of his leisure in the compounding of a currant duff. Nor, when opportunity for proof arrived, could Cole and I withhold warm commendation of the outcome of his culinary industry.

"Well," the skipper's modesty permitted him to observe, "a bit of puddin' like that stands by yer, don't it?"

It was, I found, even so. Nay, sweets on a bawley being served before meat and vegetables (though all are cooked simultaneously in one saucepan), I found myself, after demonstrating approval of Gotty's pudding, looking with small favour on the meat which, with its gnarled embroidery of fat, lay beside steaming potatoes in (for the skipper turned all things to account) my large photographic bath. His perplexity at my failure to follow two healthy examples was the greater because, as he explained, It was the best salted scrag, and he had been at the pains to tie a piece of rope around the same, and tow it astern for a dozen miles or so, the more surely to minimise its saline properties.

A breeze presently coming to our assistance, we ran to Beachy Head, and the sight of that dreary stretch of shingle prompted Cole to do what, in our experience of him, he had never done before, and never did again. He told a story.

"During that March blizzard a few years ago," he related, "some of our fishermen got ashore over there. It was daytime, but it was so thick they didn't know where they were, and hadn't any idea land was near till they went aground.''

"Was the wessel lost?" asked Gotty, always impatient to know the worst.

"No; she was got off a few days afterwards. But you may know what the weather was like, for one of the coastguards, who must have started to try and walk down to them, was found dead next day, half buried in the snow. When they got ashore they climbed up the bank, which was all snow, and then they started this way and that way, one of them getting up to his waist in water; and afterwards they found his boots was full of hob nails.''

"Full o' what?" asked the perplexed skipper.

"You know them little black things swimming about in ponds— big heads and all the rest tail.''

"Tadpoles?" I suggested.

"That's it," said Cole. "Well, the pore chaps walked miles and miles—hours they were at it, and nearly perished with cold. At last they came to a house with a light in it, and they knocked, and asked for a cup of hot tea. But, would you believe it, the people said 'No,' and sent them away.''

"Them parties ought to 'ave six months!" was Gotty's indignant interjection.

"They had to walk all the way to Seaford, and the first person they saw was a shopkeeper standing at his door. He asked them who they were and where they'd come from, and when they told him he made them come inside by the fire, and gave them plenty to eat and drink, and did all he could for them.''

"Don't that jest show you the dif'rence between people," exclaimed Gotty, his further comments on the varied character of human nature being interrupted by a sudden appreciation of the fact that a welcome breeze was springing up. Ten minutes later, indeed, we were making steady progress towards Newhaven, and I was instructing my mind as to features of that harbour. But I did not then know which local fact, among the many supplied by the chart and book, was destined to prove the one sure and indispensable guide to our destination.

Sailing in clear sunshine, we heard distant fog signals, only to wonder what they could mean. But soon a great fog bank had blown up and enveloped us in its wet whiteness. With the coast all blotted out, and our outlook restricted to a few yards of indistinct sea, we fetched up the compass and started to blow our dismal horn. For miles we groped our uncertain way, and once—putting a little premature north in our course, from a belief that Newhaven must surely be near—we came within sound of waves breaking on the beach, and had to put about in guilty haste.

The pilot, you will observe, had lost touch with the position of his vessel. That is where steamboats, with the mechanical regularity of their propelling machinery, have such an advantage. To ascertain just how fast a sailing craft has travelled, through tidal variations and in a changeable wind, is a matter, if the reader will accept my word for it largely of guesswork. Yet I dare say that is where a little experience and training come in useful to a pilot.

During a fog, my invaluable book stated, a single blast is sounded every thirty seconds from the head of Newhaven breakwater. Watch in hand I sought, from amid the tangled clamour of horns, to detect that local signal. Standing out from all the other moanings was a strenuous blast repeated four times in sixty seconds. Timing those sounds again and again, I discovered while the minute invariably contained them all, there was a want of uniformity in the intervals dividing them. Bringing my observation to a further perfection, I was able to dissociate the blasts into two distinct pairs; and attributing one pair (now becoming less emphatic) to an ingoing steamer, I was able to identify the other pair (growing more audible, and of precise recurrence every thirty seconds) as unmistakably the breakwater signal.

For that sound, then, we steered, and anon the extremity of the great wall loomed upon us out of the fog. A run to the north brought us to the head of the east pier, whence a short north-west slant revealed the head of the west pier; and thus we entered Newhaven's fine harbour, which in its upper reaches proved free from fog.

While Gotty and Cole were berthing the *Betty* alongside a great Norwegian barque, I gave audience to a couple of courteous officials who came alongside in their rowing boats. One readily accepted the honest word of a fisherman that we had no excisable commodities to declare. The other merely desired twopence, this being the most modest claim for harbour dues in all our voyage.

On landing—to touch briefly upon a matter of domestic rather than nautical interest—Gotty and I, as the outcome of some earnest consultations in which we had privily engaged, set forth to do some shopping of more than ordinary importance. His reports to me of an element of unrest in the cabin had been frequent and bitter; and while he mentioned no names, and, indeed, scrupulously abstained from expressing any personal suspicions that might or might not lurk in the recesses of his mind, he made no secret of his conviction

161

that they were Folkestone fleas.

While incidentally mentioning a pennyworth of powder, his main proposal, as the remedy commanding his confidence in fullest measure, was six-pennyworth of sulphur, to be left burning under closed hatches.

To purchase the suggested quantity of that mineral we visited a leading grocery establishment in Newhaven's main thoroughfare, my companion stating our requirements, and I goading him to take that manly course; for, be it understood, on finding several other customers, in that spacious and brightly lighted emporium, a diffidence arose from a sense of what we wanted the article for.

Having secured the sulphur, Gotty was on the point of precipitate exit when I held him back with urgent arguments on the importance of making doubly sure. Nor was this appeal to his better self made in vain, for he screwed up his courage to return to the counter, and—as I inferred from the furtive way in which he leaned across that obstruction—whisper his further need to the obliging shopman.

After we had beat a retreat down the road, Gotty, recovering from the awkward sense that everybody was looking at him, betrayed legitimate pride in the complete measure of success that had attended our expedition.

"They give yer a tidy lot for a penny , not 'alf they don't," he remarked with gratification, as, there being no inquisitive folk about, he drew the precious packet from his pocket. "And tell yer 'ow ter sprinkle it about seemin'ly," he added, making a shrewd guess at the purport of all the little print which, by the light of a street lamp, he observed on the label.

Taking it from him, I read, instead, in one of the most embarrassing moments of my life, how many spoonfuls should go in a stew, and the precise quantity needed for thickening soup. And, indeed, "Pea Powder" bears so close an acoustic resemblance to the article Gotty had asked for, that the mistake was one easy to make. But both of us lacked the fortitude to go back and get it rectified. We were content to concentrate our hopes on sulphur.

The measures taken by my skipper were simple, scientific, and—as time was to show—successful. Having stuffed an old shirt in the flue, he ignited his remedy on an iron plate in the cabin, and, abruptly emerging thence, put on the top and screened all apertures. To give the imprisoned fumes ample opportunity to do what was expected of them, the cabin was left thus sealed till the morrow.

Gotty and Cole, declining my hospitable offer of floor space in the hold, slept that night on deck.

XXIV

THE SCHOONER'S PERIL

NEXT night, in the absence of wind, we anchored off Brighton, Gotty and I going ashore to visit the Aquarium, where, besides being weighed, he saw his first alligator, and was equally awed by an electric Lady of Mystery.

On the following morning we resumed our voyage in a haze; the day yielding some anxious experiences in navigation. Ere we reached Worthing I had read myself into so lively a dread of Selsey Bill that I directed my skipper to shape a south-westerly course, and not deviate therefrom until we sighted the Owers light-ship. I knew the distance, but had to ask how fast we were travelling.

At first Gotty replied in knots—a measure with which his pilot did not happen to be familiar.

"Can't you tell me," I asked, "how many miles an hour we are going?"

"It can't be fur off five," the skipper certified after due rumination. "It's more than four and charnse it."

Making a careful calculation on the basis of four and a half, I announced that, assuming uniformity in our rate of progress, we should see the light-ship at about midday.

At 2 p.m. we were still looking for it, and my credit as a pilot stood in gravest jeopardy. Since one o'clock my skipper had been full of mutinous mutterings concerning the foolishness of not going more directly westward. Nay, I had found it useful to keep my own eye on the compass, to be able, every now and then, to call his attention to what may have been unconscious deviations in the direction he thought preferable.

At half-past two I caught Gotty and Cole exchanging confidences with significant grins, and I noted the latter shrugging his shoulders. At a quarter to three the situation had entered a still more uncomfortable phase. A cold silence had fallen upon the *Betty*, and when I detected Gotty regarding me, with an expression of repressed amusement, out of the corner of his eye, he ostentatiously turned away and whistled.

"We certainly are a long time coming to the lightship," I presently admitted, my eyes tired of scanning the unprofitable horizon, and a sense of incompetence and failure beginning to tell upon my spirits.

"If they ain't took it off the road," replied the skipper, allowing himself to be facetious, "we must 'ave gorn by that vessel two howers ago, and most likely ten mile to the south'ard of 'er."

"What do _you_ say?" I turned to Cole and miserably inquired.

"Oh, we've passed her right enough," he replied, with a complacency which seemed to me uncalled for.

Poor pilot! He could no longer resist the evidence. And how much wider the scope of this discomfiture than his shipmates knew. For he at least realised that, having so completely failed where all factors in the situation seemed so plain, he could trust himself no further in the business of navigation.

Nor could I find any consolation on carefully remeasuring the distance on my chart.

"It's only about fifteen miles," I once more stated, "from Worthing to the Owers."

"And we've come thirty," was Gotty's indignant reply, "if we ain't come more."

"On this course I thought we should be certain to see the light-ship."

"You thought! Yes, but—" he began, explosively, checking himself and adding, in a voice merely reproachful: "Didn't I keep tellin' yer we was too fur to the south'ard? On'y you would know best."

The resulting silence was broken by Gotty.

"Why," he exclaimed, as his eagle eye took cognisance of a speck on the horizon, "there's one of them light-vessels."

"I suppose," was my lame comment, "it can't be the one we are looking for?"

"The one we _ain't_ lookin' for, don't you mean?" he retorted brusquely. "'Ow can it be the one when we must 'ave gorn by it howers ago—and this 'ere light miles ahead on us!"

And, indeed, though that was no tone in which to address a pilot, my suggestion seemed, on his presentation of the facts, sufficiently improbable. So there was nothing for it but to search my sources of information for a light-vessel situated south-west of the Owers. But obviously they had not put it on the chart; and I was constrained to make humble confession that I did not know where we were.

"H'm! Nice thing!" Gotty snorted.

"Couldn't you manage to run near that barge," I suggested, "and ask the name of the light-ship we are coming to?"

"It ain't a barge. That's a ketch. But I don't know as that

wouldn't be the best thing to do;" and he handled the tiller accordingly.

The reply to my skipper's leather-lungs was dramatic indeed.

"Yon's th'Owers!" was the deep-toned and surprised explanation of a broad and massive man, who seemed perilously near an attack of unseemly mirth at finding a mariner of Gotty's aspect and inches so completely at sea.

Doing a little rapid arithmetic on the back of an envelope, I pointed out, for the general instruction of my shipmates, that since leaving Worthing we had been travelling, on an average, at the rate of about two and a half miles an hour.

"Yer see," Gotty explained, "it's the tide reg'lar draws yer back, so you might fancy a wessel was movin' a lot faster that what she is."

"We were laying true enough for the light-ship after all," observed Cole.

"The Guv'nor was right, and we were wrong. There you are!" exclaimed the skipper; and this was so handsome a recognition of the facts that, reinstated with strengthened authority in my office of pilot, I—by way of demonstrating a willingness to let bygones be bygones—busied myself in dishing up the delayed dinner.

Nor had that meal drawn to a conclusion ere a new interest was sprung upon us. Having done his duty by the meat, Gotty was midway in a second serving of potatoes when his alert eye detected an object intermittently bobbing into sight amid broken water away to the north-west.

"Ain't that a punt bottom-up!" he cried, not a little excited. "I lay it is. A white bottom fresh painted, seemin'ly—wery likely got adrift from one of them big yachts. Worth a pound or two—a punt like that is. Ain't this all right?" and, without more ado, he pulled our dinghy alongside, got into her, unlashed the rope, and set off to row with a zeal which revealed a determination to secure the prize ere it attracted the covetous eye of some less deserving mariner; and indeed several vessels were visible in the neighbourhood of the lightship.

Gazing after the receding boat as we peacefully concluded our repast, Cole and I experienced a sense of disappointment, heavily charged with mystification, when Gotty, on coming within speaking distance of his goal, abruptly altered his course, and started rowing back with, apparently, augmented energy.

He having returned to the *Betty's* vicinity without vouchsafing any relief to our curiosity, I assailed his tantalising taciturnity with a definite question.

"It warn't a punt," he indignantly replied—"only one o' them porpoises. Talk about dead—phuff! it fair hollers. But don't you 'ear 'em blowin' a fog-'orn on that light-ship? What's it for, I wonder. The weather ain't so thick as all that."

This enigma defied our efforts to solve it during the half-hour that the *Betty* occupied in making her slow way to the scene of these mysterious moanings. Strict obedience to printed instruction would have involved our going to the south of the light-ship; but, observing two vessels of superior tonnage on the land side, Gotty, with some idea of taking a short cut, also passed her on the north.

Within biscuit throw of the Trinity boat, we gazed up at her as we went by, vainly seeking to satisfy ourselves why she invaded the serenity of a summer afternoon with her dolorous horn, when, marvel on marvel! a tongue of crimson flame shot from her bulwarks, billows of smoke unfolded above its line of passage, and our ears were stunned by a cannon's roar.

"It's that schooner they're firing for, isn't it?" was the anxious inquiry shouted to us from a two-master tacking across our bow.

"That's it, mate," Gotty replied, in a great assured voice which seemed to suggest, not merely that he knew all about it, but that he was quite used to that sort of thing.

The stranger's inquiry had put us in the way of knowledge. We now looked with eyes of understanding at the three-masted schooner which, about a quarter of a mile to the inside of us, had ominous breakers astern, and, with all sails bent, was heading eastward with no observable sign of progress. Was the light breeze bearing her forward to deep water, or was the tide carrying her back? We could not tell. Apparently she lay stationary between those conflicting forces. Yet either wind or water was doubtless gaining the mastery by crucial inches.

"But," I exclaimed in my ignorance, "if she is going on to the sands, what good do the Trinity people think they are doing by firing to her?"

"Why, don't yer see," cried Gotty, "they want 'im ter drop 'is anchor. Then when the tide turns she'll git off all right."

"Why of course; and what a fool he is not to do so."

"That's a true word," agreed the skipper.

"He knows what he's doing," was Cole's comment. "He reckons he can weather it."

The horn went on sounding its hoarse message of urgency, and once more the cannon thundered its stern warning. But the schooner did not drop her anchor.

166

"Good-night!" ejaculated Gotty. "Ain't some people obstinate! Jest ter save a few howers, fancy any one risking a big wessel like that."

More moanings, and another report of the gun. Yet still the schooner paid no heed. It was a situation full of awe, nothing making a stronger appeal to the imagination than the thought of that self-reliant man of iron nerves who persisted in preferring his own judgment to that of the local experts.

It is a story whereof I know not the end. As we found the situation, so we left it. The horn and, occasionally, the gun were reiterating their disregarded warnings when that picture of uncertainty and hazard was blotted out behind us in the haze.

Further to the west we found more wind, and of a slant that favoured our rapid progress to Shanklin, our next place of call for letters. The pilot hit that part of the Isle of Wight to a nicety.

Evening had come when we dropped anchor off the pier, where Japanese lanterns made a tangle of waving prettiness in the moonlight. Languorous Shanklin lay under the witchery of dainty waltz music, and we rowed through water bespangled with confetti.

Unfortunately the favourable impressions thus made upon my shipmates' minds were destined to be erased by an experience following promptly upon our entry into the town.

I desired to proffer them a congenial solace after the fatigues of the day, but, having sipped the offering, I found them regarding one another with expressions in which misgiving and indignation competed for a mastery.

"I can't drink it," said Cole, firmly, as he deposited his tankard on a little round table.

"No more can't I," acquiesced his superior. Then, obeying a common impulse, they arose with puckered brows and carried their measures to the bar, bent on making a formal complaint to the young lady at whose hands they had received the liquid. The skipper acted as spokesman.

"You don't call this beer, do yer?" he asked her. "I wouldn't give it ter hogs—leave alone Christians."

The girl at once went off to fetch the proprietor, who was promptly on the scene.

"It's only fit ter poison rats," Gotty assured him, adding—though the unpremeditated juxtaposition of the two remarks was, I could not help reflecting, calculated to wound any one of sensitive disposition—"'Ave some yerself and see."

But the cautious proprietor resisted this invitation, and contented himself with the statement, uttered somewhat warmly, that he did not make the beer, and if they did not like it they could leave it.

By way of safeguarding the imperilled peace, I gave an auxiliary order for bottled specimens, by which, hailing it as refreshment of a totally different order, my companions were restored to the bearing of calm and collected citizens.

On leaving that establishment, we took a stroll along Shanklin's main thoroughfare, the excursion yielding an opportunity that the skipper was not slow in turning to account.

As we had entered Sandown Bay the light was sufficient to reveal that charming sweep of water as, in Gotty's matured judgment, a likely place for soles, and he made the suggestion, with which I promptly concurred, that on the following morning we should put down our trawl to them. Coming now to a superb fishmonger's, the prudent thought crossed his mind that it might be well, before being at the trouble of catching the fish, to make sure of a channel through which to dispose of them. Accordingly, leaving Cole and myself outside, he entered the shop to try and arrive at an understanding with the proprietor; and from animated conference he presently emerged with the springy footsteps and beaming countenance of one who has concluded an advantageous bargain. To details of the negotiations I readily lent a listening ear.

"At fust 'e wanted ter say a shillin' a pound fer small and one-and-six fer large, but I says, 'Don't be 'ard, sir, on a pore man,' I says; so at larst 'e comes round ter one-and-five all sorts, and take 'em as they come."

So that nothing actually remained undone but the catching of the soles—to which we addressed our energies early on the following morning. Having hoisted anchor and sails, we were on the point of lifting the net overboard when a distraction occurred. An elderly individual in a boat was shouting all manner of incoherencies as, with hasty and floundering manipulation of his oars, he came rowing in our direction.

When he arrived alongside, his jumbled stream of talk resolved itself into jerky sentences urgently dissuading us from our obvious and declared intention of shooting the trawl. Gotty, with deepening perplexity, endeavoured to engage our peculiar visitor in consecutive and rational conversation; to which end the old man was in the less position to bend his mind, as, entirely without authority, he had entered upon the laborious task of throwing a quantity of tattered periodical literature from his vessel to ours.

"'Ere, steady, mate, steady!" protested the skipper, as he began to return these unrequested favours. "You keep your books; we don't want 'em."

With splutterings to the effect that we could have them, they being of no use to him, the painstaking stranger continued to load us with his property, so that the senseless spectacle was presented of that cargo of old monthly magazines passing in uncouth handfuls from his boat to the *Betty* and back from the *Betty* to his boat.

Meanwhile Gotty's attention was in a subordinate degree engaged in an endeavour to extract some definite statement as to why we should not go trawling.

With a hiccoughing reference to rocks, the old man paused momentarily from his unappreciated industry and swung his arms afar, as though in comprehensive suggestion that those perils existed in all the surrounding sea.

"Well, where ain't there any, then?" asked Gotty, a trifle impatiently; whereat, raising a wobbling finger in the neighbourhood of screwed-up eyes, the old man somewhat collapsed anatomically in the endeavour to hint at rich stores of private knowledge.

"Take me along yer. I show whertfish."

I needed but this revelation of ulterior motives to bring matters to a head. The skipper, ever slow to form harsh judgments on such a point, was constrained to recognise the palpable and extraordinary fact that our visitor was grievously the worse for liquor.

"'Ere," cried Gotty, "clear out of it. D'yer 'ear? I ain't got no time ter waste over them as gets boozed. And not gorn eight yet! You did ought ter be ashamed of yerself—an ole man of your age;" and, feet assisting hands, he freed the deck of the temporary accumulation of printed matter, and ruthlessly cast the boat off. The old man dropped astern, making vain vocal efforts to be offensive.

"We ain't goin' ter be put off fishin' by a drunken ole noosance like 'im, shorely!" asked Gotty.

"Certainly not," I replied.

"Not likely," he pointed out; and two minutes later our trawl was down.

After the manner of a prudent fisherman, he was presently holding on to the tow-rope, that he might feel how his gear was travelling along the bottom. Suddenly a great agony came over him, and he cried:

"She's fast! Good-night, 'ere's a nice thing! Bear up sharp!" Then rosy hope succeeded black despair.

"Stay a bit. She's free. And drorin' over the sand nice and easy . . Why! Fast agin! Ah! she's parst it. But bump, bump. It's dirty

169

ground, no mistake. Weed, I shouldn't wonder . . . That's better. That's a lot better. Now she's fishin' . . . Hullo! If she ain't 'ooked agin. 'Ere! I've 'ad enough of this. Bear up 'ard. Quick, the runnin' pin! Look alive!"

Our anxious salvage labours were successful, and as the trawl was coming up I reflected that we had at anyrate stolen a brief haul in virgin waters, and the fruits thereof I was all curiosity to behold.

At a rough estimate we had captured a hundred-weight of brown seaweed. In the net we also found an only fish—a sturdy little whiting pollock weighing, I should suppose, about one ounce and three-quarters.

As some consolation to my shipmates, I took them after dinner, to see the Chine.

When we were in that ferny paradise, nothing filled them with greater awe than the recollection that payment had been exacted for admission, and while ungrudging in their recognition of a certain sylvan beauty in the place, they made no secret of their regret that the money had not been laid out in tobacco.

Yet Shanklin Chine was destined, as we made our exit from it, to provide Gotty with a gratifying and memorable experience. An old lady with brooches and other gee-gaws to sell detained us with an invitation to purchase of her wares, and the skipper was endeavouring to make her understand his attitude towards jewellery when his tongue went speechless, and his eyes lit with innocent delight, as he suddenly beheld, perched unafraid on a twig within two yards of his face, a robin redbreast.

An acquaintance with the bird was promptly claimed by Maggie of the pay-box and the laughing eyes, she having meanwhile joined the group, the sight of three sailormen possessing a natural attraction (as the sagacious old lady privily informed us) for one whose absent lover was steward on a barque carrying timber from Sweden to Hull.

"He is so tame," Maggie explained, in allusion to the bird, "that he will come and eat out of your hand;" at which the skipper was divided between honest scepticism and reluctance to question a young lady's word. Having tripped off to fetch crumbs of suitable size, she set him to make the experiment, at the same time imperatively enjoining quietude.

And indeed the massive palm had not been long on exhibition before it was tickled by those tiny feet. Nor did the trustful robin withdraw from that tarry platform before securing the morsels of bread deposited thereon.

"That's somethin'," exclaimed the skipper, a prey to lively gratification, "what there's many at our place 'll say it's a lie when I go and back and tell 'em."

Presently discovering that Maggie was a stranger to his exploits on the greasy pole, Gotty instructed her mind under that head; and, ere we departed, she had found courage to ask his expert opinion as to the sort of weather they were likely to be having at Stockholm.

XXV

SHADOWS OF PORTLAND PRISON

OUR journey from the Isle of Wight to Weymouth was deficient in pleasing experiences. Darkness found us south-east of the Anvil light, and we were occupied throughout that moonless night in dodging steamboats. The pilot was long in ridding himself of the gloomy fancy that each one was heading straight for the *Betty*; but he came at last to reserve his anxiety for those rare occasions when an iron monster, invisible but audible, glared at him through both her coloured eyes.

The next day was hardly worthy of the name. Through a dense wet fog we drifted westward, uttering sad and disagreeable noises with our eighteenpenny horn. To peer too intently into a sea fog is, I found, unwise. You are apt to see things that are not there. Once Gotty was sure he descried trees and a church steeple, but we sailed through them all right.

Before sunset the weather cleared, and against the glowing sky we saw dark Portland—a place which, when I mentioned its prison, powerfully engaged my skipper's interest.

"Well, all I 'ope is," he remarked, a slightly reproachful ring in the note of solicitude, "they give theirselves more trouble to air yer things over there than what they do in 'Olloway.''

Cole and I, our curiosity whetted, encouraged him to enlarge upon such matters as lay on his mind.

"Bin there! Why, ercourse I 'ave!" Gotty exclaimed, as though a little offended that the range of his experiences should be questioned. "It was along o' sellin' a pint of shrimps on the kerb at Southend— only the old lady what bought the shrimps, she reg'lar flew at the perliceman, and said I warn't on the kerb, and no more I wasn't, but jest off it. At one time I fancied she was goin' ter land 'im one acrost the 'ead with 'er umbrella, she carried on so angry. But they took me ter Rochford, where I got the charnse of a week inside or pay twenty-seven shillin's and sixpence! I wasn't goin' ter throw good money away like that—it ain't likely; so I took the 'oliday. Outside 'Olloway, me 'aving eighteen shillin's in my pocket, I says ter the perlicemen what come along o' me, 'I'll jest run acrost the way ter get a drink,' I says, "afore we go in.' 'No, you won't,' he says. 'Beggin' your pardin',' I says, 'but I know the regerlations if you don't, and a man ain't supposed ter be in prison not afore 'e gets there.' So we went inter the public-'ouse on t'other side of the road, and arter 'aving three 'a'porth of beer I give the perliceman the rest of my money ter mind till I come out."

"And how did you like being in prison?" I ventured respectfully to inquire.

"As fur as that goes," the skipper thoughtfully replied, "bein' in chokee wasn't no bother ter me, fer I didn't let it be a bother, if you understand my meanin'. They give me two pound of oakum ter pick, and when I come ter see it I says, 'No, thank yer—not stuff like that I won't pick.' So they took me afore the Guv'nor and 'e says, 'You're 'ere ter be punished!' 'I'm quite aware of that, sir,' I says. 'Then you must pick the oakum,' he says. 'Beggin' your pardin',' I says, 'but my father and mother didn't give me fingers ter pick tarry rope like that. If it was proper rope,' I says, 'I'd pick it and glad of the job.' 'Then you'll 'ave ter go in the dark cells,' says 'e. 'Wery good, sir,' I says, 'I'd as lieve be in dark cells as what I would in light.' It never made no dif'rence ter me—bein' in dark cells didn't; but on the day fer me ter come out they gave me back my clothes all dampish. That's where I do think they oughter be more careful. When you go in they do 'em up in a bundle and sling 'em up in a loft, and there they lay till you come out agin. Now don't you think they might 'ave the thoughtfulness jest ter air 'em?"

"Certainly," I agreed.

"Only, mind yer, they was jest as I left 'em, and my rings and watch was there all right. Nothin' wasn't gorn only two ounces of 'bacca and 'alf an ounce of 'ard."

"Stolen?" I asked.

"Well, it was gorn."

"Why," I indignantly observed, "that was a worse offence than you were in prison for."

"Oh, I never made no bother about the 'bacca, and I soon bought myself a bit more when I went acrost the road fer my money. And arterwards I come even with that perliceman what put me away."

"Indeed!"

"Yes, it was regatter day, and 'e was to be on the barge ter see nobody didn't put a pig on the pole same as they used ter do at one time. There was several young fellers what was goin' ter row me out ter the barge, and 'e arsked if 'e couldn't come aboard with us. So I

173

says 'Yus,' and I give them young fellers word it was 'im what put me away, and what d'yer think 'appened?"

The ecstatic light in Gotty's eyes affording no clue, both Cole and I were unable to conjecture the character of later developments.

"Why," pursued the skipper, "when we got agin the barge, them and me 'appened ter all stand up tergether on one side of the boat, and over it went, only don't you see we'd all got 'old of the barge, so none of us didn't go in the water—only the perliceman, and the pore feller didn't 'alf look a pictur' when at larst we got 'im out. 'Ad ter go back ter the station ter change 'is things, 'e did. I give those young fellers a gallon of beer betwixt 'em, and I don't know," he concluded reflectively, "as they didn't oughter 'ave 'ad more."

These instructive reminiscences, coupled with the frowning aspect of Portland,necessarily gave a criminal turn to my thoughts; and Fate seemed bent on deepening the impression thus produced.

Let me trace the incidents that led to my falling into the hands of the police.

Having dropped anchor within the illumination of the promenade, Gotty and I rowed ashore to Weymouth and visited Melcombe Regis, which fine place proved to be populated with bluejackets from Portland; for in that quarter of England, let me parenthetically observe, several towns and harbours are jumbled together in a way which, as a lover of simplicity, I do not approve. But the matter of more immediate moment was that the post-office had closed for the night; and thus, the desire for correspondence being strong upon me, I was astir early next morning. Yet not so early as Gotty, who, when I emerged on deck in a toilet lacking some finishing touches, proved to be baling out—still with my mind running on Justice and her victims, I had almost written bailing out—the dinghy. If the fastidious reader will permit me to particularise (and the details will prove not without a possible bearing on what subsequently occurred) I would mention that, besides being in old slippers, I had neither brushed my hair nor donned a necktie. Yet even in that slovenly state I joined Gotty in the dinghy, to take immediate advantage of his presence on the rowing seat; for I reflected that at so early an hour there would be few persons abroad in the town to remark my appearance.

"Arter you've got yer letters," said the skipper, as we parted at the stairs, "you might jest get a loaf of bread. If you go ter the pier 'ead and wave yer 'at, when you come back, I'll be shore ter see yer."

I had soon secured my correspondence, but several bakers told me their bread would not leave the oven for half-an-hour. The fourth

174

time of my receiving that answer occurred in a confectioner's shop rich with the aromas of toast and coffee, and, a sudden greediness taking hold of me, I decided to occupy the interval of waiting with a luxurious land breakfast.

It was when emerging from the scene of that stolen feast (not that I omitted to pay for it), with the abstracted air of one whose senses are slumbrous with sufficiency, that a detaining hand was laid firmly on my shoulder, and, turning with a start, I found a sturdy policeman confronting me with an aspect inquisitive, triumphant, and even proprietorial, Surprised, I shrank back, but succeeded in abstaining from taking to my heels—which I assume to be the first impulse of a citizen in such a situation.

"I want you to tell me who you are and where you come from."

So spake the audacious uniformed creature, with an expression of countenance I do not hesitate to describe as a leer. He did not so much as say "please."

A wave of indignation trembled along my spine and in and out of my finger tips; and I hesitated for a reply. As a matter of fact, I found myself with nothing but a vague and general idea who I was. As to where I came from—why, as I told him, from that shop.

"Where did you sleep last night?" he sternly inquired.

"On my ship," I replied.

"What ship?"

So the magisterial examination ran on. I could but tell him the truth, and the truth, as usual, sounded lame, a trifle ludicrous, and wholly unconvincing.

"What work do *you* do on the fishing-smack?" he asked, critically eyeing me from head to foot.

"I sometimes lend a hand with the sails. Then I do cooking, and washing up, and things like that."

"Are you the steward?"

"No, I'm the owner, And now," I added, "if you've finished asking me questions. I'll ask you one. Why have you stopped me like this?"

"Because," he replied with alacrity and the leer, "you're very like some one I'm looking for."

Truly a nice thing to be told by a policeman!

"Well," I rejoined, somewhat warmly, "I think you've made a mistake this time."

"Perhaps I have," he replied, in a non-committal tone; and thus we parted.

A less satisfactory interview it has seldom been my lot to have with anybody. Nay, I walked back to the harbour with an uneasy feeling that there had been remissness on his part or mine. But whether he ought to have locked me up, or I ought to have knocked him down, I leave the impartial reader to determine.

Gotty, when I gave him the tidings, was less complimentary than kind.

"Look 'ere," he exclaimed with earnest chivalry, "if anythin' more comes of it, you put it on ter me. If they want somebody, you shan't go—I'm ready for 'em."

But at the moment my attention was claimed by a matter less susceptible of postponement, and of a more unselfish complexion, than the finding of someone to represent me in connection with an unknown crime which, for anything I knew, I might not have committed.

Among the letters just to hand, was one for Cole, who, after bashfully extracting it from its envelope handed it to me with a request that I would disclose the hidden meaning. And here let me mention a delicate responsibility with which, as a shipmate of the unscholarly, I found myself clothed. Skipper and mate readily agreed with me that weekly remittances to wives should be accompanied by missives which besides giving some account of the sender's health and fortunes, would convey suitable expressions of solicitude and affection to his family circle.

At my consent to perform these literary labours on their behalf, they were sufficiently voluble with their thanks; but unfortunately I failed to make them realise that the position demanded some measure of mental co-operation on their part. I could not rid them of a superstitious belief that, because I was accustomed to use the pen, I must necessarily know what they would desire to say to their wives better than they knew themselves. Thus invariably I found myself with instructions embarrassingly meagre and monotonous; and had I conscientiously kept my communication within authorised limits, they would, week after week, have read as follows:-

"DEAR MRS. GOTTY (or COLE),—Your husband wishes me to say that he is all right, and he hopes you are all right."

Manifestly these rudimentary thoughts needed to be copiously supplemented. Knowing the members of my skipper's household, I found it comparatively easy to devise appropriate messages from him to them. In Cole's case, however, great circumspection was called for, and, as a prelude to the labour of composition, I had to ascertain, *inter alia*, his pet name for Mrs. Cole, the sex and

176

approximate age of the baby, and distinguishing charms of the other children; nor, let me add, did any Friday find me above the necessity, on some point or other, of refreshing my memory.

The letter which Cole now gave me to read was the first he had received from his wife in answer to one written by me to her on his behalf. At a first glance I was reassured to see that my string of crosses had provoked an even more liberal consignment from the lady; and, indeed, if I may say so without immodesty, her epistle was a triumphant vindication of mine. Beginning, "My Dear Darling Husband,—Thank you very very much for your kind and loving letter," it ran on, for four pages, in the same strain, and, as a crowning proof that I had done my work with judgment, my endearing allusion to the baby had provoked a few crooning words quoted from that little personage in reply.

"Did yer see 'im pipe the flute?'' gasped Gotty, pent-up amazement finding outlet when he and I were afterwards alone; and indeed I had noticed, without particularly remarking, a moisture in Cole's eyes as I returned his letter and he placed it in his pocket. "Well of the all the—!" pursued the skipper, language failing him. "We know 'e ain't left 'ome before; but ter stand with 'is eyes all runnin' over, and 'ave ter put up 'is coat sleeve to 'em! These Folkestin' chaps reg'lar beat me. Fancy if I was ter go and pipe the flute when my Missis writes ter me.''

And in truth communications from that quarter had tended to make his mouth, rather than his eyes, water. For they were commonly contained in boxes stuffed with apple-turnovers and treacle tarts of the consigner's own making, she being alive to her spouse's powerful predilection for those articles of diet: not (as Gotty would assuredly point out, were he writing this book) that the pilot was slow also to demonstrate approval of the good soul's culinary achievements.

During the remainder of our stay at those towns, I saw no more of my inquisitive policeman; but, as if the influence of neighbouring Portland were not yet exhausted, I was destined to narrowly escape being taken into custody on a totally fresh charge.

Like Sandown Bay, the Weymouth Waters had the true fishy look to Gotty, and we were minded once more to try our luck with the trawl. But, profiting by experience, I resolved on the prudent course of first taking counsel with a local fisherman. In a jerseyed veteran of benign aspect, who looked to be deeply versed in all maritime matters, I recognised the man for our need; and to him, accordingly, following on an exchange of friendly salutations, I opened my mind.

Having, with ready courtesy, given me gratifying details of the size and multiplicity of the fish waiting to be caught, he was at pains to indicate the range of waters in which we could trawl without risk of rocks and wrecks. Nay, to such an extent did he identify himself with our interests that, dwelling on moon and wind as factors in our favour, he urgently advised that we try our luck that very night. And not by word or tone did he hint a hope that, for all this useful information, I would concede him even the price of a pint of beer; so that, on observing my shipmates across the harbour, I took my departure, entertaining warm sentiments towards a man of whose nobility of character I had received such signal proof.

Having crossed in the ferry-boat, I filled Gotty's bosom with enthusiasm by apprising him of the encouraging information I had gleaned. To such a degree, indeed, was his mind engaged with thoughts of our nocturnal intentions that when, a few minutes later, we received a passing greeting from two fishermen leaning at leisure against a railing, he paused to take them into his confidence.

"Yus," he agreed, "the weather seems reg'lar set in fer fair. And jest wind enough fer our job."

"Going west?" came the politely interested inquiry.

"Not ter night we ain't. But we're goin' ter 'ave a few 'auls off 'ere, jest ter see what Leigh gear's good for in your waters."

"Trawling?" they both exclaimed, standing upright with astonishment.

"What! Ain't there nothin' worth trying after?" asked Gotty, in a voice of trouble. "There was some one give the Guv'nor word you do stand a charnse ter catch a few, and nothin' ter pull you up west'ard of them white clifts."

"Who was it?" asked the pair in unison, and with something of sternness in their tone.

I endeavoured to indicate distinguishing physionomical traits of the venerable fisherman who had so readily placed his stores of knowledge at my service.

"Old Sam!" exclaimed one, identifying the verbal portrait.

"We might 'a known!" exclaimed the other.

Then they told us that trawling in those waters had been strictly banned, during the previous six years, by the responsible Government authority, who were understood to regard the bay as a nursery for young fish; and we furthermore learnt that, while the last man to defy this prohibition was visited with a heavy pecuniary penalty, against the next transgressor loomed an official threat of imprisonment and the confiscation of his boat.

This caused a radical change in my sentiments towards the old man across the harbour; and after we had returned our sober and sincere thanks for the tidings just imparted, Gotty and I went aboard for a quiet game of dominoes before turning in for the night.

We set sail from the vicinity of Portland early next morning.

XXVI

BANKRUPT AT CORNWALL

FOR two nights and a day, in alternate calms, fogs, and squalls, we made our uncertain way to Brixham, periods of human perturbation being associated with the failure of our lamps during a high wind, and the misbehaviour of our kedge anchor in temporarily hooking itself to a rock thrice five fathoms down.

Tor Bay proved alive with small craft lining for mackerel, and we saw the little shining creatures drawn from the water in quick succession; so that, Cole having some experience in the art, we bought hooks and twine and got to work. Our success, if comparatively unsensational, at least supplied a welcome variation in our dietary, besides giving us confidence to go our fishing with the great Brixham trawlers. Like a tom-tit among ravens, we hauled with them, well to the east of Star Point, in a brisk breeze and a heavy swell.

"All them big wessels wouldn't shove their gear in tergether if there wasn't somethin' ter git." Thus, with a wink, spake complacent Gotty. "Now we'll see if Leigh gear ain't as good as what theirs is."

Noting that the Brixham boats were making one long haul, we did the same, rolling in those great sweeping billows for two hours and a quarter. Then came the grating of windlasses, and with enthusiastic impatience we hoisted our trawl also.

It was empty, not merely of fish, but of all things else; and on comparing the depth of the water, as revealed by my chart, with the length of our warp, as revealed by Gotty, I found that the *Betty's* net had been hanging fifteen fathoms above the bottom.

We had done with fishing. Thenceforward, during two sunny weeks, we cruised from harbour to harbour in that fair region which is called Devonshire in its first section, and Cornwall beyond—a region of transparent blue sea where the rocks are mottled with purples and gold; a region of apples and cream, where, rambling about lanes and moors, we accepted nuts and mushrooms from bountiful Nature, with blackberries of a size and juiciness that recalled to my delighted skipper the mulberries of his boyhood.

We were in a strange, remote world, and I was to have a sharp reminder that this was not wholly an advantage. Of the cash supply I had taken in at Folkestone, it chanced that but a pound remained when we arrived at Looe—a circumstance of the less moment as, among correspondence awaiting me there, I expected to find a letter enclosing postal orders. Yet when that anticipation was falsified, I gave the matter no further attemtion than was involved in the reflection that, for the moment, I must abstain from the purchase of stores (though ours were practically exhausted) and limit expenditure to current needs. The remittance would not improbably arrive on the morrow, or the day after; and, in any case, I had my cheque book.

Disappointed of that letter on the third morning, the necessity for taking action was suggested by a discovery that our financial resources had dwindled to two shillings and five pence. Calling at a bank, I asked permission to present a cheque, payment to await an exchange of telegrams, at my cost, with my bank. But in this procedure, which I thought would close all avenues to suspicion, the Looe banker discovered a flaw.

The telegram, he pointed out, would but prove the existence of an account in the name of the signatory; and how was he to know—he asked, beaming blandly at me through his spectacles—that I really was myself, and not some one else forging my own signature? And, indeed, the clever way in which he expressed himself induced me almost to share the doubt on that point which I realised might be actually lurking in his mind. Moreover, toilet facilities on a bawley being slender, I bethought me, in guilty confusion, that the pilot's appearance lent small support to his cock-and-a-bull story of a banking account in Fleet Street.

Nevertheless, inviting the Looe banker, for the sake of argument, to assume that I was no imposter, how, I asked him, could I gain prompt access to £5? On that hypothetical assumption, he pointed out, nothing would be easier than for my bank, on receiving telegraphic instructions from me, to at once wire such a sum through the post-office.

Two minutes afterwards I was sending the message: "Please wire me £5 immediately. Address fishing-boat *Betty*, Looe Harbour, Cornwall."

Three hours later, this reply reached me from Fleet Street: "Present cheque nearest bank. They will wire us before paying."

The vaunted resources of civilisation, it will be noted, were playing battledore with Gotty's Guv'nor as the shuttlecock. However there chanced to be a bank nearer than the one I had earlier visited; and, thither, accordingly, I went with my petition and telegram.

It was their early closing day, and the manager was on the point of shutting up shop and going home. He would have nothing to do with the matter. So I took long strides back to the post-office, and had this urgent message flashed to Fleet Street: "Local bank closing. Please wire money at once."

I returned to the *Betty*, of which my last impressions were associated with the sight of two men whose spirits I had depressed by dark hints of an empty exchequer. I now came plump against the disconcerting fact that, although it was nearly three o'clock, they had had no dinner.

As I feared, neither retained a penny in his pocket, while the outlay for telegrams had reduced my available resources to 2½d. Nor could I feel sure, in the anxious situation which had developed, that I might not be compelled, later on, to further deplete that reserve by the purchase of a postage stamp.

On looking our situation squarely in the face, I found that, while our chest contained generous quantities of soda, tea, coffee, milk, sugar, marmalade, and soap, we were otherwise reduced to half the top of a loaf, and a little of yesterday's rabbit at the bottom of the saucepan. Taking a slice of bread by way of encouragement, I bade my shipmates eat the remainder with the remnants of the rodent. But to this arrangement Gotty, with some hauteur, demurred, coldly insisting that I must have the rabbit; so that, for the time being, we all stood severely aloof from our savoury, each professing contentment with his crust.

My endeavours to make the skipper understand the cause of our embarrassment would, doubtless, have met with a fuller measure of success had his mind held a clearer conception of the principles and intricacies of banking. As it was, his politely sympathetic interest did not wholly conceal the element of honest misgiving that coloured his thoughts on the subject. In truth, I had earlier become aware that the Guv'nor's trick of beguiling good money out of simple folk, in return for slips of paper, did not command his full approval, even if he could not repress a sportsman's pleasure in the success of such cool audacity. As a way of making a living, the writing of cheques was, I am sure, in Gotty's opinion, ethically unsound; nor do I think, had he spoken his private thoughts, he was so greatly surprised to find that at last, apparently, the game was up.

Perhaps I did not greatly assist his grasp of the situation by mentioning an expectation—which, however, grew fainter as the hours dragged by—that a consignment of cash would be communicated to me by electricity. Yet when, at eight o'clock, he found his Guv'nor disclaiming against a bank that had failed us in our hour of need, Gotty's loyal bosom swelled with indignation in unison. In my anger I vowed to withdraw my patronage from the institution in question—in which purpose I found myself encouraged by his stern approval.

"I would!" he urged. "That's the way to treat 'em."

Yet in contemplating these ruthless measures against that joint stock corporation, with its seven millions of menaced capital, we were doing nothing to mend our own fortunes, which had reached a sufficiently low ebb. I had bought the penny postage stamp (to send a written application to the bank); so we were three hungry men with three halfpence, and with no certainty of receiving a remittance till the morning after the morrow.

Shrinking from the thought of so prolonged a fast, I entered upon a solemn consultation with my skipper, requesting that he would bethink him what was best to be done.

After we had discussed several ingenious schemes, and reluctantly abandoned them, one after the other, because of their impracticability, a daring thought suddenly flashed into my mind. Why not fall back on our calling as fishermen? After all, we had our vessel and our nets. Why not catch some fish, and make a little money that way?

At first Gotty thought I was joking. When he found me in earnest he seemed to think I must be demented.

"'Ow can we go trawlin'," he indignantly inquired, "when we dunno the ground? Night-time and all, and no moon!"

"Some one was saying there's clear ground east of Port Wrinkel, if you keep well in."

"And most likely go ashore! That'd do us a lot of good, wouldn't it?"

"We have our lead, and surely we should hear the breakers. It seems to me we must take a little risk, or starve. But, of course, if you think there's too much danger, that's the end of the matter."

Gotty did not at once reply, and it was a hopeful sign that, when he did so, the tone of aggrieved expostulation had given place to one of thoughtful inquiry.

"What about that young feller sayin' you ain't allowed ter trawl anywheres along this coast?"

"I don't believe it."

"Well, it don't 'ardly seem reasonable, do it—ter say a pore man shouldn't 'ave the charnse to arn a 'a'penny. Wicked crool, I should call it."

I submitted a supplementary suggestion—that we seek the co-operation of a local fisherman, offering him a moiety of such revenues as might result from our labours in the safe and fruitful waters to which he should pilot us.

Responding to this modified proposition with a grunt that might have meant anything, Gotty betook himself to the vessel's stern, where, by the light of a lamp on the harbour wall, I saw him mistily as a still, solitary figure, deep in meditation.

"Cast 'er off!" rang out the sudden injunction to Cole, who, vaguely aware of our paralysing penury, was smoking a disconsolate pipe in the cabin. He came up with a startled face, but, finding Gotty about to hoist the mainsail, he did not pause to inquire as to his superior's sanity or sobriety, but straightway applied his strength to undoing the ropes by which we were tethered fore and aft.

Next minute, having swung into the stream, the *Betty*, leaning over in the breeze, began her passage down the narrow harbour, Gotty, with an anxious hand on the tiller, projecting his eyesight into the darkness beyond.

As we raced along in the night, ignoring the well-meaning but unintelligible instructions shouted to us from the wall, I tardily recalled the stress and complications which had attended our arrival, in broad daylight, at that haven; so that, had not the time for choice gone by, I should after all have voted for an empty larder and safety, rather than for the possibility of cash with the certainty of many hours in darkness and danger.

Great was my relief when we reached the open sea; nor was the wind slow in taking us within sight of the lights of Port Wrinkel. But other and mysterious lights—eight in number—lay ahead of us, in a situation where my chart and book made no mention of any illumination on the coast. Even as we gazed askance at those eight lights, many others were added to them, until we could no longer doubt that a long line of pilchard boats lay fishing right across the area in which we had hoped to mend our fortunes.

Neither Gotty nor I knew aught of pilchards, and the way they are caught, but as Folkestone fishermen often buy their boats from the West, Cole had a certain amount of second-hand knowledge on the subject. His revelations were highly disconcerting.

"We can't be far off their nets," he ominously observed, "for they lay half a mile over the water; and if you touch 'em they can bleed you for it. If we aren't careful, we might get right in amongst 'em, and then there'd be a nice sum to pay. I wouldn't put down the trawl for £60, if it was my boat. But," he added, more cheerfully, "you please yourselves."

184

Gotty and I, anxiously conferring together, agreed in thinking we were still a good mile from the pilchard boats, which now showed lights to the number of sixty-seven (for I had counted the selfish things). On the other hand, we were not yet quite abreast of Port Wrinkel.

"Are we agoin' ter come all this way ," asked Gotty incredulously, "and then not 'ave a try? I don't think. 'Ere—in she goes."

The trawl went down, but, alas, so speedily hugged a rock that we had to pull it up again. A little farther on, undaunted Gotty tried once more, but with the same result.

"Well, this is all right, ain't it?" he exclaimed, perspiring with toil and annoyance. "Them boats," he cried, in sudden heat, "are fair on our ground;" and the aggressive way in which he glared at the yellow lights seemed to reveal him as ready, for two pins, to go back and fetch the Looe police.

"What's to be done?" I asked, dismally conscious that we were confronted by difficulties of the insuperable order.

"Oh, I ain't beat—not yet I ain't," replied my skipper stoutly, adding as an instruction to his subordinate, "shove in the anchor."

Having put up our riding light and refreshed ourselves with a pot of tea, we beguiled two hours with dominoes, Gotty ever and anon popping up from the game to keep himself informed of developments in the watery world around us. At last the time came when, lingering on the look-out, he called down to us:

"Them pilchers are movin' off—and time they did! 'Ullow! 'Ere comes a craft. Wonder what she's after so fur inshore."

Going up to look, we beheld a red light gaining rapidly upon us, and presently a great black shape, which we recognised as a Plymouth trawler, was passing within hail. West-country lungs demanded to be told the time, and I supplied the information—1.15 a.m. Then from the stranger there arose a noise of cog-wheels and commotion which conveyed a glad message to Gotty's heart.

"'E's puttin' 'is trawl down, Good enough! Up anchor. Look sharp."

In a trice we were sailing in the wake of that vessel, which was already lost to view, and although the course seemed straight for the shore, we could have no misgivings when superior tonnage led the way. Our trawl now down, on we pitched, our equanimity heightened by the sight of all those embarrassing yellow lights streaming seaward.

On spying the starboard light of the Plymouth trawler some half-hour later, we laid to and hauled; when our satisfactory

185

recompense took the form of two large soles, a young turbot, and nine good-sized plaice, with a few roker and other fish of minor marketable importance.

To sail back, and haul again over approximately the same ground, was a task of no difficulty to Gotty, who steers through darkness by some clear instinct of his own. A second and third haul were equal to the first; and on we went fishing.

At three o'clock a brilliant inspiration came upon me; and I systematically overhauled the box in which unpopular items of our original stores had been stowed. There, sure enough, I found a packet of ground rice, which the skipper had discarded with soap and soda in the belief that it partook of the same character. My hungry shipmates knew not to what end I had tarried so long in the cabin; but when I took them each a steaming plate of the nutritious diet in question, with marmalade copiously added, their eyes were opened and their hearts touched.

There being an autumnal coldness in the night air, I did a further piece of benevolence in lending each of them an overcoat. In Gotty's case the garment fitted so closely that it strongly resembled a black frock-coat, so that, a shower having caused him to don his sou'-wester, the figure of which I caught occasional glimpses in the lamplight, as he bustled about in the discharge of his successful labours, conveyed a droll dual suggestion of a general practitioner and a dustman.

The wind dropping before the dawn, there was some falling off in the richness of our later hauls; but it was two fine trunks of fish that we returned to Looe, triumphant but tired, at six o'clock. Leaving the bawley outside the jetty we rowed into the harbour, where Cole remained in charge of our fish while Gotty and I set forth to find a purchaser.

"Them two boxes," said my companion, as we hurried towards a part of the quay where we had seen fishermen land their catches, "are worth thirty shillin's of anybody's money"—at which words I saw a beautiful mental picture of poached eggs and fried rashers. For, in truth, I fain would break my fast.

That Gotty's emotions bore a close resemblance to my own was attested by his next remark:

"I tell yer what I could do with. That's a nice plate o' cold meat and onions. Not 'alf I couldn't."

Ah!" I greedily exclaimed, "we shan't have to wait much longer now."

A minute later and I should have lacked heart to utter those bold words. For sparrows proved to be the only living creature in the locality where we had hoped to find salesmen.

Walking on, we came presently to a black-bearded fisherman whom we besought to acquaint us with local facilities for selling one's catch. Readily lending assistance to brother-craftsmen hailing from a distant port, he explained that, there being no market at Looe, you had to send your fish by rail to Liskeard; and he gave us the name of a consigner from whom, he was confident, we should receive fair treatment, and a just remittance on the following Saturday.

Too proud to explain that our physical needs would not brook a financial delay of three hours, leave alone three days, we thanked the Cornishman for his well-intentioned explanations, and set off for the main thoroughfare.

The shops were not yet open, but, seeing signs of life in one of the principal hotels, I bade Gotty enter that establishment and ask if they would not like a nice lot of prime fish for their visitors.

As, having rung the bell, he stood bashfully on the hotel mat, I—lurking behind an outhouse up an alley on the opposite side of the way—awaited developments with a beating heart.

Gotty was invited within, and when at last he reappeared I drew a hopeful inference from his dignified deportment.

"Wonderful civil spoken 'e was," I learnt, "and comin' acrost ter see the fish when 'e's 'ad 'is breakfast."

We occupied the tedious interregnum in impatiently pacing to and fro upon the quay; and when we ultimately espied the glutton (for a man who took so long over a meal could be nothing else) he was strolling towards us with his hands in his pockets, as though stupidly unconscious that there may be occasions when one should hurry.

Of our fish he was pleased to speak in terms of eulogy, but, shaking a regretful head, he explained that there was far too much for him to buy.

"Twenty-five shillin's wont 'urt yer," observed persuasive Gotty.

"No," the hotel manager was good enough to say, "that's not much for all those fish. But I could never get rid of so many. Look here, you go up to one of the other hotels and see if they won't take half. Then I'll have the rest;" and by way of showing that this was his ultimatum, he departed.

Without a word, Gotty shouldered the box of prime, and he and I set off to find another hotel. The skipper's exit therefrom was almost simultaneous with his entrance and I gathered that the proprietor's manner of declining business overtures had been abrupt. At another hotel he lingered longer, but finally emerged with a woeful countenance, and still bearing his burden.

"She fingered 'em all over," he told me, scarce able to contain himself with indignation, "and then she said she'd 'ave three pair of soles and give me sixpence a pound for 'em. 'What!' I says, 'you pick out all the best. That's not reasonable,' I says. Then she up and said she 'adn't got no more time ter talk with the likes of me. So I says, 'Good mornin', lady,' and come away."

The shops were now opening, and, faint from the want of food, sleep, and a little human sympathy, we wandered about in search of a fishmonger's. But a protracted pilgrimage to and fro in the streets of East and West Looe, while it disclosed a tantalising succession of butchers and bakers, failed to make us acquainted with premises of the desired character. A sausage-shop was the nearest approximation to what we sought, and, noting an empty area of its window-space, I urged my companion to approach the proprietor and point out that, even though he were not in the habit of selling fish, he might advantageously utilise his marble slab in introducing that feature as a supplement to his ordinary business.

At first the skipper was shy of submitting this suggestion to the sausage-maker, but I murmured "Cold meat and onions," and in he went.

However, my ingenious scheme for benefiting that Looe shop-keeper came to naught.

"Says 'e don't want no fish," Gotty on rejoining me explained, his tone testifying to a temper somewhat ruffled. "When I said he might do worse, seein' 'e'd 'ave all the compertition to 'isself, 'e turned saucy."

Nor did my next proposition serve to restore the equanimity which that interview had disturbed. It was this: that we should dispose of our catch piecemeal, letting the lady have her three pairs of soles, inviting the hotel-keeper whom he had first approached to supply his limited requirements, and then seeking customers for the remainder.

"But that's 'awkin'!" cried the scandalised Gotty.

"'Where's yer licence, my man,' one of them coppers'd be askin'; and then where'd we be? You're allowed ter sell all yer fish tergether, but ter go from door to door, a few 'ere and a few there—why, didn't you know that's 'awkin'?"

But indeed my conscious knowledge was limited to the one strident fact that I was an hungered. "Tommy," I cried, turning to a little boy carrying a pail of milk, "where is there a fish-shop?"

The open-eyed youngster explained that there wasn't one. He added that, if we wanted to buy some fish, we could do so from a cart that drove into Looe every morning. We eagerly inquired the probable hour of its arrival. The boy thought it might come at any moment now.

For three-quarters of an hour, as two pathetic figures sitting on the stone bridge, we closely studied the vehicular traffic. Two carts of uncertain aspect Gotty ventured to stop. One proved to contain meat, while the other was the property of a farmer, and in neither case were our apologies very graciously received. At the second of these disappointments my skipper so far forgot himself as to petulantly proclaim a disposition to fling all our fish in the water.

Desiring him to do no such thing, I proposed that he carry our prime to the hotel-keeper we had interviewed on landing, and let him have the lot at his own price.

On this errand he was so long gone that, walking up and down outside, I allowed my mind to foster an ugly suspicion that he had accepted an invitation to stay to breakfast. But this unworthy misgiving was banished in the joy of beholding him issue from the hotel with the empty fish-box poised sideways on his head.

"Yes," he explained, "'e's took 'em. But you dunno what a job I 'ad ter git 'im to;" and exhausted Gotty passed a coat-sleeve across his damp brow. "Fust 'e said no; 'e didn't want 'em. 'Beggin' your pardin', sir,' I says, 'but you promised ter take 'alf. 'Yus,' says 'e, 'but since then four of my wisitors 'ave gorn away, so now there's no one to eat 'em.' 'Well, there you are,' I says, 'take the lot fer fifteen shillin's.' No, 'e wouldn't. So I come down ter twelve-and-six. But it wasn't no good; and after a lot more talk, I says 'e could 'ave 'em fer seven-and-six, seein' I was fair sick o' carrying 'em about. And at fust 'e says no ter seven-and-six, so I 'ad ter reg'lar go down on my 'ands and knees and beg and pray 'im ter take 'em. Then at larst 'e give way. But jest fancy, a nice lot of fish like that fer seven-and-six!"

Gotty seemed broken-hearted. But I cared nothing about the disproportion between price and value. Rather let me say that I was prepared to welcome any current coin, silver or bronze, as more precious than rubies, leave alone fish.

"Where's the money, Gotty?" and I held out a tremulous palm.

"'E never give it me," was the appalling answer I received. "Says 'e'll bring it out when 'e can find time ter go to 'is cash-box."

For half-an-hour we hovered about that hotel; and once when I saw the proprietor step to his threshold, smoking a cigarette at full leisure, I had it in my heart to run across the road and do him a personal injury. Finally, losing all patience, I sent Gotty in for the money, with which he promptly reappeared.

It was characteristic of my skipper that, having seen this matter to a conclusion, his disengaged thoughts at once turned to the bawley.

"I'll go ter the 'ead of the pier and see if she's all right," he anxiously remarked, "if you wouldn't mind doin' the shoppin';" and, having handed me five of the dear-bought shillings, he hurried away.

Darting into a fruit shop, I laid out three half-pence in a luxurious William pear, and its flavour, should I live to be a hundred, is likely to endure as a thrilling memory.

Afterwards I bought two delightfully warm, sweet-smelling loaves of bread, half a pound of delicious-looking butter, and a quarter of a pound of tobacco.

Having tried us so sorely, Fate had indeed relented, how completely I realised when, on calling at the post-office, I found £5 from my banker and the postal remittance which, by travelling from town in an ill-directed envelope, was the cause of all our trouble.

XXVII

HOMEWARD IN A HURRICANE

AND the day came when the *Betty* passed from heaving waters of the open sea, and glided into a river that was broad and still and beautiful—a perspective of repose and velvet hills where, travelling through green reflections, we were among the little singing birds.

This was Helford River, the western limit of our voyage—a fairy region with foregrounds of fern and purple rocks; and beyond a headland smoothly clothed with oak trees we found an ancient ruin of turreted masonry, grey and peaceful. All others things were also tranquil: elms and their cawing population; three homely houses with frontages of sunshine, limewash, and ivy; a little white boat that lay on the shore; and five pink pigs.

Gotty paid this Cornish paradise the supreme compliment of recognising it as the very place where, given the opportunity, he would elect to live in pensioned retirement.

"With a pound a week," he explained, in a flight of fancy foreign to his usual style, "and pick up a oyster or two, or it might be dig a few worms, I could make a do of it, it's a fact I could."

And indeed, with all that end of England, so far as we explored it, he, Cole, and I were highly pleased. Each place left its vivid impression. Falmouth, that panorama, we entered at night, and only escaped the Black Rock by accident—the erring pilot supposing it where it was not. At Fowey we anchored beside Lord Brassey's *Sunbeam*, and were soon in conversation with a talented Polruan parrot. Spotless Polperro, visited on a Sunday afternoon, looked prosperously picturesque. At Mevagissey we were courteously conducted over premises where, by workers and ways faultlessly clean, two million pilchards were being cured and packed for humble, discerning Italians. Nobler Plymouth proved to contain a fish market that appalled us in the morning and a music hall that delighted us at night.

And now the autumn was well advanced, so that Gotty grew concerned for our comfort and safety in returning; and each was sick for a sight of his home.

Our programme was to provision for three days, hoist the dinghy

191

on deck, and then, getting out into the Channel, run to Folkestone without pausing on the way.

But the wind blew strong and contrary; and after tacking for fourteen hours we were glad to find shelter at Fowey.

"It ain't no good," exhausted Gotty admitted. "We must wait till the wind gets round."

But two days later, though the weather had not altered, our impatience caused us to try again.

We made a good fight of it, but after a day and a night of monotonous misery we revisited Plymouth with certain details of our rigging snapped and hanging.

"Everlastin' turn and turn," deplored the indignant skipper, "and what good is it? We don't make no 'eadway, and everything strainin' and flappin'? Why, we shan't 'ave a rag left flyin' if we ain't careful. I shan't leave this 'ere 'arbour not till the wind gets round ter the west'ard—there you are."

And the set jaw revealed an emphatic determination to abide by that wise decision. Two depressing and annoying days went by, and still the wind blew from the east. It seemed to be doing so on purpose.

"What d'yer say," said Gotty, feverish with home sickness, "if we 'ave another try? If it's only a few miles, that'll make it less fur ter go when the wind does shift round; and we ain't gettin' no nearer 'ome all the while we lay 'ere, are we?"

Cole and I, suffering acutely from the skipper's complaint, eagerly endorsed his reasoning; and once more we set forth to wrestle with the elements.

Ten hours later the *Betty* was contending against a great grey sea that raged around the Start. We ran aslant in parallel lines to and from the shore, obstinately refusing to admit defeat until a rope snapped with a shriek, and down came the mainsail, a goodly portion whereof, with the end of the gaff, drooping over into the water. In some anxiety we dragged our property on board, and then, turning tail, flew before the wind.

We had urgent need of the nearest harbour, but I was too good a navigator to suppose myself a match for the rocks of Salcombe. However, we ran within shelter of Bolt Head, and a local pilot came out and took us in for half-a-crown—this being the only occasion of our following the Woodbridge Haven precedent.

Even the exquisite scenery of Salcombe could not reconcile us to delay. Blackberrying expeditions were marred by constant denunciation of the east wind, with which, indeed, Gotty became so vexed that he passed unwarranted criticisms on Cole, who was goaded into an expression of regret that he had ever come with us, at which I sought relief to my feelings by giving them both a good lecture; to such deplorable lengths did a love of home impel the three retarded mariners.

We had once more vowed not to resume our voyage till the wind veered round; and once more we were forsworn. Having spliced our broken ropes, we adventured out again in the teeth of that hostile wind, and set ourselves to round the Start. That the task demanded a certain amount of doggedness we had received a hint prior to our recent experience. For a torpedo boat that arrived at Plymouth while we were there, reported broken crockery and other small misfortunes; and, Cole having an uncle in the town whose son was one the crew, word reached us that the iron craft had incurred that internal derangement while rolling in boisterous waters off the Start.

It took us all day to do it, but we got past, and—grim disappointment—found worse water on the other side. It was the sea's cruel whim to break upon our vessel and deluge us with spray; so that, after three more hours of obstinate endurance, all spirit was blown out of the three saturated adventurers, and they ran for shelter to Torquay.

Completely baffled, there we lay, impatient and petulant, for three nights and two days. Then came the morning when I awoke to what seemed a dream. Gotty was singing—not merely humming a hymn, as was the poor level of his recent vocal efforts: but singing with all his throat, like a blackbird. And the hold opening—my window in the ceiling—had lost some of its breadth.

Sitting up in bed to clear my wits, I guessed the truth. Our dinghy was on deck. The wind had changed. It was twanging our rigging to the tune of "Home, Sweet Home."

Away we went, not tarrying for fresh stores, for time was more valuable than new bread, and what if the water cask were half empty?

"Why," exclaimed Gotty, as having curved out of Torbay, we charged the open sea on a strong straight line, "if the wind keeps in the west'ard, and don't fall away too much, we oughter be in Folkestin' the day arter termorrer. It blows wonderful steady—reg'lar walkin' through the water she is. In by Wednesday mornin' I shouldn't wonder. Yer see, she don't feel the punt now it's aboard. Goes twice as easy, she does, not 'aving all that dead weight ter pull. If the wind don't drop. That's all I'm afraid of."

On that point he spoke Cole's thoughts and mine. Because perfection seemed too good to last, we feared a diminution of zeal on the part of the wind.

But these timorous misgivings proved without warrant. So far from lessening, the aerial velocity increased. Our mast ofttimes stood at a considerable slant, and the sea came on board at the bow in gurgling mounds of frothy unrest, then streamed down the deck and escaped hissing through the scuppers. Some passed into the hold, where on going below to consult my chart, I found disconcerting patches of wetness on my books, my clothes, and my bed. But we were going home fast. And faster and faster.

Being well out in the Channel, we had no occasion to concern ourselves with navigation subtleties, and this was just as well, for the pilot did not feel quite himself. He was cold and wet, for one thing, and he was beginning to have a headache, for another.

When day faded, Portland was far astern, and we were south of the Anvil light. All the reefs were taken in. The weather showed no signs of abating its boisterousness.

The question of running for shelter to the Isle of Wight was raised, but only to be unanimously negatived. No one was more prompt than the poor pilot in resisting the suggestion. He now makes frank confession that he would joyfully have gone into harbour if only his swimming brain had been equal to the task of reading up the necessary particulars. The lesser evil was to continue sitting, damp and impassive, on the provision chest, dully wondering if the storm would never cease.

At midnight he put forth a great effort, and bestirred himself to the extent of thrusting an inquisitive head into the open air. St. Catherine's light shone brightly in the north; and no sooner had he made that observation than about a quart of sea water leapt over the dinghy and smote him on the head, icy trickles running down his spine. Stung into a certain amount of life, he fumbled about until he found his lamp, with which having succeeded in lighting it, he scrutinised his apartment, if haply he might find a dry spot on which to deposit himself. But, with moisture dripping everywhere, the place had rather the look of a grotto than a hold.

My bed was saturated, and a sheet of water was ebbing and flowing across the oilcloth. Boxes and my smaller belongings were passing harshly to and fro, in obedience to the rolling of the vessel. A special lurch deprived me of the support of a chest, and abrupt developments were associated with the extinction and loss of my lamp. Extricating myself from those difficulties, I once more protruded into the open air, just in time to receive about a bucketful of cold sea at the back of my neck.

In oilskins, sea-boots, and sou'westers, Gotty and Cole were encased against those sharp discomforts; my own wardrobe including nothing appropriate to a gale. But I submitted the less rebelliously to the disability of reflecting that my better-clothed companions were doing all the work.

Another subject of my unspoken envy was the way in which, clutching at this and that, Cole succeeded when occasion arose, in traversing the deck without suffering himself to be borne overboard. Fain would I accomplish a gymnastic expedition of the sort; for my inclination lay towards the cabin, which did not leak, and where a fire was burning. Ultimately, and with great circumspection, I essayed and achieved the feat, much as a monkey climbs a tree.

There was no comfort in the cabin. I put coal on the dying embers, and Gotty must have noted the augmented smoke, for Cole struggled to the hatchway, and bade me suffer the fire to die down. Before that could be, the *Betty* indulged in a shuddering spasm which emptied the grate on to the floor, besides working mischief (as the din attested) in our crockery locker.

Afterwards came many upheavals of the sort. Water dripped through the deck, and spray came down the hatchway like rain. I sat or squatted in several situations, but always the lawless lurching of my apartment threw me elsewhere. Lying embedded in a heap of sails, I finally found stable quarters, and I remained there, listening to the roar of wind and water, for many hours.

It was my opinion that the bawley would not founder. Getting into that cold water seemed a thing so pitifully distressing that, by a piece of sublime egotism, I could not believe I should be called upon to do it. And, indeed, physical discomforts apart, there is a sense in which I was, so to speak, enjoying myself. It was drama, bold and spacious. Above, below, and all round, Nature was in a passion—the same Nature which had ofttimes lulled me with rosebuds, blue sky, and linnets. In weak moments, during that awful night, how I longed for the sight and feel of land—if it were only a little in a flowerpot.

At about ten o'clock I came half-way up the hatchway and looked about me. The moist world was tinted in degrees of grey. Swollen masses of water ran towards us in unending succession, and each on drawing near loomed down upon us; but it got underneath the *Betty*, and rolled her about, and hurried on its way. At certain angles of the pitching I saw Beachy Head. We were going home at a pace far outstripping our most hopeful anticipations.

Astern, there were my shipmates, figures of rigid endurance, Gotty still at the helm. At about noon, to get within earshot of them, I clambered across to the hold.

On the previous afternoon we noted a schooner putting back into Portland. Since then the Channel had seemed empty of sailing craft. But we saw many rolling steamers, bravely breasting the weather.

In the early evening we were being hurled towards Dungeness. Suddenly, to the confusion of the helmsman, land was blotted from sight as by a fog. Having been continuously drenched all day by spray, we did not recognise that now we were also in a torrent of rain.

On the other side of the headland we encountered our worst weather. The *Betty* only carried her mainsail, storm-reefed, and a small jib. Yet so nearly did she heel over that Gotty perceived the necessity of lowering the former. Tackling his urgent and difficult task with spirit, Cole soon had the gaff on deck. The sea all around us was churned into whiteness. With only a little triangle of canvas over the bowsprit, the *Betty* flew across Dungeness Bay.

Would there be water in Folkestone harbour? Gotty shouted in my ear that I must learn the time of the tide. Somehow I got to the cabin; and, to save me the hazard of a return journey, Cole came crawling to the hatchway for that vital information.

It wanted two hours to high water. With my head out of the cabin opening, I anxiously awaited Gotty's solution of the difficulty. He gave the helm to Cole, and himself came forward and lowered our remaining sail. Then so considerable a volume of water rose from the side and descended upon me that I withdrew into shelter. The next minute our vessel received a blow that sounded like a clap of thunder; a tremor passed through her framework, and I heard an avalanche of water fall on deck.

Amid the howling of the gale, Gotty's agonised shout could not have reached Cole. But the wind carried it to me, and also I heard the skipper fling himself back to the stern. The less expert hand had held the helm and to ship two seas of that character in quick succession might have meant disaster. With our dinghy sprawling across the opening, we could not—as now I realised—batten down the hatchways. Cole was slaving at the pump, and, when I judged his strength to be spent, I clambered across and relieved him.

With bare rigging, for an hour and a half the *Betty* staggered in that raging sea. Impatient to the point of pain, with the wind assaulting all my senses, I lived through a long experience of swinging on and on, and still for ever on, in a lost equilibrium of air and water madly mingled. But at last (for the tide bore us towards the shore) I beheld the harbour lights—rigid stars of composure; comfortable reminders that, with good luck, we soon should pass from that quaking realm of boisterous upheaval, and return to the dear old solid land, where roads and kerbstones and houses remained obediently still.

Hoist by Cole, our jib stood against the might of the wind; and, all athrill, we ran for the entrance lights, the tiller in Gotty's tough grip. Then came the sudden relief of sheltered water, and the *Betty*, at peace at last glided among the multitude of moored luggers in Folkestone harbour. A lifetime had elapsed since we left Torquay— but a lifetime of only thirty-two hours.

Into the public bar of a little inn went Gotty and I—two haggard and dishevelled figures, dripping with salt, water and rain. I think it was not the rum we met with, but the reception, that put warmth into my companion. That group of veteran fishermen, socially assembled under shelter, broke into exclamations of honest astonishment when we went splashing into their midst.

"You've come through it, then!" cried one.

"So that little boat o' yourn," observed another, with respectful eyebrows raised, "can stand a bit o' weather!"

"Evenin'," replied Gotty, in friendly greeting to one and all; and not till he had swallowed the first dose of my prescription did he vouchsafe any relief to the curiosity our appearance had excited. Then he casually let fall one crisp, comprehensive sentence:

"We've jest run up from Torky."

At these tidings the Folkestone men exchanged expressive glances; then bent their eyes anew on the pair of storm-stained mariners.

"Not sorry to be in harbour, I dessay?" one presently ventured.

"Not sorry!" cried Gotty, depositing his tumbler on a table, to be the better able to unlock the inmost chamber of his soul; "not sorry! Look 'ere, mate! I wouldn't go through that lot again not fer a 'undred pound—nor yet two 'undred; there you are. I've seen a bit o' wind, and I've seen a bit o' weather, at our place sometimes; but talk about larst night! It wasn't water—it was boilin' froth, and all round yer the same! There was times when I thought she was goin' ter shut the door—that's the truth I did. . . . 'Where's the Guv'nor?' I says to Joe, fer I 'adn't set eyes on 'im all day. 'Is 'e dead or alive?' I says. "E was when I see 'im larst,' says Joe. 'Thank Gawd fer that,' I says."

.   .   .   .   .   .

Next day the storm was over; and on the evening tide we entered upon the last stage of our voyage.

197

Restored to his delighted family, Cole had exhibited a complacency that rather jarred on Gotty and the Guv'nor. So we scorned to ask his further assistance, particularly as we had no hope that he would concede it. We two took the *Betty* back.

Passing the Foreland next morning, I rolled up my chart. The pilot's work was done. We had re-entered the old familiar estuary—Gotty's world.

Four hours later, with Essex still invisible, I was aghast to feel our keel bumping submerged solidity. As Gotty seized an oar and plunged on both sides for the depth, his face was dark with agony.

"Clumsy old duffer!" I gasped.

"Oh, dear," he whimpered. "We ain't goin' ter be pulled up, are we? Shorley—shorley we ain't!" Suddenly his countenance brightened, and he shouted: "Parst it! Bray-vo!"

"Yes, but—" I began, indignantly.

"I fancied," he explained in excitement, "there'd be a fadum over that bank. Not quite there wasn't. But jest enough. That's saved us five mile and charnse it."

So I forgave him.

They saw us coming. Mrs. Gotty stood waiting and waving on the jetty.

Well, sir," she exclaimed, as our dinghy touched the stairs, "I hope he's been behaving himself."

"Don't talk so silly!" said Gotty.

APPENDIX

THE sailing bawley as finally evolved and built at Harwich, at Brightlingsea, at Maldon, and at the Thames, Medway and Swale fishing ports was powerful in hull form and rig and a distinctive type. A typical boat built during the twenty years prior to 1914, such as the *Betty*, was between 35-42 feet long overall; a 35-footer having a 12 foot beam and 5-foot or 5-foot 6 in draught. The hull had a straight keel, straight stem, slightly rounded at the forefoot and a transom stern with slight rake but often surprisingly delicate shape. The sheer was very high forward and swept down to little freeboard aft, in the manner of the finer lined Essex smacks. The hull had a very hollow entrance with bold "shoulders" about the mast and usually considerable shape in the beamy hull sections which made the bawleys rather stiffer sail carriers than the smacks, in smooth water. Construction was heavy and cheap, with sawn oak frames, beams and centreline structure, pitch pine bottom planking and pine topsides, decks and spars. Low bulwarks and a heavy oak wale belted the sheer. All the six or seven tons of iron ballast was carried in the bilge and ceiled over. Below decks they were arranged with accommodation for four in the forecastle, which usually extended aft of the mast and was entered by a hatch from the deck. The crew slept on locker tops and cooked on a coal stove. The hold occupied the remaining aft space. In a shrimping bawley it was divided from forward into a net and gear store space, room for the shrimp boiling copper and its coal and general stowage of the catch and a steering well at the aft end. The hold was served by a long, narrow and slightly tapering hatch with wooden covers for bad weather, leaving wide side decks for working trawl or stowboat gear and sorting the catch. A handspike windlass with pawl post was fitted across the foredeck and many had a simple, geared hand winch or "wink" mounted on a post amidships, to haul the trawl warp.

The boomless cutter rig was the bawley's most distinctive feature. The mast was rather short but a long, fidded topmast was carried and in a 35-foot boat the topmast head would be about 48 feet above deck. Standing rigging comprised two shrouds a side, with single

199

topmast shrouds passing over wooden spreaders and set up midway between the lower shrouds. A forestay led to the stemhead and the two fish tackles for handling the nets could be, and occasionally were, set up as backstays in heavy weather. The bowsprit stood 17 feet 6 inches outboard, without shrouds, but had a running bobstay and a topmast forestay led to its end. The sail plan was tall and comparatively narrow but efficient and handy to those accustomed to it. A 35-footer would set a 500 square feet mainsail, often referred to by bawleymen as the "trysail"; a 200 square feet topsail; a foresail (staysail) and a 117 square feet working jib; the rig totalling 912 square feet. A spitfire jib or a large light weather jib could be set to suit varying weather conditions and a jib topsail and balloon foresail could be set in light weather, when a bowsprit spinnaker was sometimes set to the topmast head and was boomed out for running or was sheeted in as a balloon jib. The jib sheets had no purchase and led in through holes in the bulwarks, the forward to make fast to the bitts, but the balloon foresail sheet was led aft, outside everything. The length of the gaff averaged 25 feet and this was hoisted, smack-style, by peak and throat halyards. The mainsail leech was almost parallel to the luff and the boomless foot of the sail was very short. The luff was hooped to the mast and the main tack could be triced up with a tackle and a single brail was fitted, running from a block at the throat, around the leach and back again to another throat block and down to the deck. Both truss and brail were in constant use when working gear, to regulate speed. Two or three rows of reef points were also fitted. The mainsheet had three parts and two blocks and a bearing-out spar was used when running in light weather. The foresail sheeted to a horse across the foredeck and the fall of its halyard was made fast to the neck of the lower block to retain it when lowering in haste. The topsail was often diagonally cut and its luff was laced, hooped or set on a leader to the topmast. In light weather the topsail often remained set above a brailed mainsail for ease of working or when brought up for short periods. In winter the bawleys often struck their topmasts and some removed them altogether. When the mainsail was lowered it was made up along the gaff, which was stowed with its peak on deck, to one side.

With the square forefoot and long keel, bawleys looked after themselves when sailing or hove to. The tiller had a pin rail across the after coaming, called the "old man" at Leigh and with the foresail just a'weather these boats held their course for miles while the crew were culling, cooking and packing the catch.

A bawley took about six months to build and over the years many